ZOO *Animals, People, Places*

ZOO *Animals,*

by BERNARD LIVINGSTON

ALSO BY BERNARD LIVINGSTON

THEIR TURF   *America's Horsey Set & Its Princely Dynasties*

People, Places

ARBOR HOUSE   *New York*

"At the Zoo" © 1967 by Paul Simon, used with permission of the publisher

For Nina Martin
without whose encouragement
this book might not have been

FOREWORD

Everybody, young and old, goes to the zoo at least once in his lifetime—indeed, some sixty million Americans do it each year. Europeans do it, Australians do it, the Chinese do it, even Africans do it. That's because the zoological garden is the "greatest show on earth"—older than the circus, with more behind-the-bars drama than a police precinct, more fun than a Broadway show, and yet, as serious an educational institution as any university. Indeed, the zoo is nature's penultimate university, at least with respect to the animal component of the natural world, for, practically the whole of nature's panorama of living creatures is presented for study at the zoo.

Moreover, as man is further separated from nature by expanding urbanization and technology, attendance at zoos spirals, and to its traditional role as a recreational and amusement facility the zoo adds the service of providing a link back to nature and a concern for conservation.

The latter role, conservation, is a swing back to that of the original zoo, Noah's Ark. Myth or not, the Ark is a lesson for all times in how dangerously close to the brink man periodically goes in decimating the very things that give nature its balance and him his life.

Thus the zoo (or menagerie, its original name) has since earliest times been a *social* phenomenon, a saga of man's inhumanity—or humanity, if you will—to beast, whether for idle pleasure, civic enlightenment or ecological good. The zoo story, accordingly, is a story not only of animals but of the human species as well, and every bit as fascinating as the world of man.

In this book the author will present a study of this world which treats it as social history. But the style will be a light-handed one similar to that of his previous social study, *Their Turf*, the story of the world of the racehorse and the people involved therein. It is to be hoped that the fun, drama, humor and, yes, enlightenment inherent in the world of the zoo will not be lacking in this work.

—Bernard Livingston

CONTENTS

	Foreword	11
1	Beginnings	15
2	The Typical Zoo	37
3	The Private Zoo	71
4	The San Diego Zoo	93
5	The Safari Zoo	121
6	Carl Hagenbeck	137
7	Animal Traders	153
8	Capturing Wild Animals— From Queen Hatshepsut to Frank Buck	171
9	Breeding in the Zoo	185
10	Superstars at the Zoo	205
11	Yeas And Nays—Including the Case of New York City's Central Park Zoo	231
12	Zoo of the Future—for Example, The Bronx	263
	Index	283

1 *Beginnings*

Man is historically both decimator and conservator. Long before "Buffalo" Bill Cody and his comrades-in-arms had exterminated the American plains bison, the cave dwellers of prehistoric Europe—despite the primitiveness of their weapons—had already found ways to annihilate immense populations of wildlife. Generally it is assumed that they were able to do so by stampeding great herds of panicked animals over cliffs; but whatever the technique, the bones of fifty-thousand prehistoric cave bears found at the site of a Cro-Magnon settlement in Austria are ample proof that man has always had a genius for mass destruction.

On the other hand, the Biblical story of the Ark testifies to mankind's concern for conservation. Noah, the First Zookeeper, with his ark of gopher wood and his collection of breeding pairs for each species, took unto himself responsibility for saving the animal kingdom from extinction. With this commitment he became a symbol for the saving force in man, and his ark a kind of "Ship of Hope" for endangered species. The First Zookeeper was thus the first con-

15

servationist and the archetype for all the St. Francis's, Thoreaus and Schweitzers who came after him.

But zoos were not always committed to the cause of salvation. In their earlier history, far from being a place of animal refuge, they were actually animal prisons, whose main purpose was to flaunt imperial power. Indeed, the story of the captive animal is as old as the history of imperial power and as much an expression of power as are the Pyramids of Egypt.

Consider what is generally regarded as man's first formal zoo. In the fifteenth century B.C., there was a Queen of Egypt by name of Hatshepsut, daughter of Thutmose I of the Eighteenth Dynasty, a group that did things in a big way. Among the trifles that these Pharaohs conjured up with the Temple of Amen-Ra at Karnak, one of the seven Wonders of the World, into one room of which the whole of New York's St. Patrick's Cathedral could have been placed with room to spare. So it is not surprising that Queen Hatshepsut, a woman who ruled the empire by forcing her husband into the background, would want to display her power by queening it over a horde of wild beasts imprisoned in her gardens.

Not content with the usual wildcats, hares and lynxes that were a part of lesser Egyptian menageries, the Queen dispatched history's first animal-collecting expedition through the Red Sea to the "Land of Punt" (Somalia) to bring back exotic monkeys, leopards, birds and wild cattle. These went into the palace zoo, where, with her courtiers, she could indulge a whim for feeding snacks to jungle beasts.

Queen Hatshepsut's menagerie may not have been as large as New York's Bronx Zoo, nor as streamlined as San Diego's, but for its time it was every bit as showmanlike as many modern zoos. Like Phineas T. Barnum, the Queen had a taste for the unusual. Giraffes, for instance. Today that tallest of animals is commonplace by virtue of wide exposure in film, art and zoos. But in the ancient world the giraffe was a thing of wonder. Called the camelopard because it was spotted like the leopard and related to the camel, the first of these beasts ever to be seen in Egypt was imported by the First Lady of Zoos. She also introduced another rarity into her country: the greyhound, a dog that hunts by sight instead of smell, being deficient in the latter. Thus, as a result of the Queen's lead, two of the rarest and most graceful of animals became fashionable in the menageries of the ancient world. One Chinese monarch even dispatched an expedition halfway around the world for the single purpose of securing a giraffe.

That the world's first zoo goes so far back in time (some historians place it farther back in Old Kingdom Egypt, others in China) may come as something of a surprise to many people. Generally, the zoo is considered a relatively modern phenomenon. But the fact is that the ancients had all the know-how and their rulers all the resources to create and maintain the most complex wild-animal collections. By Queen Hatshepsut's time, man already had long experience as a hunter and therefore as a student of wildlife. Those famous paintings made by Stone Age man on the walls of the caves at Lascaux, France, demonstrate how well he understood the bison, the rhinoceros, the deer and the wild horse. Even farther back in time, Early Stone Age man had domesticated the dog, a feat that was aided by his understanding of the peculiar psychology of that wild animal. Pups of some wild canine species will, when captured, accept man as a surrogate parent and relate to him as they would to a dominant member of their own group. The tail will be placed between the legs as a gesture of submission to the human master just as it would in the wild to a leader of the pack. (In mythology the surrogate relation is exactly reversed, with a she-wolf acting as *parent* to Romulus and Remus.)

Other wild species, notably the goose, also came under the domination of Stone Age man as a result of his discovery of physical characteristics which made their capture possible. Adult geese lose their flight wings during the summer. The warm months are also the time when their young are running, preparatory to growing their own flight wings which will mature by the time the parents are ready to fly again. But it was during the "grounded" period that primitive man was able to capture and domesticate both goose and gosling.

By the time of the full flourishing of ancient civilizations, man the tamer had the capability of being man the zookeeper. The great royal menageries were, of course, not public zoos. Mostly they were regal indulgences set aside for pure pleasure and political use, such as the entertainment of foreign potentates.

In China, for instance, there was by at least the twelfth century B.C. a great proliferation of zookeeping among the ruling classes. Confucius writes that the Empress Tanki built for her own pleasure a deer house entirely of marble. Later on, Wen Wang, an emperor of the Chou Dynasty, set aside what he called a "park of intelligence" in which he kept exotic animals. These included the giant panda, a species on which the Chinese today have a monopoly, and which, some three thousand years later, another Chou was to present to an American president for his country's national zoo. Parks of intelligence became commonplace in ancient China for the nobility and the ancient tradition of "intelligence" endures to this very day in the form of the most stringent wildlife-conservation laws in the world.

In the next few centuries, as more great cities arose, royal menageries began to spring up with them. Israel, under King Solomon, had now risen to its highest peak of splendor. Solomon in Hebrew means peaceful, and the King had a reign that was indeed eminently peaceful, supported as it was by a strong system of foreign alliances that gave him time to accumulate enormous wealth. He was thus free to indulge himself in the pleasures of peace, which, of course, he did on a scale that made him legendary: "his throne, of ivory and gold, had twelve lions on the one side and on the other [twelve lions] upon the six steps . . . there was not the like made in any kingdom."

Moreover, Solomon stocked his land with immense herds of cattle, sheep, deer and fowl. For his horses and chariots he constructed over four thousand stalls, each with running water. Fourteen hundred chariots and twelve hundred horsemen were stationed in waiting, both at Jerusalem and in cities around the country. Whether he had seven hundred wives and three hundred concubines, as the Bible credits him with, is open to question, but there is no doubt that he staffed his palaces with a respectably large harem. And of course he collected an appropriately royal zoo.

But Solomon was no ordinary zookeeper. He was, after all, the King of Kings, wisest of the wise, and a man with a keen interest in trade. "For the King had at sea a navy of Tarshish (ocean-going vessels) with the navy of King Hiram of Tyre," says I Kings 20:22. "Once in three years came the navy of Tarshish bringing gold, and silver, ivory, and apes and peacocks."

This establishes Solomon as one of the first great wild-animal traders. He not only swapped animals with his neighbor, King Hiram, but also did business with his father-in-law, the Pharaoh of Egypt, as witness I Kings 28–29: "And Solomon had horses brought up out of Egypt. . . . And a chariot came up and went out of Egypt for six hundred shekels of silver and a horse for one hundred fifty." That would be, respectively, something like $1,000 and $250 at current prices, no small market at any time, considering that the King dealt with quantities such as twelve hundred horsemen and fourteen hundred chariots.

In addition to being an active trader in animals, Solomon is reputed also to have been wise in their ways, that is, a zoologist. It is even asserted that he understood their language well enough to have been able to communicate with them in the way some people currently claim they can talk to plants. Some writings in the Old Testament, attributed to Solomon, do in fact demonstrate an understanding of the ant, the lizard, the spider and the coney (a species of rabbit which, in colonial times, swarmed over a New York beach in sufficient quantity to give Coney Island its name). But some Biblical scholars point out that not only is there great question as to whether Solomon really was the author of this material but, even if it is so, the writings are at best only "wisdom literature": material of the most elementary nature used as a basis for fable. By no means are they to be regarded as scientific treatises, these authorities claim, for there was no objective observation of nature at that time. That was to come some five centuries later, with Aristotle.

In any event, whatever one might say about Solomon's role as a trader or as a sage, he was nothing if not kingly in his choice of specimens for his zoo. In the days when he was trading in peacocks with Hiram of Tyre, that ornamental fowl was the oldest and most exotic of birds. It was also the costliest, one of the chief reasons being that in India, where it originated, it was sacred. A peacock sold for about two thousand times the price of an ordinary cock. Acquiring a breeding pair was like taking a prize of war; monarchs went to great lengths to get them. Peafowl were also eaten by the very rich, particularly in Rome where the practice of roasting the bird and serving it in its own gorgeous plumage became a status symbol. Great numbers of this proud bird—so proud indeed, that it will not mix with other fowl—graced the aviaries of Solomon's zoo. To his credit, as far as is known, they never reached his table.

Up to this point in history, most of the kings and nobles who kept zoos had little interest in the scientific aspects of zookeeping. Their chief concern was with the usefulness of wild animals as puffs for their ego. But, along with the spread of writing in the early pre-Christian era, a cultural upsurge took place. People in different countries were now beginning to exchange knowledge of animal behavior, among other things, and a more scholarly approach to zookeeping was becoming evident.

This set the stage for Aristotle's pioneer work in natural history and resulted in man's first encyclopedia of zoology. Alexander the Great, a pupil of Aristotle—and probably the first man in history to turn the zoo into an educational institution—made the royal menagerie available to his tutor for the study of wild animals through direct observation. Up to Alexander's time Greek animal collectors were interested chiefly in birds, and, to some extent, in monkeys and apes. But when Alexander began to conquer the world, he sent back to Greece specimens of each country's local fauna. Whether or not his primary interest in the collection of animals was more utilitarian than scientific, as in the case of his adapting the Indian elephant for military use, is open to question. But the fact is that, whatever his concern, he implemented it in true Alexandrian fashion. Along with his armies marched a unit whose sole mission was to collect from conquered countries all the living animals and zoological knowledge it could lay its hands on. In addition, when he conquered Egypt, Alexander set up that country's first public zoo.

Back in the mother country the attention of one of the world's greatest minds now became focused on the zoo which the conqueror's zoological brigades had assembled. Aristotle was a true zoo man. He concerned himself with all of nature's production; no animal was beneath him. To his students he said:

It remains to now talk about the nature of animals. So far as possible we will not leave out any of them, mean or noble. For if some do not charm the senses, yet for scientific knowledge the nature which fashioned them provides a pleasure to all who can know their causes and are by nature philosophers. Indeed, it would be strange and absurd if we took pleasure in looking at likenesses of animals, because we were seeing the art of the craftsman, the painter or the carver, yet failed to delight much more in looking at the works of nature itself, provided we were able to discern the causes of their generation. We must therefore not draw back childishly from examining the meaner animals. In all natural beings there is something of the marvelous.

Out of this first-hand study of living creatures came the master's *History of Animals,* an encyclopedia which classified and described some three hundred species of vertebrates, about as many as any average modern zoo contains. Aristotle knew enough about animals to have easily qualified as the curator on Noah's Ark. Certainly he could have served as head of any modern zoo.

In another few decades mankind arrived at one of the great turning points in the history of its relationship to wild animals. And once again, in the third century B.C., in the new, Alexandrian Egypt, the course man chose did not go forward along Aristotle's scientific road; the zoo now made an abrupt turn. Instead, wild animals became "show business" on a scale never seen before or since.

In part this may have been due to the fact that Alexander himself had mounted a kind of "greatest show on earth." In what was history's most brilliant military career, he had thrust his sword across the major part of the civilized world, farther than had any man before. He had lived thirty-three incredible, all-consuming years, and he died, according to some reports, in similar style: consuming thirty-three quarts of wine. But, before his death, he had succeeded in getting himself accepted as divine. As a result, the Ptolemaic Dynasty he installed as the new rulers of Egypt might well have felt constrained to carry on their god's style of doing things, for the zoo they assembled was undoubtedly the greatest show on earth.

Imagine one of those great parades contemporary Russia traditionally stages in Red Square on May Day, which take all day to pass the reviewing stand on Lenin's tomb. That, as they say in show business, would be Dullsville compared to the parades that Ptolemy II put on in Alexandria in the third century B.C. His processions also took all day to pass the reviewing stand. The only difference, however, was that Ptolemy's paraders were animals— not people.

The most stupendous of these processions, and very likely one of the greatest spectacles ever mounted by man, was the animal parade Ptolemy II staged for the festival of Dionysus. Given in honor of the god of wine and fertility the event was probably the world's most magnificent orgy. Twenty-four chariots drawn by ninety-six elephants, four to a team, with the lead elephant harnessed and garlanded in pure gold, headed a mile-long parade into the city stadium. These were followed by chariots pulled by the most unlikely combination of draft animals imaginable: lions, oryxes, ostriches and wild asses.

In addition, there were birds, many thousands of them, exotic and ornamental, carried along in cages by slaves. Big cats too, in the dozens: leopards, cheetahs, lynxes; a "white" bear, brown bears, camels laden with cinnamon and the tusks of 600 elephants, 130 Ethiopian and 300 Arabian sheep, a snake reported to have been 45 feet long, and 24,000 Indian dogs (Ptolemy Philadelphus of Alexandria had so immense a number of Indian dogs—believed to have been produced from a bitch and a tiger—that four Babylonian towns were exempted from all other tax but that of maintaining them). Bringing up the rear were two of the rarest species in captivity at the time: the giraffe and the black African rhinoceros. Apart from the inconceivability of staging so colossal a spectacle with the primitive transport technology of those times, Ptolemy II can take the prize for assembling the greatest zoo the world has yet known—and almost certainly a collection surpassing that of any modern zoological garden.

With the rise of Rome, the zoo had moved into the big time, a kind of animal big business, albeit show business to be sure. Up to this point, two of the greatest Mediterranean civilizations had related to the wild animal world in different ways. Alexander, in the tradition of his scholarly master, Aristotle, had made his collection available for the advancement of learning; Ptolemy II had turned his vast zoo into spectacular public shows. Now came Rome's turn.

Egyptian Queen Hapshepsut, XVIII Dynasty, as a sphinx. (She died in 1468 B.C.). Despite the fact that women did not normally rule Egypt in that period, Hapshepsut displaced both her stepson and nephew from the throne, and ruled as Pharaoh of the Two Lands. She also established what many consider mankind's first formal zoo.

Montezuma (1480?–1520)— Aztec emperor. Hernando Cortez first seized Montezuma as hostage and attempted to rule through him, then later killed him. The Emperor maintained one of the largest zoos ever known, which included retarded and deformed humans in its exhibits.

Two views of the Ménagerie du Parc at Versailles, the zoo of Louis XIV (1643–1715). It was beseiged by a mob during the French Revolution and many of its animals were set free.

The imperial Roman Barnums began to comb their farflung empire for specimens of every conceivable type. At first wild animals were presented merely as curiosities; for instance, the giraffe, the crocodile and other unusual beasts and birds, in addition to, of course, the elephant and the big feline predators. Then the Caesars turned to what became their chief "contribution" to the world of the zoo: slaughter—slaughter on a scale that amounted to holocaust.

Neatly departmentalized by Roman pragmatism into three businesslike categories, the massacres took place in huge amphitheaters.

First there were the "hunts." Here people were allowed to seize and secure what they could for their own use, such as deer, hares, sheep, boars, oxen and all kinds of birds. A natural forest was created by trees transplanted into the amphitheater, the beasts were let in from their dens, and, at a sign given by the Emperor, Roman citizens fell to hunting the animals. Each carried away what he killed. Tablets and tickets had been previously scattered among the mob, entitling those who caught them to the animals inscribed upon them.

A second form of entertainment was the combats. Combats were deadly contests between animals. Sometimes an elephant was matched with a bull, a rhinoceros with a bear, a lion with a tiger, a bull with a lion. Deer were also hunted around the arena by packs of dogs. "But the most wonderful sight," according to Calpurnius, "was when by converting the arena into a lake, huge aquatic animals, crocodiles, were introduced to combat with wild beasts. At the Games of Carinus:

> Not only did I see wood-monsters there,
> But sea-calves also tugging with the bear.
> And that misshapen ugly beast withal,
> Which we, not without cause, the 'sea horse' call.

In the third category, men engaged in death struggles with wild animals, and the men had the common name of *Bestiarii*. The vilest criminals were doomed to such combats. Others hired themselves out at a set pay, as did the gladiators, and attended schools where they were instructed in such conflicts. Some of the nobility and gentry voluntarily took part in these encounters. Even women were infected with the frenzy.

> Sometimes, with naked breast, the sturdy whore
> Shakes the broad spear against the Tuscan boar,

wrote Juvenal in his account of the games. The safety of the combatants consisted in nimbly turning and leaping to elude their adversaries while attacking them at the same time with darts and
spears. One gladiator was known to have killed twenty animals let
in upon him at once. The beasts, however, were generally the victors
over the men. But eventually they were dispatched by missile weapons
thrown by spectators from the higher parts of the amphitheater,
safely out of reach of the animals. Frequently, in one show, three
or four hundred animals might be slaughtered.

There were of course some people in Rome of that period who
devoted themselves to zoological study rather than to slaughter.
Pliny the Elder, for instance, was a dedicated natural scientist; he
wrote a book on natural history that is still used today. But most of
the emperors and nobles were concerned with games and killing.
Octavian Augustus, perhaps greatest of the Caesars, was one of the
outstanding butchers—during his reign, which paralleled the early life
of Jesus Christ, ten thousand men and countless numbers of animals
fought and died in the arena. Octavian's zoo was almost as big as
that of Ptolemy II, but he spared nothing, not even rare animals sent
to him by other kings as diplomatic gifts. A shipment of tigers, a
species never before seen in Rome, was received from India and
quickly wound up as targets for the Augustan games. Six hundred
African animals were butchered in 11 B.C. in honor of Marcellus, the
Emperor's adopted son, who died in the imperial spa at Baia. Nine
years later, 260 lions went to their death in the amphitheater and
thirty-six Nile crocodiles were slaughtered while splashing about in a
pool specially built for the occasion.

And Augustus was not alone. Julius Caesar, who invented the
classic bullfight, sponsored the killing of four hundred lions and
twenty elephants in one day. To guard spectators against injury
from the animals, which were maddened by force-fed intoxicants,
the man who himself protested the unfriendly stabs of Brutus dug
a ten-foot-wide moat around the arena.

But the most frightful killer of all was the young Emperor Commodus (161–192 A.D.), who acceded to the throne at nineteen. He liked to do his slaughtering on his own.

"In the arena," writes Edward Gibbon, in *Decline and Fall of the Roman Empire,*

> Commodus intercepted the rapid career, and cut off the long bony neck of ostriches, a thousand of which had been released in the arena, with arrows whose points were formed like a crescent. The dens of the amphitheatres disgorged at once a hundred lions, which he laid dead by his unerring shafts. The elephant, the scaly rhinoceros, the camelopard of Ethiopia and India's most extraordinary animals were slain.
>
> Commodus, who debased himself in every manner imaginable, appeared in the amphitheatre to please his concubine, Maria, in the habit of an Amazon, a dress in which he most admired that favourite. He killed great numbers of gladiators, who were afraid to exercise all their dexterity or strength against the Emperor. The senate, even when he killed a lion or other animal, added their applauses to those of the people, servilely crying out: 'Thou overcomest the world, thou art the conqueror, O brave Amazonian!'

So colossal was this thirst for blood among the Roman masses (political leaders used the games as a vote-getting measure) that the Roman amphitheater, one of which was able to seat an incredible total of 485,000 sweating, screaming individuals, became a vast slaughterhouse whose traditions survive even to this day in the bullfight and to some extent in the rodeo.

The result: a good part of the earth's wild animals were exterminated by the demands of the Roman amphitheater. Elephants were no longer seen in Libya nor the hippopotamus on the Egyptian Nile; lions disappeared totally from Europe, as did the aurochs (wild bison) and the wolf. Where was the memory of the she-wolf that had given the milk of life to the very founders of Rome? Their sons were devastating the earth with their "greatest shows on earth."

Eventually, with the decline of the Roman Empire, the animal massacres ended. And with their end came a decrease in the number, size and comprehensiveness of zoos. Most of the menageries that remained were in the hands of royalty and the newly powerful Catholic Church.

Slowly the concept of the zoological garden began to emerge again. In Eastern Europe, both at Antioch and at Byzantium (Constantinople) where the first Christian Roman emperor, Constantine, had moved the Empire's capital, excellent animal parks were established. These were maintained as public zoos and were visited by great numbers of people until the Persians destroyed them in 538 A.D.

By the eighth century, Charlemagne, first emperor of the Holy Roman Empire, had three menageries of his own spread around his domains. His collection was heavy with exotic birds, including, as he was an ardent hunter, thousands of falcons for use in the then-fashionable sport of falconry. Bishops and monks in the Empire were charged with responsibility for maintaining animal parks on monastery grounds. One order—the friars of St. Gallen in Switzerland—built a zoo of surprisingly modern design, with roomy quarters for the carnivores, work spaces for the keepers and well-kept outdoor paddocks for the hoofed animals. At this point in history, the Persian overlords in Constantinople were disposed to deal a little more kindly with wild animals than they had in 538 A.D. Perhaps it was not kindness so much as the deterrent of Charlemagne's military might, for instead of exterminating animal populations, their ruler, Haroun al-Raschid, sent the Holy Roman Emperor elephants and monkeys for his zoo. Other monarchs presented him with bears and camels; the Pope, whose throne he had saved, sent him a lion.

Now enters Britain into the picture. By the twelfth century the Roman Caesars had long since departed the far-off British Isles. The primordial dukes and lairds had grown prosperous enough to have acquired great private parks whose animal stocks required security against the likes of poachers—such as Robin Hood. It was time for the local Plantagenets to doff their primitive deerskins for elegant silks and satins from the East. It was now meet to have that other symbol of power: the royal menagerie.

The first of the British Henrys, the youngest son of William the Conqueror, assembled a modest collection which he kept at Woodstock. Nothing much happened in England's zoo world, however, until some hundred years later. In 1230, Henry III, who became king at the age of nine, decided that Woodstock was too provincial a residence for a King of England and moved himself, his retinue and his zoo into the Tower of London.

Those pink-cheeked and kindly looking "Beefeaters" who today play ceremonial games at the Tower of London for the benefit of tourists, such as locking the ancient doors of the Byward Tower to the accompaniment of an armed escort, did not always close those portals on such sweetness and light. Apart from Anne Boleyn, Lady Jane Grey, the two "Little Princes" and others who were executed within the Tower's walls, a great number of wild animals also met violent death there. Most of England's kings entertained their guests with lion-versus-tiger fights, modeled after the old Roman games, to decide the age-old question of who really was the King of Beasts. The English never quite resolved that issue, however, unless some Shakespeare or Marlowe who was present might have muttered that the "King of Beasts" was in fact the host himself, for the savage custom persisted even up to the days of Elizabeth I. Today the Beefeaters will point out the spot near the Tower's present ticket office where the old Lion Tower once stood. It was in the cages surrounding the Lion Tower—part of whose foundation is still visible —that the animals were housed to wait their day of execution.

But Henry III, founder of the Tower of London Zoo, did not devote himself only to animal contests. He imported into England the first elephant ever seen in that land, a present from Louis IX of France, who had made the animal a souvenir of his crusade in Egypt. Droves of people came from all over the British Isles to stare at the strange beast so far from its native land. This caused Henry's zoo to become one of the first municipally supported zoos in history, for he made the City of London pay for the construction and upkeep of a shelter not only for the animals but also for the visiting tourists.

Indeed, Henry had already established the practice of making the royal menagerie a municipally supported institution. Earlier on, he had been presented with another rarity, a polar bear. A royal decree was issued declaring that the City must pay for the care of the bear, an order whose implementation came under the authority of the Lord Mayor. The buck was passed to the sheriff, who shoved it on to the keeper, along with a budget of twopence-a-day for the animal's rations and the keeper's wages, a niggardly appropriation by any municipal standard in almost any historical time. The keeper simply took his bear down to the Thames River each day and had

the animal catch his own dinner. He then used the twopence allot-
ment to provide himself with food.

At about this time over in Asia, Chinese civilization had reached
the zenith of its splendor. Under Kublai Khan, a man who lived on
a scale of grandeur probably never equaled in all of history, the
Mongol Empire exceeded in wealth and territory even the Roman
Empire. Marco Polo, the Venetian who saw it firsthand, never
quite got over it, which is understandable when one reads in his
diaries about what happened when the Grand Khan left his fabled
Xanadu to engage in a simple hunt:

> When His Majesty has resided the usual time in the metropolis,
> and leaves it in the month of March, he proceeds in a northeasterly
> direction, to within two days' journey of the ocean, attended by full
> ten thousand falconers, who carry with them a vast number of ger-
> falcons, peregrine falcons, and sakers, as well as many vultures, in
> order to pursue the game along the banks of the river . . . He has
> likewise with him ten thousand men of those who are termed
> 'taskaol,' implying that their business is to be upon the watch.
>
> The Grand Khan also has many leopards and lynxes kept for
> the purpose of chasing deer and also many lions. They are active
> in seizing boars, wild oxen and asses, bears, stags, roebucks, and
> other beasts that are the objects of sport. It is an admirable sight,
> when the lion is let loose in pursuit of the animal, to observe the
> savage eagerness and speed with which he overtakes it. His Majesty
> has the lions conveyed for this purpose in cages placed upon cars
> and along with them is confined a little dog, with which they be-
> come familiarized. The reason for thus shutting them up is, that
> they would otherwise be so keen and furious at the sight of the
> game that it would be impossible to keep them under the necessary
> restraint.

Moreover, Marco Polo points out, if this vast army of birds and
beasts of prey were not enough to bring down what the Grand
Khan thought was a proper bag for the day,

> His Majesty has in his service two persons, 'masters of the
> chase,' having charge of the hounds fleet and slow, and of the
> mastiffs. Each of these men has under his orders a body of ten
> thousand chasseurs: those under the one wearing a red uniform, and

those under the other, a sky-blue, whenever they are upon duty. The dogs of different descriptions which accompany them to the field are not fewer than five thousand. The one, with his division, takes the ground to the right hand of the Emperor, and the other to the left, with his division, and each advances in regular order, until they have enclosed a tract of country to the extent of a day's march. By this means no beast can escape them.

When his Majesty makes his progress in this manner toward the shores of the ocean, many interesting occurrences attend the sport, and it may truly be said that it is unrivaled by any other amusement in the world. He is borne by four elephants, upon the backs of which is placed a pavilion of wood, handsomely carved, the inside being lined with cloth of gold and the outside covered with the skins of lions, a mode of conveyance which is rendered necessary to him during his hunting excursions, in consequence of the gout, with which he is troubled. In the pavilion he always carries with him twelve of his best gerfalcons, with twelve officers, from amongst his favorites, to bear him company and amuse him. Those who are on horseback by his side give him notice of the approach of cranes or other birds, upon which he raises the curtain of the pavilion, and when he espies the game, gives direction for letting fly the gerfalcons, which seize the cranes and overpower them after a long struggle. The view of this sport, as he lies upon his couch, affords extreme satisfaction to His Majesty, as well as to the officers who attend him, and to the horsemen by whom he is surrounded. After having thus enjoyed the amusement for some hours, he repairs to a place named Kakzarmodin, where are pitched the pavilions and tents of his sons. The tent of His Majesty, in which he gives his audiences, is so long and wide that under it ten thousand soldiers might be drawn up, leaving room for the superior officers and other persons of rank.

As if the above animal collection were not enough to impress a visitor, Marco Polo saw rhinos, hippos, bears, boars, camels, porcupines, monkeys, civets and many fishes. He also saw the rare Milu stags, now known as Père David deer, named after the missionary-naturalist Father David, who, some five hundred years later in Peking's imperial gardens, saw the few remaining survivors, blessed them and added them to his list of souls to save. Much of the Grand Kahn's collection was housed in a style appropriate to its master's exalted position on earth. It no doubt served as a model for a later

"Chief," whose palace at San Simeon, California, with its private zoo, was often called Xanadu, although it was of course not one ten-thousandth the size of the Grand Khan's. But, like the Grand Khan's, William Randolph Hearst's Xanadu was available for viewing only by a select few.

By the time Marco Polo returned home, new dynasties, such as the Medicis, were already on the rise in the individual Italian city-states. The Vatican, some thirteen hundred years after Christ, was now a great secular as well as spiritual power. Indeed, as in the case of the Medici family, princes of the church and dynastic family members were often one and the same, even up to the level of Pope. The Medici dynasty, for instance, rose from obscure origins to immense wealth as merchants and bankers, married into the major houses of Europe and, besides ruling Florence and Tuscany, produced three Popes, two Queens of France and several Roman Catholic cardinals.

Cosimo de' Medici, first of the family to rule Florence, helped Italy return to the days of the Roman amphitheater, at least for one special occasion. In the process of cultivating another powerful Italian family, the Sforzas, whom he helped to seize Milan, Cosimo staged a revival of the Augustan slaughterhouse in a stadium which he built at his own expense. There he released Florence's menagerie of lions, bears, bulls, wild boars, wolves and mastiffs to rip each other apart for the pleasure of the Sforzas and their guest, Pius II, Pontiff of the Holy Roman Church.

The whole thing, however, wound up a fiasco. Those who had mounted the production for the Duke erred in their expectation that there would be plenty of blood flowing. The animals—even the lions—tired by a long parade through the streets, simply lay down and went to sleep when they reached the stadium. This was a fortunate thing for succeeding generations of wild animals in Florentine zoos, inasmuch as it discouraged the Medici from ever again thinking of entertaining VIP's with scenes of slaughter. When Cosimo's heir, Lorenzo, assumed the Dukedom, he turned his attention to the more humane aspects of zookeeping. Under him, Florence's menagerie became immortalized by the great poets and painters of the Renaissance.

The zoo fever was now spreading throughout Italy; other Popes and cardinals began to make collections of wild animals. Alexander VI, a Borgia Pope, whose greatest claim to immortality, perhaps, was having fathered Lucrezia Borgia, the Renaissance duchess of poison, assassination and incest fame, even reintroduced into Italy the bullfight which Julius Caesar had invented. Leo X, the Medici Pope who succeeded him, went even further. He set up a menagerie in the Vatican itself, with monkeys, lions, leopards, camels, wolves, African civets and Indian elephants. Many other cardinals followed the lead of the Pope, some going in for gauche displays, such as staging a wild-animal pageant for Eleanor of Aragon, which featured Orpheus charming the savage beast with music, followed by Bacchus bounding around on a chariot drawn by a team of leopards. But another Medici, Ippolito, bastard son of Giuliano de' Medici, and a cardinal of the Catholic Church when he was twenty, topped them all. He kept a *human* zoo filled with slaves: Africans, Indians, Tartars, Moors and Turks. Let it be said, however, that Cardinal Ippolito was at least sympathetic enough to the human condition to have maintained over three hundred needy Renaissance poets at his own expense.

Such were the zoos and zookeepers of that period when civilized man saw the full flowering of art and culture in the Old World. What then of the New World, that vast Garden of Eden, North and South, populated by animal species which, in many cases, were more varied and certainly more impressive than the fauna in the jungles of Africa? The largest snake in the world, for instance, is not the African python but the anaconda, which can be found in lengths of up to thirty-seven feet in the forests of South America. What was the relationship of wild animal to man in the sixteenth century, that golden era when civilized Europe was dispatching its discoverers, its missionaries and its adventurers to the far corners of the globe?

The Indian of North America, to be sure, considered his wild-beast neighbor an instrument for survival—just as the animal predator looked upon his own prey. But the Indian also believed that the wild animal was a kind of brother, never to be treated as an object for amusement and certainly not for senseless slaughter.

Whether this made the North American Indian's civilization more advanced than that of his cousin to the south is a question for debate.

But the fact is that there were in Mexico and South America civilizations that in many respects were more advanced, particularly with regard to ecology, than those which sent missionaries and adventurers to "discover" them. The Inca, the Aztec, and especially the Maya—whose history dates back to 1500 B.C.—were masters of abstract knowledge. Writing, astronomy, arithmetic, calendric development, recording of history, to say nothing of art, architecture and engineering, were already highly developed in these civilizations when many European peoples were still savages.

Thus it will come as no surprise that one of the best zoos the world has ever known existed in Tenochtitlán (now Mexico City). This was the royal menagerie of Montezuma, Aztec emperor of a great civilization which flourished for centuries in Central America. In 1591, a small body of Spanish soldiers led by Hernando Cortez became the first Europeans to see the zoo. They were escorted through the palace as honored guests by Montezuma himself, because the Emperor thought they were descendants of the Aztec god-hero Quetzalcoatl. The Spaniards reciprocated two years later by destroying not only the zoo but Montezuma and his empire as well.

On that first visit, however, they saw things that made their eyes bulge with wonder, as Bernal Diaz del Castillo, a Cortez soldier, recorded in his *Chronicles*. The zoo was a part of the Temple of Montezuma, the Emperor being also the Aztec religion's chief priest. It contained practically the whole list of Central American fauna in addition to great gardens of shrubs and flowering trees. Its aviaries were beyond belief, so vast that they alone required the services of three hundred keepers. Birds of prey in the collection—hawks, condors, falcons, eagles—consumed a daily ration of five hundred turkeys. Besides the cages and pits, there was a huge lake, ten ponds for waterfowl and paddocks for llamas, vicunas, deer and antelope. Jaguars and pumas, which were "fed the flesh of dogs and human beings" were penned inside intricately wrought bronze cages. In addition, Diaz del Castillo mentioned another kind of lion (also reported by Columbus ten years earlier in a letter to Ferdinand and Isabella) which "had a face like a man," suggesting that there were anthropomorphists even in those times. There were also monkeys, sloths, bison, bears, armadillos and, unfortunately, human beings. These included bearded women, dwarfs and deformed people who were displayed in cages and had their food thrown to them as if they were animals, something that brings to mind the zoo of another priest-ruler: Ippolito, Cardinal de' Medici of Florence.

If Montezuma's mammal collections made Cortez's men gasp with wonder, his reptile exhibits were enough to make them shudder. Looking down on the pools and rocks the Spaniards saw iguanas, caymans, giant turtles and, as the fascinated Diaz del Castillo wrote, "wild vipers and poisonous snakes with something on their tails that sounded like castanets." Added to these were enormous anacondas and boa constrictors.

The entire enterprise was operated with meticulous efficiency, with trained nurses to attend sick animals and attendants whose chief function was to gather the gorgeous feathers dropped by the enormous collection of ornamental birds, feathers which went into the making of ceremonial costumes. But less than a year after Montezuma had graciously shown Cortez the wonders of his zoo, the world's greatest collection of animals suddenly was no more. In 1520, after failing in his attempt to govern through Montezuma, whom he had taken hostage, Cortez laid siege to Tenochtitlán and reduced the entire city to rubble. During the course of the battle the starving Indians were forced to kill and eat most of the inhabitants of the zoo. Montezuma too met his death, but his vast treasures of gold and silver, which was really what the Spaniards were after, never reached their destination in Spain. They lie, according to legend, at the bottom of the sea, irretrievably lost in a shipwreck. For centuries thereafter there was no zoo in Spanish-governed Mexico City. But today, because Mexicans are the most ardent zoo-going people in the world, that situation has been remedied with the building of one of the best zoos of modern times.

The next century saw the great expansion of empires, and, with it, the spread of the royal-zoo idea throughout Europe. Almost every court, large or small, in addition to its royal orchestra, court theater, court laureate, had its court menagerie. And out of the "divine right of kings" thesis—that most private of all outlooks—came, oddly enough, the foundation for the first public zoo in the modern era.

The most impressive of these "divine-right" zoos was that of the most impressive of the Grand Monarchs, Louis XIV of France.

His menagerie, though a long way from being the scientific and educational institution that zoos were to become in modern times, was nevertheless innovative in many ways. The number-one interior decorator of all time, Louis with his 66,000,000-livre palace at Versailles had a little garden that needed some livening up. But instead of installing a *trompe l'oeil* of sculptured fauns and pixies in the manner beloved of some present-day decorators, Le Roi Soleil peopled his backyard with living things, which, of course, he could well afford to do. These were animals, exotic and wild, in goodly enough number to please the eye of a man who himself regularly summoned an audience of sycophants to watch him dine alone.

There was, of course, nothing new about a king in the seventeenth century having a menagerie outside his window. What was unique was the fact that Louis XIV, with his passion for depleting the public treasury with experiments in architectural extravaganzas, decided to make his animal enclosures fan out from a central courtyard like the spokes of a wheel from a hub. This was a plan that Napoleon later used in rearranging the streets of Paris. In addition, Louis camouflaged the ugly cages and pits by planting flowers and trees and shrubs around them. Here indeed was something new in zoo design. Never before had anybody concentrated all their animal exhibits in one area, as the hub design of Louis XIV required. (Cages and pits were generally spread all over the place in conformity with the random pattern of the terrain and their owner's desire to give an impression of size.) It was also the first time that a zoo had been designed with an eye for beauty, with landscaping made a part of the plan. So here in the Ménagerie du Parc at Versailles was not only the then-largest collection of animals in existence (Louis didn't need to give an impression of size, he was a synonym for the word) but also the world's first zoological *garden.*

How that private French menagerie became the foundation of today's public zoo is another story. Many private things would eventually become public as the French Bourbons headed inevitably down the road to revolution. For one thing, so imperial was the court of Louis XIV, so heavy was the traffic of visiting princes with enormous retinues of servants who could not tactfully be barred from the Grand Monarch's menagerie, that the gates were already opened to a much larger public than had ever been intended.

By the time the unfortunate Louis XVI occupied Versailles, Paris' lower-class lackey leaven had begun to rise into that "cake" which his wife had suggested that the Parisians eat. The mob, however, opted for the venison on the hoof that was housed in the Ménagerie Royale. In October 1789, it descended on Versailles, demanding that all the animals in the zoo be released in the name of the Revolution. And they made no bones about the fact that, under the new regime, they considered that animals were for eating. To this, the director of the zoo, Monsieur Laimant, tactfully agreed. But when he pointed out that among his charges were some that could easily turn the tables and do some eating themselves, the mob changed its mind and let the zoo alone.

Three years later Louis XVI, who had gracefully supported one revolution—the American—only to be overthrown by another—was condemned to the guillotine by a majority of one. The Ménagerie Royale de Versailles was dissolved and the great French naturalist, Cuvier, undertook its reorganization after the animals were transferred to the Jardin des Plantes in Paris. The Committee for Public Safety decreed that henceforth the zoo was to be open to all citizens. In 1798 one of the world's first experiments in animal psychology was conducted in the new public zoo. An elephant was serenaded by an orchestra and his reaction to the music noted. The big beast is reported to have swayed in time to the march music, fidgeted at the trumpet blasts and dozed off during the symphonies. Since then the Jardin des Plantes in Paris has been the scene of as many ups-and-downs as that of the French Republic. Once it was the home of a giraffe that debarked at Marseilles, as a gift from the Pasha of Egypt, and walked all the way to the capital. In 1870, the zoo survived not only the German siege of Paris, but also the fact that many of its edible animals had to be sacrificed to feed the starving people. After World War II it did the same thing: put itself together again after the bombing by Adolph Hitler. Today, in Versailles, Louis XIV's palace still gleams in splendor, thanks to gifts of the Rockefeller family. But its royal menagerie was never resurrected.

2 *The Typical Zoo*

Someone told me
It's all happening at the zoo.
I do believe it,
I do believe it's true.

It's a light and tumble journey
From the East Side to the park;
Just a fine and fancy ramble
To the zoo.
But you can take the crosstown bus
If it's raining or it's cold,
And the animals will love it
If you do.

Somethin' tells me
It's all happening at the zoo.
I do believe it,
I do believe it's true.

The Monkeys stand for honesty,
Giraffes are insincere,
And the elephants are kindly but
They're dumb.
Orangutans are skeptical
Of changes in their cages,
And the zookeeper is very fond of rum.

Zebras are reactionaries,
Antelopes are missionaries,
Pigeons plot in secrecy,
And hamsters turn on frequently.
What a gas! You gotta come and see
At the zoo.

—Simon and Garfunkel
"At The Zoo"
lyrics by Paul Simon

37

Mickey, a 2½-inch-long fluffy white mouse with carmine red eyes is also part of the zoo. He arrives crated in a wooden cage together with 143 others of his species. But Mickey is not an exhibit specimen; on his cage is posted no identifying marker—*Mus Musculus* in his case—and certainly not the usual "DO NOT FEED" sign. Mickey himself is feed, a laboratory creation bred to be eaten by other animals in the zoo. In addition to weeks-old chicks, white rats, rabbits, suckling pigs, horsemeat, fish and a great variety of fruit, vegetables and grains, Mickey is a part of the daily menu of a typical big-city zoo. In a place like the federally operated National Zoo in Washington, which all of us own, a gross or so of live Mickeys is delivered every month for those occupants that fancy delectable little mice, while literally tons of dead fare go to the rest of the population.

Mickey is destined for the Reptile House of the particular zoo to which he has been delivered. That is where the snakes, lizards and crocodiles, in addition to amphibians such as frogs, salamanders and turtles, are housed. For a few days, Mickey will enjoy life bobbing in and out among his 143 companions, lodged in a crate behind the exhibits where the reptiles that will eat him are displayed. Some reptiles will take their food dead; others insist on killing it themselves. If Mickey is lucky the reptile keeper will do him the kindness of taking him by the tail and knocking his head on a board. Then Mickey will be offered up to the reptile dead. Or he might mercifully be ensconced in a deep freeze to wait for the day when the cobra has an appetite for him. But if he is marked for live deposit in the cage of his natural enemy, he gets a brief reprieve and waits.

Finally comes the day for Mickey's rendezvous with death. He is placed in the cage of *Eryx johni*, the Indian sand boa, an individual that could do him in with the flick of an eye. But to the amazement of a novice visitor to the backstage world of zoos, little Mickey shows not the slightest fear. Unbelievable! Just a few inches away in the same enclosure lies the monster that will strike him dead, and Mickey is busy flicking a flea out of his fur. In a moment he will be up on his tiny haunches calmly sniffing the air of his new digs and then down poking around in the crushed gravel in search of tidbits. Super Mouse!

Innocent Mouse . . . the truth is that Mickey, having been bred in a laboratory, has never had the slightest contact with a predator. To him the reptile that will devour him is just another part of the scenery, an external thing like the wall of his crate or the hand of the keeper. Thus no fear and, mercifully for him, not even time for fear: when the snake decides to strike, death comes in a split second. None of that slow, torturing crushing-to-death business as envisioned in popular legend: the python kills its victim instantly by suffocating it in a vice-like grip. Nature is generally more merciful in killing than is man; the act is perhaps even less cruel for the mouse than it was for the chicken on our dinner plate. Such is the way God designed his universe: either the mouse dies as food for the snake or the snake dies of starvation. Nature plays no favorites.

Where zoos do feed live, or at least some of its reptiles feed live, as in the Baltimore Zoo, the Reptile House is closed to the public for the day. Zoos have a difficult enough time coping with people who will not accept the workings of nature, let alone inviting them in to watch her in action. In these instances, generally once a week, the live prey is presented to the predator and the only witness to its fate is the reptile keeper. The snake kills and consumes its food —taking about a week to digest it—and then stays in a relaxed state until the next Monday, whereupon it will be ready for another Mickey. But occasionally Mickey is lucky. The two and one-half-inch rodent will kill the six-foot snake.

"That's right," said Frank Groves, Curator of Reptiles at the Baltimore Zoo. "Inconceivable as it sounds, we've lost valuable snakes from the little teeth of a laboratory mouse. Oh, there's nothing like a battle or anything like that. What happens is this. . . . A snake has a very primitively developed nervous system. When it falls asleep, as it often does in the cage, it's not very sensitive to external sensation. What I mean is that you can touch it and often it won't even feel it. Well, the lab mouse doesn't know it's a snake. If it stays in the enclosure long enough it will of course eventually come into contact with the reptile. And since the mouse never has had contact with a predator it will start to nibble on the sleeping snake just as though it were food. Rodents have been known to chew away all down the spine without waking the reptile up. We've had several valuable snakes killed this way. If the reptile doesn't take the mouse in three or four hours we take the mouse out. We certainly don't ever leave it in the cage overnight."

Such high drama does not, of course, characterize the task of feeding all members of the diverse population of the typical zoo. Mostly it is a simple but arduous exercise in logistics, the National Zoo, for instance, annually handling over two hundred tons of hay, seventy tons of crushed oats and thirty tons of corn, in addition to enormous quantities of processed "chows," fresh fruit, fish, meat and grain. Occasionally some member of the public will add a fillip to a zoo animal's diet by tossing into its cage such delicacies as razor blades wrapped in chocolate candy or fruit stuffed with crushed glass. Some years ago when a 6000-pound river hippopotamus died at the National Zoo, his stomach contained a plastic wallet, one hundred pennies, a lipstick case, a quantity of marbles, some subway tokens, a 22-caliber cartridge case and other indigestible items that thoughtless admirers had thrown him for amusement. But this kind of feeding is extracurricular, as are the home-baked Easter bunnies that lonely old ladies bring to the bears in frayed shopping bags. Public feeding of animals in zoos is generally prohibited, but circumvention of the injunction fills a lot of ego needs, such as a taste for power ("a bear feeds out of *my* hand!"), and the "DO NOT FEED" sign makes the violation all the more enticing.

Although the standard diets that have been worked out over the years are normally adequate to satisfy the wide variety of appetites found in a typical zoo, sometimes there are special problems. The anteater, for instance. This is an animal which, over millions of years, developed an eating apparatus that is designed specifically for the consumption of ants, as its name indicates. It has a long, narrow snout containing a two-foot-long sticky tongue that darts out to scoop up the insects. The job of supplying such a creature with enough ants for his enormous appetite would be insurmountable for a zoo, and so some of them, such as the National, have occasionally succeeded in turning his fancy to the more prosaic menu of chopped steak with a side dish of eggs and milk, and a few ants thrown in for dessert. Other zoos have not always been as successful in reversing a million years of dietary specialization, and that is the reason why an anteater may occasionally be exhibited for a few weeks, only suddenly to disappear—either to the mortician or to another zoo in some kind of a trade.

The King Cobra, most venomous of this deadly species, dines only once every two weeks. Then it becomes a case of cannibal against cannibal, for the cobra will eat nothing but another snake. His *pièce de résistance* is the indigo snake, which makes the long journey from a Texas snake farm only to disappear alive, and in a flash, into the cobra's mouth. And the mistake must not be made of putting the indigo snake in the cage with both the cobra and his mate at the same time. The male cobra often will grab the prey at one end while the female starts swallowing it at the other; when the two mouths meet at the center, the larger mouth, generally the male's, may keep on going and wind up with his own mate inside his belly. When this mistake has been discovered before the male eats his mate, a keeper has to enter the cage and slice the indigo snake apart at the middle, an act involving great nerve but little danger, because, with the prey in its mouth, neither cobra can bite him.

The National Zoo's giant pandas, Hsing-Hsing and Ling-Ling, also require a special diet. These two animals are native to the dense bamboo forests high in the hills of Western China, and their natural food is chiefly bamboo, which they eat fresh, by uprooting the stalk from the ground. The giant panda has been well equipped by nature for eating as tough and stringy a texture as bamboo stalk. Its head has evolved into a giant crunching machine, with heavy muscles connecting a broad blunt-toothed jaw to an enormous skull. This makes the panda capable of biting through a one-and-a-half-inch bamboo stalk and milling it down for digestion by a stomach extraordinarily adapted to handle such food. The giant panda requires its natural food (nearly half of its diet at the Washington Zoo is fresh bamboo) in order to do well in captivity. The National Zoo was therefore compelled to grow enough bamboo on its own premises to provide the two animals with their daily ration of twenty pounds of fresh-cut stalks. There are also the stalks the zoo grows in pots in the pandas' gardens. These fulfill the animals' need to pull down a certain number of stalks by themselves in order to "keep their hand in" on an action that their species has done for millions of years in the wild.

Then there are bats demanding a special nectar; birds requiring mealworms, which must be raised by the thousands at the zoo; lizards and frogs who eat flies and wax moths because their mouths are too tender to chew the bony carcasses of even tiny worms; and, in one case where a bird of paradise went "off his feed," the pupae of ants native to the Black Forest of Germany.

But although, as with Napoleon's theoretical army, a zoo population "marches on its stomach"—and an unbelievably complex stomach it is—feeding a collection ranging from a thimble-size hummingbird to a twenty-foot-tall giraffe is only one of a typical zoo's problems. (The Baltimore Zoo, though perhaps not the most outstanding, is a representative big-city zoo, with positives as well as negatives—so considerable research was done there.) Like all living things, wild animals can fall victim to a great number of diseases, particularly when removed from their natural habitat. This becomes evident in the inspection of the zoo population which the director or his delegate must make each day.

Dr. Ted Roth, a veterinarian and assistant director of the Baltimore Zoo, takes what many old-time zoo people used to call the "morning walk" (which can be compared to a physician making the rounds of patients in a hospital). Dr. Roth, however, does it not on foot but in a heavy-duty panel truck. Down the back roads where the hoofed animals are grazing, on past the cages where the big carnivores nervously pace, into the mammal house, the elephant house, the hippo house—all the enclosures where zoo animals have spent the night—his rangy Ford bounces. Every living thing in the zoo must be given the once-over for signs of sickness; wild animals, unlike humans, have no way of telling you that they feel bad. Even more, the feral beast will instinctively try to conceal his sickness. In the wild a sick animal would be easy prey for his enemies, a fact that has caused him to develop a self-preserving tendency to hide his vulnerability. So, in addition to his keen veterinarian's eye, Dr. Roth must bring to his "morning walk" a sharp skill at detecting, almost at a glance, anything untoward in his animal charges.

"After a while in this business you get a second sense about animals," he said in his cultivated Mittel-European voice.

"You mean a psychic insight, a kind of ESP?" a visitor asked.

"No, not that," he laughed. "Nothing metaphysical, no psycho-analysis here. It's just that familiarity with the individuals gives you a certain sense about them. Also, the animals get to know *you*, and you can often tell from their reaction to you if anything is off the beam. Besides, there are the feces—one of the most important exhibits in the zoo.

"If an animal has an off-normal stool, that's a danger signal. The same if it goes off its feed. Just like on the outside with humans: intake and output, intake and output, those are the basics."

There is hardly a place for Sigmund Freud in the world of the zoo, at least in the animal side of it, but Dr. Roth's anal and oral allusions did make him sound just a bit like his famous Viennese compatriot, an impression that was strengthened by the way he held a cigar in front of his goateed face.

"You might call those fellows up there on the hill mental cases though," he said as his truck thomped over the rough road past some llamas in isolation pens. "Those are our neurotics. They're 'prisoners' now, committed to the 'sanitarium.' That's because they're maladjusted individuals. They bite, kick and spit at the public."

Ted Roth was referring to the new practice of permitting certain groups of docile animals such as llamas, guanacos, deer and aoudad to roam free among the public, a practice in which Baltimore was a pioneer. Under this arrangement, people walk among the animals (not *ride* as in a "drive-through" zoo) and the animals walk among the people. Although the great majority of the beasts take well to their freedom, some few show a profound dislike for the human race and seem to prefer being segregated to their own paddocks. Those that do accept the option to free-roam have the opportunity to feed on pasture grass, flowers and twigs, including, of course, the omnipresent peanut and pretzel offered by a delighted public. One white-tailed deer in the Baltimore Zoo even comes up to the snack stand each noon on the dot for his handout of a hot dog "with everything on it," with no obvious harm from his renunciation of vegetarianism. "Calico," a baby llama marked like a cat of that name, hangs around the Hippo House whining for her surrogate mother, Senior Keeper Nancy Pegelow, to feed her the warm milk she has been getting since the day she was abandoned by her real mother. If the petting by small boys and dawdling old ladies gets too overwhelming, the animals have plenty of room to retreat, for the entire park section of the zoo is their home. Except for the human interlopers this is about as close to natural habitat as a zoo can get (there are no moats or ditches—only the zoo's peripheral fence—to prevent the roamers' escaping into the city). And the prolific rate at which the free-roaming population breeds shows that natural grazing and free movement is the responsible factor.

By now Ted Roth's Ford was chugging along past the old "Stone Shed," those ancient stone-and-steel cages where the big cats, bears and baboons are housed (Baltimore, like many other big-city zoos, possesses the space but still lacks the funds for the moated enclosures that it one day hopes to have.) Here the doctor looked lions, tigers, jaguars and pumas in the eye. The big Kodiak bear, an animal that can reach twelve feet high, knew him on sight and showed off his good health by executing one of those odd pirouettes that bears are so fond of doing. Or, perhaps in this case, the bear was expressing frustration—anger at being separated from his mate who, with her young cub, was in the new bear house that featured an Olympic-size pool donated by a wealthy local family. Next the Doctor abandoned his Ford and strode through the elephant house—the first time his "morning walk" had been on foot. Here he found his first case of the morning. Big Minnie, with a baby by her side, had had diarrhea during the night, presenting rather a sizable chore for the young keeper, who nevertheless accepted it with good grace. "Input, output," Dr. Roth joked with him, "that's what it's like in a zoo."

At this point, the doctor huddled with Head Keeper Ben Gary, a zoo man of the old school, a kind of army first sergeant that knows everything going on in the entire regiment, in this case numbering nearly a thousand animals and some eighty humans. Ben Gary, now with forty years at the zoo, had been a high-school dropout who came directly from the farm to the zoo, as so many keepers of his period did. His trim, hard figure and his great crown of reddish-gray hair gave him the look of a lion in mufti, and he presided over his staff, many of them college graduates, with an authority nearly equal to that of the king of beasts.

"In the old days many municipal zoos were nothing more than a drop for worn-out circus animals," he said. "This one was a special prize dump. You had your lions, you had your tigers, you had your bears—I don't know if the City even owned the animals. I think they just boarded them for somebody. It was more like some old menagerie with maybe three or four people working, and a pretty sorry one at that—till Mr. Watson took over." What Ben Gary failed to mention was the role that he had played in building the zoo into a first-line operation, for he was that archetypal backbone of any good zoo: its first sergeant, drill master and banger-together-of-heads, its head keeper.

Ben presented Dr. Roth his own morning report of activities, as any army first sergeant does for his company commander, and the doctor resumed his morning walk. Now he was in the Mammal House, where are housed most of the primates and other small animals, and where the infirmary is located. Here he met Senior Keeper Mary Wilson, a strong woman who occasionally acted as mother for orphaned chimpanzees in her charge.

"It used to be hard for a woman here. The men resented it . . . But it's getting better every day," said Mary, "especially with these, what you call 'em—liberated—young people coming to work here. These kids are all right, believe me—long hair, liberated, hippie or whatever. They love animals and they love people too. Me, when I first came, I didn't know what the word "liberated" meant. The boss said, 'Ms. Wilson, you're not afraid of mice, I hope. Because you'll see plenty of 'em around a zoo. And you can't scream out in the Mammal House, you know, because a scream can start a panic in a zoo.' Well, you know something—gorillas, tigers, hyenas don't scare me. But first day I was here wouldn't you know a mouse came in on me, and I let out a scream you could hear clean up to the Mansion House. That's how liberated a woman I was."

As if in response to her words, a little brown mouse ambled in, and Mary tightened her legs a bit around the high stool on which she was sitting.

"See what I mean," she said. "I don't scream anymore, but I sure want to. Don't kill it!" she ordered one of her long-haired assistants as he picked up the mouse by its unprotesting tail and took it out to release it.

Before he made his last stop, Ted Roth went down to the basement to check the infirmary. There, among a number of patients

in various states of indisposition, lay a week-old chimpanzee sound
asleep on a criblike table. The chimp had been diapered by Mary,
an act one visitor considered a silly anthropomorphism. But no, it
was simply an act of kindness (a motherless chimp can be rather
messy when confined to a crib) and no more anthropomorphic than
placing an animal in an infirmary bed. Besides, it was springtime
now, the season when zoo babies are born, the time when news
photographers plague the director for pictures of the new arrivals.
Two weeks ago a pigmy hippo and a new tapir had come into the
world, both of which were safe with their parents. Last week a
polar-bear cub arrived: it was alone in the enclosure with its mother,
for the father considers his own offspring legitimate prey. And last
night three tiger cubs, which must also be protected from the male,
were born. In a zoo, as in a field, a river, or a ghetto dump, birth
represents the same marvelous reaching out for life, the all-embrac-
ing grasp of the external world. A visitor was permitted to take
hold of the diapered chimp, to feel the vicelike grip of the week-old
hands, the pulse of the tiny feral heart and experience first hand that
familial bond which unites all living things.

This was the next to the last stop. Farther down the hall was the
final station—the morgue. As in the human world, death usually
visits the zoo during the dim hours. Dr. Roth opened the iron door
to a small, lightless closet, and the glare from the hallway filtered in.
Down on the floor stretched an old bull yak that had lived out its
years in the zoo, while up on a shelf lay one of the three tiger cubs
that had been born last night—no great tragedy for the zoo, really,
as tigers breed well in captivity. The cub came and went in a
brief moment. It will never make the Sunday magazine sections in
cute pictures with its siblings, nor will the old bull yak taste the
hard wine of another mating season. But neither will the two be
torn to pieces by jungle predators as surely they would have been
in the wild. The cub on the shelf, the old bull on the floor: birth
and death in the zoo—the cycle was complete and the morning walk
came to an end. That is, except for the act of authorizing the autop-
sies. In the afternoon the two carcasses would go to Johns Hopkins
Medical Center for certification of the cause of death. The modern
zoo is, after all, not just a place where junior comes with dad to
toss peanuts at Smokey Bear. The typical big-city zoo, to greater or

lesser extent, is committed to the cause of science. No longer are dead zoo animals buried without a proper investigation. Each case of death in the zoo might, as a result of an autopsic investigation, yield some new medical knowledge which could mean a better life not only for animals but also for humans. One zoo veterinarian was so dedicated to the cause of research in animal pathology that he resolved to eat a bit of every animal that died in the London Zoo. On one occasion, when he was absent, a leopard died in the zoo; on his return, several weeks later, the doctor ordered the carcass dug up so that he could sample a leopard chop.

Animals in a typical big-city zoo must be protected not only from the sicknesses visited on them by nature but also from the violence wrought by man. One of the greatest problems, as one keeper puts it, is not keeping the animals but rather "keeping the public." Vandalism, which ranges all the way from feeding innocent monkeys camouflaged rusty nails to climbing over fences and flailing fallow deer to death, has something of the same enchantment for certain members of the modern public that watching amphitheater slaughter had for the Romans.

"When we put the fence up around our two hundred acres of ground in Druid Hill Park," said Arthur R. Watson, director of the Baltimore Zoo, "there was a great squawk about depriving the poor of access to an open zoo. Well, it is true that we do charge an admission now, except of course for children. But that's one way to cut down on the vandalism. An individual who shells out an admission is less likely to be mischief-prone. It's almost axiomatic that troublemakers are the freeloaders. An open zoo is an invitation to violence. Remember the recent deer killing in Central Park or that business with the polar bear sometime back."

Watson was referring to the time, some years ago, when a tipsy couple, capping a night of party-going, swung into Central Park Zoo and tried playing patty-cake with the caged polar bear. The young lady paid dearly for her amusement, having had her right arm torn from its socket by the enraged animal. But that did not deter another man, sometime later, from climbing over the guard rail and poking a Good Humor into the polar bear's paw. In this case it was the bear who paid dearly for the intruder's misdemeanor, for in order to extricate the man from the bear's grip the animal had to be shot—a classic example of the unfairness of the zoo vandalism that causes caged and disadvantaged animals to pay the price for human sadism.

"Our fence cut down the incidence of human vandalism considerably, no doubt about that," said Watson. "And a fence can also keep out animal predators too. There is a sizable feral population right in the middle of almost every city that preys on the smaller zoo mammals, did you know that? You can find even in the middle of Manhattan or Washington—wild dogs, foxes, opposums and other predators that make the zoo an occasional hunting ground."

Arthur Watson puckered up his pink cheeks, peered over the rim of his spectacles and out into the cloud of smoke his Meerschaum was raising. A thin, fiftyish man, dressed in English tweed, Watson's professorial look belies his formal education. With only a high-school diploma he made his mark in the zoo world as an employee of the Cleveland Zoo while still in his twenties by putting together a personal collection of reptiles that at the time was considered one of the best in the country. In 1948 he took over direction of the Baltimore Zoo and built it from a row of squalid rusty cages into a top-drawer modern zoological garden, mostly by gentle but stubborn public relations. And, as with most reptile collectors, there was a gentleness about him that made you certain he wouldn't harm a fly.

"A great many of us are antipeople, you know," said Watson. "Zookeepers see enough mischief in individual human beings to, rightly or wrongly, turn them off people generally. It's a fantasy of course, but I guess deep down many of us dream of a zoo without visitors. In any event, it's a gross mistake to consider us as anti-animal because zoos deprive wildlife of its freedom. What's closer to the truth is to think of us as fantasizing that kind of limitation for people. When you find one of your deer has had an arrow shot through his neck by some sadist practicing archery, then you wonder who it is should be caged."

The range of public nuisance in the typical zoo ranges from open violation of the prohibition on feeding animals food that is deleterious to their health all the way to suicides who break into the cages of dangerous beasts. Among the most common pests at the zoo are the "dirty old men" of the zoo (not the male bears or monkeys but rather those male humans who peep on the bears and monkeys). These voyeurs hang around the zoo for hours on end hoping to see animals copulate. Every zoo has them and mostly they are harmless except for an occasional exhibitionist.

"As a matter of fact they are even a kind of asset," said Dr. Roth, half in jest. "They spend so much time at their occupation that they are often better informed than we are about when some females are in estrus and thus become a barometer to us. They spy on the animals and we spy on them."

Another type of sexual pervert who occasionally plagues zoos is the sodomist. The wild ass, the deer, the aoudad, young llamas and other more or less docile hoofed beasts are usually the choice for this night-visiting predator, chiefly because these animals are similar to the kind of animal he victimized on the farm where the habit often started. Also they are kept in open paddocks in the zoo and thus can easily be reached by climbing over fences. And there are now the free-roamers. One wonders to what extent the sodomist might have been the cause of the "neurotic" personality in those prisoner llamas that Dr. Roth had pointed out on his morning inspection.

Heini Hediger, director of the Zurich Zoo and one of the world's foremost authorities on animal behavior, comments on the public nuisances that plague the typical zoo, in his book: *Man and Animal in the Zoo*.[1] Among the most annoying, he said, are the practical jokers . . . "who are also very stupid. On April Fools' Day—which fortunately comes only once a year—men and women who happen to have the name of an animal, e.g., Miss Bird, Mr. Bear, Fish, Lion, etc. are asked to ring a certain telephone number, which is the number of the zoo. In the smaller zoos this may mean that the whole day's work is wasted in the office. Over one hundred calls of this nature were received by Zurich Zoo on April 1, 1964. In a previous year I tried to warn everyone with likely names by an announcement in the press; the net result was that the number of these senseless calls was if anything larger than ever."

Hediger then goes on to group the negative elements among the public into typical groups, adding to the sexual perverts mentioned

1. New York: Seymour Lawrence/Delacorte Press, 1969.

above "the type who concentrates not on the animals but on women, young people and children, eying them in dark and secluded corners of the zoo. There are also people who apparently are sexually stimulated by the sight of some particular animal or other, e.g., a long-necked terrapin, and consequently visit it with inordinate frequency."

Among others on Hediger's list are thieves, publicity seekers, and murderers and suicides. "Thieves are often pet-keepers with an obsession who are interested in rare species, and, as a result, such people are confined to a small circle. Rabbits, birds and animals known to be edible are stolen for quite different reasons, namely for the pot. Strictly speaking, intruders who open cages or smash them up out of a desire to 'free' certain animals—birds are often involved—can properly be described as psychopaths."

As for the publicity seeker, he "commits some gruesome act or indulges in some dangerous piece of mischief that may well be completely unpredictable, in order to read about his deeds or misdeeds in the papers the following day and thus achieve 'fame' through notoriety."

The murderer and the suicide, on the other hand, "make use of the special conditions of the zoo, which provide opportunities that are not available elsewhere, in order to carry out their crime under cover of the zoo's routine, thus making it less easy in some circumstances to detect the crime. Suicides usually want to let themselves be killed by large carnivores that are alleged to be dangerous or by animals such as elephants that are presumed to be carnivores, either at night in the absence of witnesses or even in broad daylight in the presence of horrified spectators."

"Comparative psychology," adds Hediger, "is indeed forced upon one in the zoo. Both sides of the bars have to be kept under control and it is the side where the humans are that usually causes the most trouble. This state of affairs was particularly brought home to me in the anthropoid ape house at the Zurich Zoo when glass panes were fitted in front of the bars. To make the glass visible and thus prevent visitors from knocking their heads against it, we had circles of colored paint put on the inside of the glass. The chimpanzees, however, scratched the paint off, so we then painted them on the side of the public. It was now the turn *of*

Homo sapiens to scratch them off with his finger nails. The division between the two was only a third of an inch thick in this case."

There are of course many other aspects of a modern zoo's relationship with the public it serves. Indeed, those functions related to vandalism are the least of its responsibilities. The typical modern zoo, although incalculably more animal-oriented than the private menagerie of old, is also considerably more public-oriented. Today's big-city zoo is by its very nature designed to perform a public service, as are other municipal organizations such as fire and police departments. Firefighters and policemen are often pressed into service to deliver emergency babies and take would-be suicides off bridges, but if any citizen has a problem involving a wild animal, particularly a snake, the call goes out to the zoo.

"The snake calls are the ones that give us the most trouble," said Frank Groves, the Baltimore Zoo's Curator of Reptiles. "I guess it must be the same in every big city. Most people detest snakes—they're the low man on the totem pole. They *do* look slimy, although they're actually not. They're also secretive: snake and sneak are cognate words, you know, they both derive from the same root. And maybe the fear of snakes goes back to our cave-man ancestors who must have lived in mortal terror of hidden reptiles. Anyway, most people will have nothing to do with snakes. But there are always those who get dangerously involved with reptiles, sometimes in far-out ways. Once the zoo got an emergency call about a drunken rattlesnake. An old Chinese man was in the habit of using rattlesnakes for an ancient Oriental remedy. He'd take these big glass jars, fill them with gin and then stick a rattlesnake inside. The alcohol would of course kill the snake but he'd let it pickle a while and then he'd drink the gin. Claimed it cured almost anything—and he *was* doing pretty well, because when we caught up to him he was already a good seventy. But one day one of the rattlers broke out of the jar before the old man could get the top on and bit him. The old man survived the bite but we had one damned time trying to catch that half-tanked rattler."

And how was it that the rattler's bite didn't prove fatal to the old man, Groves was asked.

"Who knows? Sometimes a bite won't be deadly because the snake doesn't coordinate. When a venomous snake strikes, he sinks his fangs into you and at the same time exerts muscular pressure on his poison gland to inject the venom. Occasionally these two actions aren't coordinated and you get the bite but not the poison. Maybe this particular rattler couldn't coordinate because he was in his cups.

"Then there are the stripteasers who dance with snakes. They take these big boas on the road with them, and zoos all along the circuit are plagued with their troubles. Most of these babes haven't the slightest idea about reptile care and most couldn't care less. But we had one that kept us on the run even though she should have known better because she'd been a Girl Scout and grew up with snakes. Her name, that is her stage name, was Naja—that's the generic name for cobra. She was a German war bride, married a G.I. who brought her over here, dumped her in a trailer camp and then left her. Naja became very depressed but she was adaptable. She learned the language, became a stripper and then branched out into specialty work with snakes where there was better money than in straight stripping. At first she worked with pythons, which are relatively harmless because they're not venomous. But then she decided to dance with cobras, which are deadly. I'm convinced she had a suicidal complex. She was hung up on this guy who left her, and began boozing heavily and didn't seem to give a damn about anyone. I used to go down to see her perform and when she told me about the cobras, I said, 'Look, Naja, don't be crazy. If you insist on using cobras, let me teach you how to tape up their mouths, so you have some protection.' But she refused, said snakes had taken her to top billing, and she wanted the real thing. Well, she had the real thing all right. Twice she got bitten but was lucky— probably because of that lack of coordination I mentioned. And once the cobra disappeared and we were never able to find it. But she kept at it with another one and finally the snake got her. They put her in an iron lung, because cobra bites affect the nerve centers that control breathing and kill by suffocating the victim. But she died within twenty hours. She was only twenty-five years old. We got the cobra as a specimen for the zoo. That's what happens with many of the snake calls that zoos go out on."

These are some of the things that take place in terms of the people on the outside of the cages, that is, the public. As to the people on the backside of the cages—the animal keepers—their relationship with animals is quite another story.

Consider the typical old-time zoo employee, as represented by Keeper Leon Dunn of the Baltimore Zoo. Leon brings to his work a love for all living things which has in no degree been dimmed despite considerably rough treatment by various occupants of the cages over which he has charge. With his slow-moving, bulky figure and his close-cropped hair, Leon, a sixty-year-old black man, is the diametric opposite of the idealistic long-tressed youth that has recently come to work in zoos. At present he is assigned to the Bird House, not necessarily because he is partial to feathered creatures but because his loving encounters with certain more dangerous animals have taken their toll.

"A Himalayan bear was the first thing that caught me," said Leon. "December the thirty-first I got caught, 1962. A Himalayan caught me and mauled me."

"What do you mean, a bear caught you?" Leon was asked.

"It was snowin' and slippery an' I fell into the cage. An' he grab me."

"How can anyone *fall* into a cage? It has bars on all sides."

"The back door to the den was open and the other door that opens to the cage has got bars but they were far apart. He just reach through the bars and grab me an' I fell in."

"What did the bear do to you?"

"Well, he stood up there an' look at me an' I look at him. I used to feed him every day an' by me feedin' him I thought maybe he would lissen at me. So I talk to him. I say, 'Chop, let go! Let go of me, Chop!' That's how I done, because he was just holdin' me. But after a while somethin' come to me, say, 'Now relax yourself a few minutes, Leon, then jerk, fast.' An' I done that. Relax myself a few seconds and when I went to jerk he tightened up on me. Then I started to holler, 'Murder! Police! Help! Murder! Police!' Man, I was hollerin'! Because I knew now I cain't git away from him. First thing jump in my mind is holler for the police 'cause they got pistols. But nobody heard me. Not a livin' soul around. Finally I broke away, but I was all tore up. He rip my hand and chew up the fingers."

"How is it a bear you feed every day would want to grab you?"

"Well, let me explain somethin' to you about wild animals. You can treat a human being well, like him, an' you've proven it to him you like him. A human being that's got a mind to think—you can treat him well and he'll turn around and knock you in your head. That's a human being. Now what do you expect an animal to do that can't think like a human being?"

"It looks like you've had a real case of 'bite the hand that feeds you,' Leon."

"You can say that again. And then that big Kodiak bear, Casper, broke his door. I was feedin' him one day an' he broke the door. An' when I turn around and look, he was standin' in the cage with me."

"What do you mean he broke the door? It's made of iron."

"Don't make any difference. He hit the door and the door broke. Somebody hollered, 'Look out, Leon!' An' when I turn around there was Casper standin' there and lookin' down on *me*! I said, 'Jeezus Chrise Awmighty! I know I'm dead now!' Because he was in there with me an' I'm lookin' up at him an' he's lookin' down on *me*. Meantime it come to me just that quick: if you don't panic, you'd be surprise, you can git out of a thing sometime. But if a person panic, he cain't think too good. He do the wrong thing."

"They say if an animal knows you're panicking, it's bad. Does the bear know you're panicking?"

"I don't know about that. The oniest thing I knew . . . he was standin' up, an' he hit at me and couldn't hit me. Then it come to me: in order for him to git me he gonna have to come down on all four."

"Why couldn't he hit you?"

"Because at the distance he was from me he couldn't reach me."

"Why couldn't he move in closer to you then?"

"By him standin' straight up he cain't maneuver on two feet like he can on all four. Looky here, if he had jump into the den with me an' stayed down on all four he coulda caught me. I couldn'a got outta his way. But when he jump in he stood up, an' that gave *me* the break. I had a bushel basket an' when he come on all four I throwed it right in his face. An' then—boom boom—I went flyin' through the door and close it real easy. Because if I pushed it hard it would bounce back open. But when I pushed it easy it stuck, and he doubled up right there. That gave me the chance to shut the outside steel door, an' just as I shut it he hit the door—wham, wham!—but I had him locked in. Then I got scared."

"You got scared *after* it was all over?"

"Man, I trembled so bad the Boss said, 'Leon, take off, go home for a few days. I don't want you unlockin' no more doors around here today.' "

One might expect that after such unkindly encounters with animals that he had treated well, Leon Dunn would bear a grudge, especially since one had maimed the very hand that fed him. Zoo people have been known to take subtle retribution on beasts that have savaged them. How did Leon feel about the bear that hurt him? Did he want to kill him?

"Naw, not afterwards, no. I was invadin' his privacy, he thought. Ain't no sense in me goin' back an' tryin' to hurt him after it was over. If I was goin' to hurt him I shoulda hurt him right then when he was doin' somethin' to me. Because what the bear thought was by me slippin' and fallin' off into the cage, I was tryin' to git in there where he was at, tryin' to invade his place. So he was probably fightin' back. You understan'? It'd be the same thing with a lion in the jungle if he saw you walkin' by. If you didn't go over where he was he wouldn't even bother with you as long as he wasn't hungry."

Leon Dunn, animal keeper without a high-school education was showing he understood the rudiments of animal behaviorism even though he probably had never heard of Robert Ardrey and the territorial-imperative hypothesis (which claims that all living things are genetically motivated to defend their own territory even to the point of war). Even more, he was fellow with Aristotle, who advised his students that in all animals, even the meanest, "there was something marvelous."

"I like everything that's on earth," Leon said. "They all have been put here for a purpose. An' to me everything is beautiful. Never seen nothin' ugly in my life. I hear people say, 'Ain't that person ugly, ain't that animal hideous!' I never say that. You know why? It's beautiful. If you look the way you're supposed to look then you're beautiful."

Down on Rock Island in the Baltimore Zoo there is another kind of keeper. Janet Gailey is assigned to the Bird Department, as is Leon Dunn; Janet cleans cages, she feeds and treats her charges well, as did Leon his Chop and Casper. But with Janet's animals there is no question of "me lookin' up at him and him lookin' down on me."

First of all, Janet Gailey, in an odd coincidence of name and personality, is full of laughter—a red-haired, open young woman standing nearly six feet tall—and she looks *down* on her charges, a colony of two-foot-high water birds known as *Spheniscus demersus* or, more commonly, as South African penguins.

Additionally, Janet Gailey is well acquainted with Robert Ardrey's "territorial-imperative" thesis, as well as with Ashley Montagu's rebuttal. Not only does she hold a B.S. degree in zoology from the University of Oklahoma, she has also published scholarly papers in her field of ornithology, notably a study of the behavior patterns of the Andean Condor *(Vultur gryphus)* made at the Oklahoma City Zoo while she was a college sophomore.

After her daily chore of "policing" the cages in the main Bird House, twenty-six-year-old Janet Gailey applies herself to the acquisition of a graduate degree in zoology under the sponsorship of Johns Hopkins University's Dr. Wm. Sladen, an eminent authority on penguins. This pursuit takes the form of an in-depth study of the behavior patterns of the South African penguin, which she undertakes in connection with her full-time job as keeper of the breeding colony at the Baltimore Zoo.

Many modern big-city zoos are notable for one or another specialty. The Bronx Zoo in New York, for instance, has its unique World of Birds exhibit, San Diego stresses the size and variety of its collection, the National emphasizes science and breeding, Philadelphia has its outstanding reptile collection. In Baltimore the breeding colony of penguins is the specialty; it is considered by many to be among the finest in the world. Undoubtedly the zoo has the most successful breeding group of penguins in the United States, for it is the first to have succeeded in raising second-generations of this species. Its Rock Island Penguin House, with its large pool and its piles of craggy rocks and interior nesting houses, is a gem among penguin habitats.

Newborn hippopotamus and mother. The young, born and nursed under water, sometimes climb on the mother's back to sun and rest while she is afloat.

Pigmy hippopotamus.

The Spotted Hyena—scavenger and largest of the species—has jaws so powerful they have been known to crush the limbs of an ox.

Zoo workers can easily control a formidable fourteen-foot python by stretching its body out. This is a method used in restraint and transportation of reptiles.

The Komodo Dragon, world's largest lizard, from the Indonesian island of Komodo and surrounding smaller islands, has large darting yellow tongues and fiery red eyes that give the reptile a dragon-like appearance. They roam as king of their domain, preying on deer, wild pigs and even buffalo. There are only three in the U.S., two at San Diego, one in the National Zoo. *(Photo credit: Ron Garrison, San Diego Zoo)*

Przewalski horse—the only true wild horse—is now practically extinct, except in zoos. It once roamed the plateaus of Northwestern China and Mongolia by the thousands.

Most species of squirrel are active only by day, but the flying squirrels are usually abroad at night. They have the ability to scale through the air. *(Photo credit: New York Zoological Society)*

Hoffman's Two-toed Sloth, found from Nicaragua to Colombia, does well in captivity. In the wild it spends most of its time in the trees, hanging suspended by claws as it feeds on leaves. *(Photo credit: New York Zoological Society)*

Gibbons are slender apes that are remarkably adept for swinging through trees. Leaps of thirty feet or more are common. Their cries, emitted from great pouches that look like balloons, can be heard for a couple of miles.

Ball Python of West Africa, a snake, which when alarmed, rolls into such a tight ball that it can be "bowled" across the floor. *(Photo credit: Ron Garrison, San Diego Zoo)*

The West African Crowned Crane—symbol of Uganda—is a majestic bird that travels in pairs or small flocks, generally near water. Its numbers have been reduced in some areas by draining of wet places. *(Photo credit: New York Zoological Society)*

Monkey-eating Eagle from the Philippines. Its favorite prey is the Macaque monkey. Seriously endangered by over-trapping and hunting, the bird exists in numbers of less than one hundred on the islands of Mindanao and Luzon. *(Photo credit: New York Zoological Society)*

Asiatic Elephant. Only the male Asiatic elephant has tusks that extend beyond the lips, and even these are shorter than those of the African Bush elephant. The Asiatic species is the one generally used for work or performing.

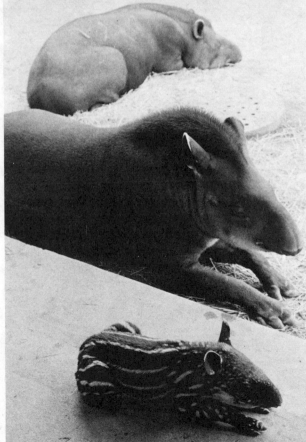

A baby tapir (foreground) being ignored by its parents.

"These are water birds that traverse vast distances at sea," said Janet in her twangy Oklahoma drawl. "Yet even a zoo as prestigious as the Bronx—which has that gorgeous World of Birds exhibit—puts their penguins in a tiny hole-in-the-wall exhibit with a pool the size of a bathtub. This, in effect, changes them into a land bird which is essentially what they are *not*."

With its outstanding penguin exhibit, Baltimore can thus be considered a classic example of the typical big-city zoo in the respect that it outdoes the top-drawer establishments in at least one area. And Janet Gailey is a classic example of the college-educated person that is currently coming into the zoo world.

"I guess I kind of prepared myself for this type of work early," she said. "At ten I was already a member of the local bird club, where I met Dr. George Sutton, who taught at the University of Oklahoma. I started bugging him—me a ten-year-old snip bugging a world-famous ornithologist for information about birds. Later, when I came to Baltimore and saw the penguins in this colony down here it was love at first sight."

The conversation was punctuated by a loud noise that sounded like a donkey's hee-haw which echoed through the subterranean passage under the Penguin House where Janet has her quarters.

"You have donkeys here?" her visitor inquired. "I've seen some odd combinations these mornings in my excursions behind the zoo scenes. But donkeys in the Penguin House? I just heard a hee-haw."

Janet laughed a country-girl laugh. "That's the jackass call," she said with a look of love in her eyes. "That's why these birds are sometimes called Jackass Penguins. It's their mating call. Only they haw-hee, not hee-haw. They're back in the nesting boxes now. I've heard that call a thousand times. It's music to my ears, I just love it."

She tossed several handsful of six-inch-long smelts into a bucket in preparation for feeding time. Smelts are a main staple of a penguin diet in captivity.

"Penguins are free-swinging pelagics—birds that spend most of their time at sea and come on land only to reproduce and moult. Parents leave the young when they are about three months old and never see them again. When the chicks become fully feathered they finally make the plunge into the sea. That's when the adult–chick bond will have been broken for good. There's an example behind you."

Taking a foot-high, down-covered little creature from his nest, Janet cradled him in her lap as though he were a kitten. "C'mon, you little dummy, you know you want it," she said and lovingly presented him with a large smelt, which the tiny fellow gobbled down with ease.

"You see, we've artificially broken the adult–chick bond by separating this fellow from the parent," she pointed out. "He's a month and a half old and has already learned to take artificial food. The penguin's natural food is live, but here it learns to take the smelt dead. In another month when it's fully feathered it will go out and join the rest of the juveniles."

Another loud haw-hee from the adjacent meeting boxes; the chick responded with a movement of its head.

"Oh yes, the chick reacts to the calls," said Janet. "Besides being imprinted on the adults, the young are also imprinted on their vocalizations. (Imprinting is to regard an object or individual as a parent or member of its own species.) That's how birds learn to identify one another. When a bird calls or whistles in the wild he's not just whistling in the dark. He's addressing himself to a particular individual, usually his mate, telling her where he is."

As Janet fed the chick more smelts the visitor had a moment to look around. The work quarters beneath the penguin exhibit were sliced in two by a long, narrow tunnel. It was cold, clammy, windowless and smelled of brine and fish. Long rows of overhead pipes, cramped passageways and a silence broken only by the hum of refrigeration machinery gave the feeling of being in a submarine.

"It's like a U-boat down here," the visitor remarked. "You must get the willies in this place all by yourself."

"Good heavens, no. I love it. I never even go up on the Mansion House steps to join the rest of the guys for lunch. I got all my little sailors down here with me in this submarine. C'mon, let's go out the hatch for feeding time."

Some of the penguins were inside the nesting room and others were out on the rocks as Janet surfaced to the pool. A few of the birds in the nesting boxes lagged behind.

"Ok, you all, let's go and eat," she urged them in her high-soprano voice. "C'mon, out the back door, you little dummies. Where the hell are you? Oh, here they come parading around the corner. Here comes the penguin parade!" Most of the birds began diving into the pool as she tossed the smelts into the water. But one juvenile, a kind of cocky little bantam, came up on her lap and Janet's eyes took on a special look as she offered him a smelt.

"Who is that?" the visitor asked.

"That's a character I call Romeo. He follows me around like a pining lover. I guess it's because he became imprinted on me as a result of separation from his parents. Look at him—little dummy—look at those gorgeous red eyes, aren't they pretty! Little lover prefers to hang up here and be hand-fed by me. Most of the others though like to dive in after the fish. That Rock Hopper that just plunged in was raised here and is now producing a second generation. And that other female over there is mated with that pinkbill here: Mr. Grand Old Man. He's the top in the pecking order. Nobody gives him any lip."

"What do you mean by mated?"

"Husband and wife. Penguins stay together for life."

"Don't they ever change mates: No other sexual adventures?"

"Never. Well, I should say, knock on wood, practically never. Because we have had one divorce here."

"What happens when they get a divorce?"

"You see that fellow up there on top of the rocks? Well, we now have a hermit because his wife deserted him. In fact the mother of the chick you saw in the nursery, that female I just pointed out, is the divorcee . . ."

"Don't tell me there was adultery. . . ."

"Right, she's now ignoring her previous mate—that's the guy up there on the rocks—and she's now carrying on with another."

"So what happens to the ex-husband? Does he seek another mate?"

"He probably would. But it's tough for him because at this point we have a shortage of females. I'm sure the shortage of females was the original cause of the divorce."

"Some of them have to go into a kind of priesthood then, huh?"

"Or become a hermit, like that one up there. You know, he

always nested there on the top of the rockpile. He and his mate chose that site on top of the rock instead of in the nesting room. My boss said that he and his mate fought several battles with the Grand Old Man over that place and apparently won out. Then, in 1970, his mate started having this affair with boy friend here. So she would go up on the rockpile and lay eggs, get husband on the eggs and then come down here and start nest building with boy friend. And she would move back and forth between husband and boy friend."

"You mean he'd be stuck with the job of sitting on somebody else's eggs?"

"We often wondered if she'd lay two eggs up there and put him to work and then lay two eggs down in the nesting room too. But it never got to that. What finally caused the full break though was hubby got ill. Malaria—that's one of the penguin's chronic problems. I had him in the hospital a month. But then we brought him round, and they discharged him."

"It was all over?"

"Yep. He goes running very happily up to her: 'Here I am,' but she just walked off: 'Get lost, kid!' "

"So, he's still in a state of bachelorhood?"

"That's right. He's the hermit in the cave. Here comes another second-generation producer. C'mon Martin . . . she was born the day Martin Luther King was assassinated. We named her Martin."

Janet Gailey went on to point out how Martin's problems as a young bird had led the zoo to the discovery that her difficulties derived from not breaking the parent–chick bond. The season after she was born and the parents were once again nesting, Martin would come creeping back into the parental fold.

"This made it practically impossible to feed her dead fish, the kind of artificial food that a bond-broken zoo chick will readily take. Even now at five years of age she's a poor feeder. Poor feeders make poor breeders. She's really an example of why the bond should be broken early in captivity."

This was a significant discovery in penguin behavioral science and perhaps one of the reasons why this particular zoo was making such progress in raising second-generation birds.

"Moreover, the bond-broken chick, as compared to birds from

the wild, has absolutely no fear of people," Janet continued. "Because the bond was not broken early enough, Martin can be a real martinet, as it were. When you try to catch her, she has no fear—she can destroy your hand in one fell swoop. Come here, Martin, show us your weaponry. You see, they're adapted for catching slippery fast-moving fish. The edges of the beak are razor sharp."

"And what of the public? How do they react to the penguins?"

"Oh, people just adore penguins. More than any bird except maybe the talking mynah they love the penguin. That's maybe because of the upright position and the tuxedo look. It's mentioned by everybody. The public loves to watch when they play tag, and never leave till the birds quit. One penguin will initiate the game by nipping another. Then the nippee will go back to the nipper and the race is on. And they deliberately collide. I know it's deliberate because penguins are so adept in the water."

Janet led the way into the nesting room and back into her submarine. But her accompanying visitor was not welcome. Several males lunged out of the nest boxes and made passes with their beaks at the intruder. For a moment he felt a little like Leon, fallen in the cage with "him lookin' down and me lookin' up."

"You see," said Janet, "you've invaded their territory and they're defending it against you. But me, they just take me as part of the woodwork. That's why this breeding colony is so ideal for a behavior study. They go through all their courting ritual, copulate and everything else right in front of me. We could never make this study in the wild. Wonderful birds, wonderful mystery! They spend most of their life at sea, emerge for a brief period to reproduce and refeather and then back into the ocean to travel thousands of miles. To this day nobody knows just where they go."

Janet Gailey and Leon Dunn can be said to represent the two extremes of types of keeper that today does the nitty-gritty work behind the scenes of the typical modern zoo. In between these two types are a great number of others filling a wide variety of jobs necessary to the efficient functioning of the zoo. But, for the most part, the "old codger with his rum bottle showing . . ." is gone, Simon and Garfunkel's song to the contrary. The typical big-city zoo of today is, after all, a far cry from being the "drop for worn-out circus animals" that Head Keeper Ben Gary once knew. And paralleling the enlargement of its functions has been an expansion of its need for dedicated and multi-talented people.

Since one of the prime jobs of a zoo is to handle dangerous wild animals, there must be people working in the zoo who know how to move them around and, more importantly, what to do in the event of an escape. Take a giant King Cobra, for instance. What happens if he breaks out, as one did from the Baltimore Reptile House.

"He was a fourteen-footer, and the most deadly of his kind," said Frank Groves. "His cage was left wet after cleaning and this annoyed him, because, contrary to legend, snakes—except water snakes—aren't slimy. Somehow he managed to slip out unnoticed and he wound up lodged in between walls. It took us three hours to flush him out into the lobby. Meantime we had a police cordon of sharpshooters ranged around with loaded shotguns. But I was less afraid of the snake than I was of the police with those cocked triggers. A nervous cop can accidentally blow your brains out, but catching up a big snake involves a fairly predictable technique. What you do is use long poles with nooses on them. You get one noose over the center of his body then you slip another on up at the head. Then you rush in and grab him behind the head. It's a ticklish job, of course, but once you have him by the head he can't bite. Then you stretch him out and he's rendered helpless, provided you have control of his body. That's important, because if you don't keep him stretched out he can whip around and get out of hand. You can do it with two or three men, but six or eight is better— one every two feet—so that you don't break his bones."

Then there is the keeper who has a talent for another aspect of animal-handling, that is, hand-raising zoo babies whose mothers have died or disowned their offspring. Generally, this job is taken up by women, although some men have done pretty well at it. Throughout the zoos of the world there must be any number of women keepers who have, in one way or another, acted as foster mothers for orphaned wild animals ranging all the way from tigers to gorillas. Patty Cake, the gorilla born in New York's Central Park Zoo in 1972—whose parents broke her arm in a hassle over the infant —is one of the more celebrated young ones that had to be mothered by a woman during her hospitalization period. Eventually, after her arm had healed, she was returned to her home and is now the object of adoration by both her parents and thousands of visitors to Central Park.

One of the more interesting examples of skillful simulation of motherhood for a zoo animal was the experience, some years back, of Marion McCrane in hand-rearing a two-toed sloth born at the National Zoo. The two-toed sloth is a nocturnal creature that spends practically its whole life—eating, sleeping, traveling—suspended upside down in the trees by its limbs. The infant lies on the mother's abdomen as she lethargically moves about the forest. Ms. McCrane, as a zoologist on the National staff, had hand-reared everything from monkeys to snakes, but as far as they knew nobody had ever hand-reared a two-toed sloth before. First of all, since it requires a very special diet that is not easy to furnish, there are not many of this species in zoos. But the main problem is that the infant, if orphaned or rejected, is almost impossible to feed. Because of the upside-down position in which the sloth spends its life, its trachea is arranged in such a manner that milk fed to it in an upright position can cause death through inhalation.

Ms. McCrane was equal to the challenge. After experimenting with a number of techniques that did not quite work she managed to succeed in simulating the precise position that an infant sloth assumes while nursing in his upside-down world. And a bottle of half-strength evaporated milk did the trick for little Mary Jane.

But that was only half the job. The two-toed sloth may be an upside-down creature, but it is not so upside down that it does not require the conventional contact with the mother that most infant mammals need. In addition, it is nocturnal, arboreal and slothful (sleeping about eighteen hours of the twenty-four). Ms. McCrane solved the material-contact problem by housing Mary Jane in a strong basket packed with towels, blankets, hot water bottle and a muff to which the infant clung as a substitute for her mother's abdomen. The waking nocturnal hours were filled in with feeding and a bit of clinging to Ms. McCrane herself.

"She is a very affectionate little creature," Ms. McCrane reported. "She knows my voice and moves toward me when I talk to her. She also rubs noses with my Persian cat. At night she races around in her basket home in a way no sloth is reputed to act."

Result: an extraordinarily well-adjusted zoo orphan.

Another function of the zoo, in addition to handling and rearing animals, is education, that is, education as distinguished from entertainment. Into this category falls an entire array of activities, including lectures, guided tours, exhibits, demonstrations and other information-disseminating functions. One of the most important of these, and an area in which even many of the best zoos fall abysmally short, is the informational sign posted on the front of an animal's cage. These signs are as vital to informing the zoo visitor about what he is seeing (and generally just as lacking in essential facts) as is the road sign in advising the highway traveler where he is going. Indeed, the effectiveness of a really good animal-identifying sign is illustrated by the very existence of this book; the inspiration to write it came from reading a marker on a cage in Central Park:

"OLIVE BABOON (*Papio cynocephalus*)"

"Several male baboons, with their huge teeth, can usually scare off their chief enemy, the leopard," the sign said. "If the cat does make a kill he must flee the scene quickly or be killed in turn by an angry baboon mob. . . ."

At this point a very ancient man joined the author in the reading. "Baboon society," the sign continued, "is very militaristic. Twenty to eighty individuals organize into a troop. Young males act as sentries and dominant old males stay in the center of the group to protect the females and the young. Every baboon in the troop knows his place, whom he can order and from whom he must take orders. They never fight each other.

Range: rocky cliffs, forests and bush country of Africa."

"Those baboons are really something, aren't they?" said the old man. "Never fight each other, huh? Human beings could sure take a lesson from them." The author agreed.

Today one of the most important workers in the zoo is the person who is dedicated to ending the outworn menagerie-oriented way of identifying and describing exhibit specimens. Acquainting the zoo visitor with who and what the animal in the cage actually is, how it fits into nature's scheme of things, where it stands on the endangered list, what its salient characteristics are, is critical to an understanding of the world we live in and vital to a positive man–wildlife relationship. The day of posting on the zoo animal's enclosure a sickly green square of metal containing such extensive information as "American Bison, *Bison bison*" or "Axis Deer, *Axis axis*" is about finished if the new educational specialist in the zoo has his way.

"What we're trying to do," said Ray Faass, a pony-tailed, animal-loving photographer/writer who is helping to create some of the new exhibits for the Baltimore Zoo, "is show people how they're all part of one great family: the animal kingdom. People just don't really relate to animals as kin to themselves."

"How can they relate to something sitting in an iron cage?" said his associate, Adrian Brayton, a young lady with voice and eyes that could tame the most ferocious beast.

"We'd like to tie in the animals we have with the displays we're doing—that is, use the animals as live examples, like a living museum," said Ray. "Right now we're working on birds: what makes a bird. And as you go through the Bird House, the display will tell more about what a bird is, how individual species adapt to their environment, how birds relate to mammals, particularly to the human, with all the differences and likenesses between us. When a person comes out of this kind of bird house, he will have a feeling he is also an animal just as the bird is. People have a long way to go in understanding the animal world."

Terri Shanahan, a tiny, fragile hummingbird of a girl who, in her spare time away from painting zoo exhibits, runs an organic food stand in a local farmer's market, laid down her brush and joined in. "You talk about lack of understanding," she said. "The other day I was out by the hornbill cage and a man came up to me and asked me about the mynah birds. You know they've been taught to say, 'Aw, shut up,' and 'Go take a bath,' and 'Hello, Oscar' and things like that.

" 'Why those birds are just incredible!' " the man exclaimed.

"Oh, they just parrot," I replied. "In the wild they imitate other birds' calls."

" 'Really?'

"I said yes, and you know he actually was convinced that he was having a *conversation* with the mynah bird. Because he said,

'When I walked past his cage he whistled and when I walked back he said "Goodbye!" ' The man had no idea that it was simply a coincidence. He really thought the bird was addressing him personally!"

"That's the level we're coming from," said Adrian Brayton. "These signs here. Did you ever see anything more ridiculous? Tami II, Tizzy, Andy Pandy. What we want to hang are signs that show them to be animals. Not this kind of cutie-pie, anthropomorphic stuff."

"What about Sylvia and Hercules?" asked Terri Shanahan. "Or Patty Cake in the Central Park Zoo? Imagine a gorilla going through life with a name like Patty Cake!"

"What would you name a gorilla, then?" the visitor inquired.

"I wouldn't name them," Adrian said. "Not officially, at least. Oh, the keepers give them names, of course, but those are not registered anywhere. And usually they're named for characteristics —not Tippi, Patty Cake, or Andy Pandy, or one of the prize ones: Gnancy for the last gnu born here. Janet Gailey has penguins named after their markings like 'Redbill.' Even names like Grand Old Man or Husband are okay, because they're pet names between keeper and animal. But Tizzi . . . once we post that up and make it official, the public will relate to the animal as a Tizzi."

"We understand why people name them," said Ray, "and we don't condemn them because anthropomorphism is a useful tool in bringing people closer to animals."

"But that's been the only tool used—making the animal human," said Adrian. "We want to show that animals do things that are worth respecting, not because they are humanlike but because they are animal things to do. Otherwise, it's just silly stuff."

". . . and animals aren't cute," Ray added. "We're past that. We've almost eliminated them from nature. 'Cute' is no longer the word. *Acute* is more like it—deadly serious. We're going to be losing them all if we don't recognize them for their own values. It's time to stop that."

It was also time to pause for lunch and the three put aside their brushes and trimmers and paste.

"We don't know if we'll ever accomplish what we want," said Ray. "Even though we have the backing of the director and some people in the Zoological Society, it's still plenty tough. Every week we're quitting and going someplace else. But it's pretty much the same most places so we stay here and watch it slowly but painfully improve."

Meantime they have at least found a use for all those cutie-pie signs left over from animals that have passed on.

"Yes, they're useful," said Terri Shanahan. "There is a whole roomful of them. And we paint out all the Tizzis, and Picky-Poos, and Randy Pandies with a good basic white and use them for signs like . . ."

"Like 'Olive Baboon (*Papio cynocephalus*),' which organizes into militaristic troops of from twenty to eighty?" the visitor asked.

"Yes!"

A third function of the typical modern zoo is conservation. Many wild animals would in fact be totally extinct were it not for the remaining members of their species that have been conserved in the zoo. So it is not surprising that many of the young people who are coming to work in today's zoological parks are committed members of the conservationist movement.

But conservation in the zoo is not concerned exclusively with the preservation of endangered species. Conservation of useful material resources is also an important item on the typical zoo's agenda. Ecological recycling of waste, for instance, is considered, in these days of natural-resource shortages, just as necessary as are protected habitats in a period of species endangerment. And Arthur R. Watson, maverick director of the Baltimore Zoo, is typical of the zookeeper who practices conservation down to the last detail. Watson believes that zoos should indeed set an example to the general public by leading the way in conservation. To this end he has instituted a novel experiment in conserving energy at his zoo, novel in concept, that is, but actually employing a product as old as the history of living things: animal feces.

Watson's experiment is directed at the conversion of animal feces into fuel gas. Initially he is using only a fraction of the several daily truckloads of droppings which, because of health problems with giraffes and other tropical animals, must be dumped on the zoo grounds. The fecal mass is processed through a prototype "digester," set up behind the Hippo House, that, with the aid of water and bacteria, decomposes it and releases gasses, one of which is methane, a substance that burns like natural gas. Preliminary analysis has already shown that Watson's methane has a higher octane rating than some aviation fuels. In addition, the residue of the degassed manure is a fertilizer with a high nitrate and ammonia content.

"Our fuel bill runs about $13,000 a year," said Watson. "If we can cut that by one-half we will be conserving a considerable amount of energy. Apart from the economics of the process, which is not necessarily our main objective, we are mainly interested in establishing the zoo as an educational example of conservation. Another plus from the manure conversion would be insuring ourselves a backstop of fuel for heating the Hippo House or the houses of other tropical animals that might die of cold in a fuel emergency."

The success of Watson's conversion/conservation experiment could mean that the hippopotamus might one day wind up having his own waste product not only fertilizing his food but also heating the house where he consumes it. This is a closed-loop process that is not so far-fetched; in India nearly twenty-five hundred home/farm-style converters have already been made and some twenty thousand are in the planning stage.

So runs the daily cycle of activity behind the scenes of the typical big-city zoo, from the morning walk of the director to the closing of the gates at end of day. But what of the night, that time when, as zoo people say, "the wild rats take over?"

"The midnight roars and screeches," wrote Amelia Young, in a report on the nocturnal scene for the *Washington Star,* "may give rise to stark imaginings in the people who live and sleep nearby. But the Washington Zoo at night is not as eerie as it sounds.

"When the sun goes down and the gates are closed, this parkland for three thousand wild creatures becomes a kind of enchanted version of what its visitors see by day.

"It's darker than the world outside because there are no streetlights. The familiar peanut-littered terrain takes on the look of a genuine wilderness and the homely barriers between beast and viewer are less intrusive. The animals seem more agreeable, as well. Usually too glutted with company during the day to be responsive, most of them look up with interest at the rare nocturnal caller. Some give out with ear-splitting welcomes—the monkeys, for example.

And the dingos, wild Australian dogs, jump around in their pens wagging their tails. . . .

"The midnight hours sometimes also give rise to fights, which bring the keepers running with high-pressure hoses. There are occasional escapes, which send the zoo police flying with nets and fire extinguishers. There are births, lots of them—in less than a month on one occasion, a Grant's Zebra, Nile hippo, pygmy hippo, water civet, Dorcas gazelle, black spider monkey, reindeer, llama, De Brazza's guenon, Cape buffalo, and a ring-tailed lemur.

"The keepers check all the animals with flashlights," Ms. Young reports. "If two bright eyes stare back, where an animal is supposed to be, 'we can be pretty sure it's all right. It's when they don't look up that we have to worry,' Mr. Ratliff said. He explained that while a few sleep soundly through the night, most wild creatures merely doze and come awake at the first sight of intrusion.

"Of course, the Small Mammal House contains a number of types that never look alive until after dark—South African aardvarks, Cape jumping hares, flying squirrels and other nocturnal species. The spectacle of them in motion, a fascinating sight, is one of the things the sleeping public misses.

"The curious serenity that settles on the zoo at night gives all the birds and beasts a greater appeal. A huge hippopotamus named Arusha, no beauty, swam up to the edge of her pool one night when the supervisor was escorting through two special visitors. Staring up at them, she looked suddenly sweet, and then the supervisor asked her to open her mouth. Arusha slowly parted her jaws in a most obliging, most impressive yawn.

"The supervisor speaks of the lot of his animal charges fondly. 'During the day,' he says, 'they're a bunch of clowns performing for peanuts. At night, they are more themselves.' "

3 *The Private Zoo*

The liquidation of the Ménagerie du Parc at Versailles struck a body blow at the institution of the royal private zoo, but it by no means destroyed its existence for all time. Some princely menageries such as the Schönbrunn Zoo of the Hapsburg dynasty, built by Francis I for his wife, Maria Teresa, at Vienna in 1752, continued on well after the French Revolution; other new ones, notably the Woburn Abbey menagerie of the British Duke of Bedford, came into being later. The founders of these zoos, however, were princely dynasties with a long history of power and therefore little need to flaunt their position. Their zoos had been created chiefly for purposes of individual amusement or private philanthropy. The Duke of Bedford, for instance, had rescued from extinction the père David deer by managing, fortunately, to get his hands on the few that remained after the Boxer Rebellion in China and placing them on his estate, where they have since increased their number.

Other private entrepreneurs, such as the amateur naturalist Walter Rothschild in England and the professional dealer Carl Hagenbeck in Germany, also assembled great collections of their own, but they were motivated, in the first instance, by scientific interest and in the second by the needs of trade. The practice of establishing private zoos as just another way of demonstrating the divine right and panoply of kings was dying out, along with the imperial theater and the court ballet.

But some ideas die hard, particularly those that are associated with certain basic human drives. The pursuit of privilege, the quest for power and the need to lord it over others seem endemic to human nature. Powerful lords of privilege keep popping up on one scene even when they have just been toppled on another. And, like the monarchs of old, they sometimes turn to the private zoo as a symbol of royal status.

William Randolph Hearst was one of these. Not long after the House of Romanov was liquidated by the Russian Revolution in 1918, an event which, incidentally, he spent much of his life in trying to turn around, Hearst popped up in California to revive the concept of royal privilege and power. And although he did it under a banner of apple-pie democracy, his style in some ways rivaled not only the deposed Romanovs but even the fabled Kublai Khan.

Born in San Francisco in 1863, fourteen years after the discovery of gold at Sutter's Mill, California, Hearst was no rags-to-riches phenomenon. His father, George Hearst, a farm lad from Missouri, had been one of the original "Forty-niners" and had lost no time in acquiring the treasures of the West. He wound up as one of the richest cowpokes in the country, with great chunks of California land and many millions of its dollars, several newspapers, mansions, railroads and all the appurtenances of princely position, including a seat in the center of power—the United States Senate.

Nevertheless, despite this grandeur, George Hearst never quite shed his homespun Missouri background. He never indulged in show, social-climbing or sham; even as a Senator in Washington he would not buy himself a dress suit for the fashionable diplomatic affairs. To the end, his best hours were spent with old mining cronies in a San Francisco bar.

Young William, however, was an only child and the apple of his genteel mother's eye. He early manifested a liking for an imperial way of life that eventually filled his manses with more treasures than many royal palaces. Willie was an awkward, lymphatic youth with oversized hands and feet, but he soon caught on to the fact that money had the power to win things he wanted, including the sycophancy of his more-popular peers. At school he often enticed less-solvent classmates into accompanying him to the theater with bribes of candy, soda pop and the most expensive seats in the house. This was a kind of ploy that he would use throughout his life to attract movie stars, famous personalities and world leaders to wait on his favors.

After a short stint at the exclusive St. Paul's Academy in New England, which did little to bring him into the mainstream of traditional upper-class life, Willie was placed in the hands of private tutors. They in turn succeeded in adding nothing to his assimilation of bourgeois mores, so that by the time he entered Harvard College he was already a kind of combination junior Medici, Machiavelli and Mussolini. He was expelled from the university for indulging in pranks such as sending "thunder mugs" (chamber pots) to certain professors—preparation for well-cushioned idiosyncrasy. "It takes a good mind to resist education," he was later to console a grandchild who also came home with low grades on his report card.

At twenty-three, back in San Francisco and heir to twenty-five million dollars, Willie now owned his personal newspaper, the San Francisco *Examiner*, which his father had turned over to him. In a few short years, applying his special brand of "yellow" journalism (a name derived from "The Yellow Kid," cartoon character in one of his newspapers) Hearst made himself the absolute czar of the greatest media empire in the world, in addition to one of its most powerful political figures and richest men. Nothing was out-of-order on his way to the top: "Advice to the Lovelorn" columns, violent comic strips, faked crime stories, scandal-mongering, pseudo-science articles, forged letters and phony photographs pushed his competition to the wall and built a mass circulation that, at its peak, had two out of five people in major American cities reading Hearst publications. Often this success was preceded by tremendous initial losses. But Hearst's confidence was that of a Napoleon and was aptly expressed by his mother. When informed that her son was losing a million dollars a year in the newspaper business, Phoebe Apperson Hearst replied, "Oh, that's too bad; at that rate Willie can hold out for only thirty years."

Somewhere in the early nineteen-twenties William Randolph Hearst began thinking about memorializing his long tenure as unofficial emperor of America with an appropriate symbol. After all, it was he who in effect had been the reigning sovereign in 1898 when his newspapers first declared war on Spain and then forced President McKinley to make the act official under the pressure of imaginative newspaper stories of Spanish brutality in Cuba. Now, even though an ungrateful citizenry had thrice rejected his offer to make his sovereignty official in three attempts at political office, including a try for the White House, he was still the acknowledged "Chief" of a powerful media bureaucracy throughout the world. If he were not indeed official king he was still kingmaker, as he demonstrated in 1932 by helping to secure the presidential nomination for Franklin D. Roosevelt (whom later he was to disown). He would realize his ex-officio royal status with a very real seat of empire. And it would be one that would do justice to a man who owned twenty-nine big-city newspapers and fifteen magazines with a combined circulation of eighteen million, in addition to eight radio stations, four movie companies, five mines, two canning factories, a retail store, forty million dollars in real estate and two million acres of land. In 1924 the decision was made: Citizen Hearst crowned himself the Emperor of San Simeon.

It was no surprise that William Randolph Hearst would have on his royal preserve at San Simeon the world's largest private zoo. Everything he did on the estate was conceived in superlatives. The land itself, cradled among the Santa Lucia hills halfway between Los Angeles and San Francisco, spread over 295,000 acres and fronted a fifty-mile stretch of Pacific Ocean, an area nearly one-third the size of the State of Rhode Island. In effect, San Simeon was a kind of sovereign city-state, a kind of papal enclave in the middle of the State of California with a Swiss Guard of resident cowboys who policed its hills and canyons, including even a village owned by the master in the castle. His castle, La Casa Grande, was perched as near as it could get to heaven on its particular hills, some fifteen hundred feet above the sea, and was built from the components of several castles shipped in crates from Europe. In it were thirty-eight bedrooms, fourteen sitting rooms, thirty-one bathrooms, two libraries, a hotel-size kitchen, a billiard room, Roman swimming pool, movie theater, assembly hall and refectory, in addition to a complete broadcasting and teletype system to all points of the empire. Visiting courtiers, after landing at the private airport, were accommodated in the three adjacent guesthouses, La Casa del Mar, La Casa del Monte, and La Casa del Sol, which, together with the Castle, provided a total of one hundred and forty-six rooms. The Castle's furnishings provided everything that a monarch requires except a throne room, although it did boast Louis XIV's chair and the bed of Cardinal Richelieu. It even housed a modern Madame DuBarry in the person of Miss Marion Davies, the blonde movie star who shared the glories of San Simeon with Hearst for some thirty years while Mrs. William Randolph Hearst lived in her own mansion three thousand miles to the east.

Life at San Simeon was, for the famous guests who were invited by Hearst, one continuous round of high merrymaking, all expenses paid. President Coolidge, Winston Churchill, Greta Garbo, Charlie Chaplin, Bernard Shaw, Howard Hughes, Charles Lindbergh and hundreds of other celebrities from all over the world were made free to indulge themselves with its regal amenities while the host appeared and disappeared according to whim.

Only one command appearance was required of the fifty to sixty guests usually present. That, as reported by Oliver Carlson and Ernest Sutherland Bates, in *Hearst, Lord of San Simeon*,[1] meant that:

". . . everyone must come to the Great Hall of La Casa Grande every evening. First, there is the cocktail hour when guests are, if necessary, introduced to each other by an active and efficient major domo. Sooner or later, Hearst appears, accompanied by Miss Davies, after which there follows something like the grand march in *Aida* to the monks' refectory beyond, where the guests are duly seated in the order of wealth or importance, the two, of course, usually coinciding. Hearst sits in the center and Miss Davies opposite; behind the latter stands a special servant throughout the meal, holding her powder, rouge and lipstick; beside her sits her dog, 'Gandhi,'

1. New York: Viking Press, 1936.

who also has a special servant to bring him his sliced turkey or
ham on a silver platter. A most unusual diet for the namesake of a
vegetarian and ascetic. The china and glassware are varied from
gold. Menu cards are at every place as in a hotel or restaurant.

"Hearst's well-known democratic spirit is shown in several ways.
Formal evening dress is not required. San Simeon must always be
referred to as 'the ranch.' No tablecloths are ever put on the table,
and paper napkins are always served. Homemade preserves (for
which Hearst has a veritable passion), sauces, and condiments are
put upon the table in their native bottles. As Mrs. Older would say,
the 'atmosphere' of a ranch is maintained as far as possible."

There was also one inflexible rule that was never permitted to
be broken: no one, under any circumstances, was ever to mention
in Hearst's presence the subject of death, under pain of "banish-
ment from the Hill."

"The hard-headed realistic journalist who for half a century has
featured in his papers the most horrible crimes of murder," wrote
Carlson and Bates, "the blatant super-patriot who has tried again
and again to force this country into war and send millions of her
sons to slaughter—this man dares not face the thought that the
common fate of humanity will some day touch him too.

"Men say that Hearst does not seem happy at San Simeon. The
guests are not his friends, if indeed he has any friends; they are
those of Miss Davies. The laughter is theirs, not his, and as the
evening passes he is likely to be almost forgotten, an old man with
stooped shoulders and sagging cheeks, seated somewhere in a corner
—but in his hand is a pad, and he is writing editorials. There he
wrote, perhaps with Miss Davies' assistance, that famous one of
October 5, 1933, signed 'An American Husband,' pleading for
the sanctities of the home now threatened by the licentiousness of
the movies."

The Hearst zoo itself, that is, the section where the large animals
were caged, was located close enough to La Casa Grande to be a
part of its general pageantry.

"Pop's zoo," recalled William Randolph Hearst, Jr., second son
of the "Chief" and now editor-in-chief of Hearst Newspapers, "was
set on the Hill just one thousand feet behind the Big House. If

you were in the Della Robbia Room or the Doge Room you could hear the lions roaring. I don't know if we had tigers down there or not. I can't recall. But I do know we had leopards and cheetahs, yeah, cheetahs and these panthers, black ones. But you could see they were also leopards when the sun hit their spots. No snakes, though, thank goodness. Hate the goddamn things."

The old Chief was visible in the blue eyes of his sixty-six-year-old, six-foot son and namesake and audible in the flinty newsman's language that his scion used. "During the day, there was not a whole hell of a lot you could do," said Willie Junior, running his thumbs down the patterned suspenders which supported his blue-serge trousers. "You could ride horseback, drive your car out somewhere for lunch, stroll around the lake, tennis for thems that did, so forth. So the zoo was visited daily, particularly at feeding time. It was fun to see them get fed."

Miss Marion Davies, who slept in the "Celestial Suite" surrounded by paintings of the Madonna, as did the Chief himself in his own suite, left behind another view of life with the wild animals at San Simeon. "Oh, it was gay, let me tell you," she told *Time* in an interview in 1964. "Guests all the time—hundreds of them. I remember we used to toss pebbles at the lions." Echoes of Queen Hatshepsut's animal garden in ancient Egypt or in the Ménageries du Parc at Versailles, where Marie Antoinette occasionally went down to the Rookery to toss maize at the wild geese, or to the *laiterie* to play at being a milkmaid.

"Pop was a great animal lover," said Mr. Hearst. "Anybody who got caught abusing animals . . . he threw them off the Hill, banished them for good. He was very soft about animals. Take the mice, for instance. Big place like the Castle, all that lumber, basements and stuff, we had a few mice now and then. But Pop wouldn't allow them to be caught with those traps that break their backs. He'd catch them in these little boxes and then take them about a quarter-mile down the field and release them. I guess some of the damn things found their way back again. But that's the kind of softie he was.

"Or dogs. Pop spent a lifetime defending dogs. He was one of the country's hardest-working antivivisectionists. Nothing was too much for him if it meant saving a dog from being mistreated. Once when we were on a trip to Gibraltar—about twelve of us, Buddy Collier, me, M.D. [Marion Davies], a couple of others—they wouldn't let us in with Helen and Gandhi. Helen was Pop's and Gandhi was M.D.'s dachshund. 'Well, we'll just go into Spain, then,' Pop said. Someone reminded him that it was night-time and the border closed. That didn't bother him any. He simply woke up the Spanish officials and had the border opened up. And all on account of those two little animals that he didn't want to stay in quarantine."

Hearst's zoo started in 1924 with a pair of lions that were given to him by movie magnate Joseph Schenck. As with any other passion, whether it was newspapers, medieval armor, Greek temples, Renaissance Madonnas or movie stars, once he started, William Randolph Hearst had to collect the best and the most. Before long he had a herd of pure white fallow deer imported from Asia. Polar bears, brown and grizzly bears, elephants, cheetahs, leopards and panthers from Africa, tigers from India, monkeys, gorillas and orangutans, eagles, condors and cockatoos—all were gathered from the four corners of the earth and placed in the cages, pits and aviaries behind the castle. Then came warring yaks from Tibet, llamas from Peru, camels from Arabia, giraffes from Africa, fighting emu from Australia and musk oxen from Greenland. To these were added zebra, cassowaries, gnus, oryxes, kangaroos, gazelles, antelopes, elk, bison, ostriches and water buffalo, all of which were free to roam in a two thousand-acre fenced-in preserve that in many ways resembled the first of the so-called safari zoos. As visitors to San Simeon traveled about the ranch in their cars, a vast assortment of the world's wildlife could be seen grazing in the fields as naturally as though their ancestors had been there for centuries. Often a kangaroo would race by, or a group of ostriches chase after the car for handouts. Camels, fond of the heat held by the blacktop surface, would sleep on the road and have to be driven off. Once a stubborn giraffe, which refused to budge, held up Winston Churchill's entourage for over an hour.

At its peak, there were sixty species of grazing animals in the fields, and another thirty species of mammals and birds in the enclosures and aviaries, a collection that rivaled many of the world's great zoos. It was run by a small but capable professional staff.

William Randolph Hearst on a carousel at his San Simeon estate in California. One-third the size of the State of Rhode Island, San Simeon was a modern Xanadu and contained a two thousand-acre private zoo. (*Courtesy of the New York Public Library Picture Collection*)

Guests came by the hundreds to lunch with Mr. Hearst in his castle at San Simeon and have a rollicking good time. One of the high points of the visit was a trip to the private zoo. At Hearst's left is Miss Marion Davies. *(Courtesy of the New York Public Library Picture Collection)*

William Randolph Hearst (fourth from left) and his sons (from left to right) David W., John R., William R. Jr., George, and Randolph. Randolph is the father of Patricia Hearst. *(Photo credit: International News Service—now U.P.I.)*

Zebras roaming free at San Simeon, 1958.

Another private zoo. Founded by a group of Baltimore Zoo employees who run it in their spare time, and with their own finances and labor, this "storefront" zoo is devoted to the collection of reptiles, particularly species that are endangered.

Two specimens from the Baltimore "storefront" zoo. There are about seventy-five species and one hundred sixty specimens in the zoo, much of which was built of discarded bakery cases and rehabilitated plywood.

The big cats, bears, elephants and other "jungle" animals were kept in cages and pits up near the Castle, and were fed twice a day. The others, the hoofed and grazing animals, wandered about in the preserve set aside for them down in the canyons. These lived mostly off the land but they also had sheds to protect against rain, and hay drops and water troughs up near the roads. It was when these animals came from the fields to get at the hay and water that visitors could observe them close up. Visitors, of course, were those guests who had the privilege of an invitation from the master.

Why did William Randolph Hearst expend such effort and money to amass so vast a collection of animals? Traditionally, as mentioned, the owners of great private zoos have been royal or noble houses. Some of these, as with the Duke of Bedford, have been motivated by a true conservationist interest. Other private zookeepers, such as the Hagenbeck family and the Catskill Game Farm, ran purely commercial breeding and trading operations, while some rich men such as Walter Rothschild had a profound love for wildlife. One wondered what Mr. Hearst's son's explanation of motive would be.

"Pop wasn't given to explaining. My guess is that he did it because it occurred to him. Because it provided something interesting for his visitors to see. He was an entrepreneur himself, you know, producer, showman, film–maker, exhibitor—not like Sol Hurok—but he felt it would add to the general scene. Make driving up and down more interesting. Here he had more than 200,000 acres and if he just turned a bunch of animals loose they'd be all over the place and nobody'd get to see them. So he penned them up in two thousand acres so his guests could see them. But I never thought of it as a zoo."

In their book on Hearst, Carlson and Bates give a further clue. "The lord of the manor has the finest collection of armor in the world, having far outstripped his nearest competitors, Henry Ford and Andrew Mellon. He has the finest collection of old silver, the finest collection of old furniture, the finest collection of stained glass, Gothic mantels, and Mexican saddles. [He even acquired some of the cannon embossed with the Spanish royal seal in the Morro Castle fortress off Cuba after his victory over Spain.] . . . He has collected tapestries and hangings and costumes, choir stalls and ceilings and fireplaces, even mummies—the Lord knows what he hasn't collected! Loot from all over the world is gathered at San Simeon. And the end is not yet. At the foot of La Cuesta Encantata [The Enchanted Hill], strewn along the valley for half a mile, are packing cases full of more treasures for which no appropriate place has yet been found. Underneath La Casa Grande is a two-acre storeroom devoted to the same purpose. And in New York City, near Southern Boulevard and 143rd Street, is an entire block of Hearst warehouses containing, among other acquisitions, a Spanish castle taken down stone by stone, each lettered and numbered, on its way to join the marvels of San Simeon.

"While Hearst's sense of ensemble seems a little defective, there is no doubt that he is a connoisseur of details and particularly of *objets d'art*. . . . He loves to look at them; he loves to pat them and caress them; he loves, above all, to *own* them.

"This is probably the reason for the confinement of his aesthetic interest to dead art. Living art, aside from its simulacrum in the cinema, has always left him cold. He has never shown the slightest concern over any contemporary movement in art; so far as is known, he has never lifted a finger to befriend a single living artist. And living art cannot be torn from its roots and appropriated in the Hearstian manner as dead art can be. The aesthetic impulse throughout Hearst's life has been wholly subordinated to the impulse to *acquire* and *exhibit*."

So the only living "art" at San Simeon would quite naturally be the "finest collection" of animals—artifactry that could be "torn from its roots and appropriated in the Hearstian manner" . . . something which one can "pat, caress, and above all, own." The shy, awkward, unsure boy who purchased his peers' affection with bribes of candy and soda pop, the man who slept with a portrait of the Madonna over his bed and spared the lives of mice and dogs would be a natural to develop an affinity for animals to "acquire and exhibit."

More like Cecil B. De Mille, perhaps, as writer George P. West described Hearst in the *American Mercury* of November 1930: ". . . the strangest and perhaps the most significant figure of our times, holding court (at San Simeon) in Cecil B. De Mille magnificence with movie actors as his courtiers." And, like any eighteenth century monarch, as he sat in Louis XIV's chair or arose from Cardinal Richelieu's bed, he could look past the turrets and guard towers and watch his captive beasts pacing and turning in the royal zoo.

Three generations of Hearsts, including the Chief, his sons and grandsons, have lived with this royal zoo. But the King is now departed and with him went the royal menagerie.

San Simeon, August 17th—"I am writing this column sitting at my father's desk, in his study on the third floor of his big castle at San Simeon," wrote William Randolph Hearst, Jr., in the August 18, 1957, editions of his father's newspapers, of which he was now editor-in-chief. "On the wall of his bedroom is the following quotation from Sir Edward Bulwer Lytton's 'The Lady of Lyons,' which could well have been written about this place:

> A palace lifting to eternal summer
> Its marble walls, from out a glossy bower
> Of coolest foliage musical with birds . . .
> And when the night came—the perfumed light
> Stole through the mists of alabaster lamps,
> And every air was heavy with the sighs
> Of orange groves and music from sweet lutes,
> And murmurs of low fountains that gush forth
> In the midst of roses.

"My heart is heavy and aching and the beautiful panorama gets blurry once in a while, as I know this is the last time we shall ever come here as our home. Later this year the castle and all of its treasures and lovely gardens will be given to the State of California, and from next summer on it will be open to the public to come and see and admire."

That spelled the official end of Xanadu. "Citizen Kane" had passed on at the age of eighty-eight six years before, and now his castle was being deeded back to the citizens of California. The ranch had dwindled by sale of some 200,000 acres to about 75,000 acres—its original size when Hearst had inherited it. What young Bill had called the "zoo," that is, the cage and pit area as distinguished from the wild-animal preserve, had been abandoned and its animals sold or given to public zoos. Now La Casa Grande, complete with its guest houses, its temples, pools, and its treasures, in addition to a peripheral hundred acres, was going to the State.

"There was just no sympathy among the executives of the Hearst Corporation to keep the thing going," said Bill, Jr., "and the cowboys were hostile to this wild-animal business. They preferred their domestic cattle. Just to keep the place in a state of repair and maintain it would have cost several hundred thousand dollars a year. The Hearst Corporation directors figured the State could do a better job. Besides, the showplaces were not native to the 'ranch,' as Pop preferred to call it."

"You mean the Castle and all the treasures?"

"Yeah, the Big House, the guest houses, the zoo, the animals in the field, all that. So the fences were torn down when Pop died, the rarer animals sold, some given to zoos, others just allowed to beat it. We sold some zebra. I know I let a bunch out that they rounded up to send off to a zoo because we wanted to keep 'em on the ranch. And I turned 'em loose one night."

"You did that on your own?"

"Yeah. We did it. My wife and I. They never did take the trouble to round 'em up again because they scattered. There was a big fuss about that, but what the hell."

Many of the animals that escaped have become part of the wildlife of the surrounding forests as did those that were released on the dispersal of that other royal zoo at Versailles. Some, like the snow-white fallow deer, easily visible to predators, were no doubt picked off and became extinct in that area. Others remained as squatters on the ranch, seventy-five thousand acres of which the Hearsts still own.

"I went back last year," said Bill Hearst, Jr. "Some zebra are, of course, still there, part of the bunch my wife and I sprang. In fact we put in a new stallion because they were becoming awfully inbred. There are some elk still roaming way out, and some tahrs and aoudad, big herds of 'em, several hundred. They're tough babies and can fend for themselves. And I saw one or two sable deer down in the canyons, a pair. That's damn near all."

So closed the reign of a man of whom *The New York Times* said, in his obituary: "It is doubtful whether any American ever lived on so lavish a scale"; a man whose granddaughter, twenty-three years after his death, was chosen as the victim of the first political kidnapping in America because an urban guerrilla army considered him "the fountainhead of an American fascist empire"; a man who, *The New York Times* further reported, " . . . often expressed the belief that his mind was the same as the collective mind of the American people, a belief that the American people did not always share."

But to his son he was "Pop" and to his grandson "Grandpop." To his friends and associates he was the "Chief," a guy who, on occasion, could "break you up." Wrote Grandson John, Jr., in the *Reader's Digest* of May 1960: ". . . there was nothing austere about Grandpop. When he was pleased, he liked to do a little dance, sort of a cross between a time step and a jig. Once a group of executives came to San Simeon for his birthday and as he walked into the room they all began to sing 'Happy Birthday.' His face lighted up and when they had finished he did an 'Off to Buffalo,' winding up with his hand outstretched like an old-time vaudeville hoofer. It broke the place up."

The owner of the biggest private zoo of modern times—a man of whose handiwork the visiting George Bernard Shaw said: "This is the way God would have done it if he had the money."

Since God is said to work His wonders in mysterious ways, it is interesting to see now He might have done it without benefit of money. . . .

"La Casa Grande" of 900 South Kenwood Street, in Baltimore, Maryland, is, as was San Simeon, built of artifacts transported from other places. Similarly, it languishes in a perpetual state of incompletion, as did its fabled counterpart on the West Coast. It also not only contains a private zoo but represents for its builders the fulfillment of a lifelong dream.

There the resemblance to San Simeon sharply ends. Nine hundred South Kenwood Avenue is being built not from the components of ancient European castles shipped over piece by piece to the hills of California, but rather from artifacts such as rain-soaked plywood and moldy two-by-fours salvaged from junkpiles on the streets of industrial Baltimore. Moreover, if South Kenwood Street's construction is perpetually unfinished, it is not because of a wealth of material pouring in that far outstrips the ability of its artisans to incorporate it, but because of the very opposite: a perpetual scarcity of money and resources.

As for the zoo, although South Kenwood Street and San Simeon are both private (special invitation is required in each case), they nevertheless represent polar extremes in the insular world of the private zoo, as indeed did the life-dream of multimillionaire newspaper czar William Randolph Hearst as opposed to that of the three Kenwood Street young men—Bob Sinners, Dave Mack and Anthony Wisnieski.

"All of us are lifelong reptile buffs," said Bob Sinners, a college dropout. "I caught my first snake at eight. Most kids beat snakes to death at that age, but I fell in love with reptiles and have been ever since. And three years ago we decided to split the college scene and do something we dreamed about since kids."

What do reptile-lovers dream about as kids that can be done in a "storefront" zoo built of soggy plywood, old bakery cases and electric wire left over from Samuel F. B. Morse? Show the Baltimore Zoo how to exhibit reptiles?

"No, we're not an exhibit zoo," said Anthony Winieski, a tall, lean young man. "The Baltimore Zoo's got a pretty good reptile house, and we're not knocking it. We all work at the city zoo, you know, but many zoos, even the biggest ones, are exhibit-oriented. Take Baltimore's reptile curator, Frank Groves, for instance. Frank's a good reptile man—knows his stuff, keeps his animals alive. Frank believes that when a person comes to the zoo he wants to see the animals. So he keeps his specimens in bare little boxlike cages where the public can see them up close. We believe just the opposite. You ought to make the animal visible, but the first interest of a zoo should be for the animal, not the public. Take that spiney-tailed iguana there," he said, pointing out a specimen that was barely visible under a rock inside an old bakery case. "That's what that particular animal likes: to hide. So we put things in its cage that it can hide behind if it wants to. When you look around this crummy-looking place you might think we're presumptuous, but what we're really trying to do here is make up for a serious shortcoming in the traditional zoo world—that is, to dedicate ourselves to the conservation of reptiles. Most zoos have to worry about the public, so they emphasize exhibition. We're private collectors, so we can do what we want. And six months ago we decided to get our own place to do it in."

Their "own place" was a decrepit, three-story building, set among the white steps of Baltimore, whose ground floor had once contained a pool parlor. At first it served as simply a low-rent base from which the three young men could pursue their collecting work, with Dave helping to defray expenses by living on the top floor, and all of them taking supporting jobs as keepers at the Baltimore Zoo. Although all of them were reptile men, Bob Sinners worked in the Bird House ("Why not enlarge your experience of the animal world?"), Anthony Wisnieski signed on as an elephant keeper, and Dave Mack took care of primates in the Mammal House. But in practically every moment of spare time, often accompanied by girlfriends, the three pursued their missionary work of saving endangered reptiles, going as far afield in vacation periods as the Everglades of Florida.

"The reptile is the forgotten one in the zoo world," said Bob. "How many groups of affluent women who donate to conservation causes do it for reptiles? It's usually birds. 'Oh, how pretty!' they say. Put a baby tiger, a chimp, a blue jay next to a baby snake and see how many people will cough up money to save the snake. Remember the Jack Lemmon movie? It was called *Save the Tiger*. You ever hear a movie called 'Save the Rattlesnake'? People who understand the ecological importance of the reptile and are interested in conserving them can be counted on the fingers of your hands. Somebody had to do something about it."

Soon 900 South Kenwood began outgrowing its role as a base for collecting-forays into that of a depository for local reptilia that the three had saved from the land-developer's bulldozer. The Muhlenberg turtle, for instance—member of a species which had almost been wiped out in Maryland by the construction of Interstate Highway 95. It was also being even more critically endangered by members of the Maryland Herpetological Society who, on the theory that the turtle's territorial instinct was so strong it would not survive removal to new swamps, were sending the few remaining specimens to the Smithsonian Institution for anatomical dissection. Bob and Dave and Anthony, however, instituted a capture-and-release program of their own and, next season, found their tagged specimens of Muhlenbergs alive and well in safe new territories to which they had removed them. Similarly, after reading a study which reported that areas in Maryland where the timber rattlesnake had been exterminated showed a three-times increase in rodent population, as compared with areas where the snake still existed, they began collecting specimens of that snake. Added to these were many other species of reptiles which they were able to buy or trade on the open market.

But what made the little storefront zoo unique was the fact that, where they were able, by capture and purchase, they stocked their collection with breeding pairs and compatible colonies instead of the "one-for-each species" that is the traditional exhibit practice of so many zoos. They also attempted to set up habitats as natural as possible for the rapidly expanding population, which now numbered about seventy-five species and one hundred and sixty specimens—the size of a major zoo collection.

"We had to scrounge around the city streets at night, foraging for old wood to build the enclosures," said Bob. "We had no money, all our salaries went into the work. We chiseled old bakery cases from the baker, panhandled some Vida–Lites from the Duro–Test Company. Dave froze all winter without heat upstairs so that the reptiles that require warmth could have it down here, and I persuaded the experimental lab where I used to work into giving us their expendable mice for our snakes. And because people hate snakes we had to be careful of the neighbors. Even now we get an occasional rock through the window, and the landlord lets the roof fall in here and there. But what would the neighbors do if they knew we had a collection of one hundred and sixty reptiles and an army of rodents in here. They don't even know the meaning of the word conservation."

The door buzzer sounded. Bob's friend Vicki, a young schoolteacher, walked in and called him aside for a few private words.

"Oh, I clean forgot!" he exclaimed, and promptly rushed outside to make a telephone call. In a few minutes he was back with a smile of satisfaction on his face.

"That looked pretty urgent," a visitor remarked. "Forgot what?"

A few hours before, he explained, a friend had alerted him that some entrepreneurs had an inventory of three hundred baby sea turtles which they were selling on the commercial pet market. Not only was the sea turtle an endangered species protected by Federal law, but three hundred was an amount whose removal from their native habitat would deal a heavy blow to the remaining population. "Like losing two of your ten fingers," he said. "Besides, the dealers sell them to people who don't even know what to do with them. They put the babies in these ten-gallon aquariums, not realizing half the time that they'll grow to over two feet in length. Then, because the adults are too big to handle, they usually let them die. They've no right to have them!"

So Bob and his colleagues, unofficial watchdogs against this kind of crime, generally contact Lee Schmeltz, a reptile man at the National Zoo in Washington who as a Federal officer knows which law-enforcement agencies to set in motion to round up the culprits.

"Incidents like this are only a small part of the picture," he said. "One day I saw a group of Boy Scouts out in the country throwing rocks at water snakes. 'What're you doing there?' I yelled, 'you're killing water snakes.'

" 'They're not water snakes,' they said, 'they're water mocassins. They're poisonous.'

" 'There are no water mocassins in Maryland,' I said, and they proceeded to tell me how their scoutmaster told them these snakes were *poisonous* water snakes. So I went over to the scoutmaster and asked him why he had told those kids that. 'Don't you know that these snakes are performing a valuable service killing off sick fish?' They feed on diseased organisms and insure the survival of the fittest —Darwin in action.

"And he said, 'I've been a scoutmaster for thirty years and I tell you they're water mocassins.'

"So I proceeded to produce a copy of *Field Guide of Snakes of the United States and Canada* and showed him that there were no poisonous water mocassins north of the Dismal Swamp in Virginia.

"And he just said, 'Hogwash.'

"Supposed to be dedicated to nature, and here he was killing off snakes that were performing a service."

Dave, who had been sleeping off a bad cold upstairs, brought on by his long winter of freezing, came down to the first-floor zoo. Later his friend Carmela came in.

"It's beginning to change a little in the community now," Carmela said. "The kids don't spray nasty graffiti on the walls anymore. And the old ladies—I've heard them gossiping—they're not too sure just what's going on in here, but they consider that whatever it is, it's a kind of minor blessing. 'The poolhall bums are gone,' they say. 'There're no more drunken fights in front of the place, and those nice young boys at least mind their own business.' "

"Yeah, we're moving along pretty good now," said Dave. "Eventually we hope to have the neighborhood people look in. I have a feeling that when they get to see what we're doing—get to really know something about what the reptile world is—many of them will lose their hostility. Just like Carmela herself did. She was terrified of snakes before she started to work around them."

What the neighbors would see, on invitation to this plywood-and-chickenwire Xanadu, is not an expensive collection of wildlife imported from the far corners of the earth for the amusement of visiting movie stars; nor a perverted concern for the life of a housebreaking mouse or the comfort of a world-traveling dachshund. Instead, they would see exhibits, assembled at considerable personal sacrifices, of micro-communities of reptiles in environments simulating their native habitats. Over here . . . a typical Asiatic exhibit, containing both the rodent-eating Burmese rock python and the lettuce-eating tortoise, animals which coexist peacefully in nature. Down there . . . a typical Central American reptile community: redwood turtles, common and spiney-tailed iguanas, and baskless lizards. "No," you are told, "that spiney-tailed iguana is *not* dead. He just likes to hide"—and in this zoo, he is permitted to do just that—under the exhibit rocks, with no concern that visitors might not be able to see him.

On the right, up above, a typical South American setup: three common boas—one male, two females—and a pair of Cook's tree boas, arboreal, from the same area. The latter grow to great length and have long, thin necks which enable them to move easily from tree to tree. And, at 900 South Kenwood Avenue, they occupy a common enclosure with six redfoot turtles, just as they do in their native South American home: a micro-community in a refurbished old bakery case.

The Florida setup? A pair of Gulf Coast box turtles, largest in North America; two gray rat snakes and one corn snake—no mate yet. Perhaps this summer, after the team's annual vacation to the Everglades, the corn snake will get a mate, but at the moment it waits in celibate expectancy.

In addition the zoo has Mata-mata turtles from South America; two Chinese softshell tortoises (2½ inches long now at one year of age, but thirty inches at eight, when they will fully mature); speckled king snakes, a pair that comes from the swamps of Alabama; tortoises from Africa. "Notice how very flat they are, enabling them to escape from predators by squeezing into narrow slits between rocks and puffing themselves up." Also, Ceylon flapshell turtles, the most primitive type: high-domed, with flaps over their hind parts, like automobile mudguards, to protect their back legs. They are so fast they can outrun a man on land. And observe—most important of all—the great majority of this "storefront" zoo's collection are grouped in breeding pairs and colonies.

"Well, as sure as we can be that they *are* breeding pairs," said Tony Wisnieski. "Breeding is one of our main activities in helping to save threatened species. But we can't afford to buy adult individuals. The difference between a three-foot and a twenty-foot python is several hundred dollars. Or this four-inch turtle here and a twenty-four-inch mature one is maybe a hundred dollars. So we buy the inexpensive baby animals and, at that age, often we can't tell the sex. It's a calculated risk. Their value increases with maturity and if we happen to get two of the same sex, we eventually sell or trade one off. So our potential for breeding is great. Only a small pocket of people are interested in the lower life forms, you know, so somebody has got to breed reptiles. I mean, we're not Noah with divine backing, or Gerald Durrell with his wealthy friends, and certainly not William Randolph Hearst with half the country's money in his jeans. Besides, like you told us, Hearst didn't like snakes anyhow, did he?"

The telephone rang in the "office" (two soggy sofas and some rickety wooden tables rescued from Sanitation Department crunchers) and Bob Sinners hastened to answer it. In a moment he was back with good news. Lee Schmeltz, the team's Washington contact for reporting violation of animal protection laws, had received their message about the smuggling of the three hundred sea turtles. The National Fish and Wildlife Service presumably had gone into action. Three private zookeepers—all volunteers, dedicated Noahs in their early twenties—could now congratulate themselves on having done another small bit in their mission to help clean up modern man's ecological mess. While others of their generation were pursuing money and driving fast cars, Bob Sinners, Dave Mack and Tony Winieski were out hunting down breeding specimens of the endangered timber rattlesnake and tracking down sea-turtle snatchers and destroyers of the "lower orders of life."

"Eventually we hope to move our zoo to Florida, where it's warm, and reptiles are easier and cheaper to maintain," said Bob. "In the meantime, money is our chief problem, but we don't let that stop us. We love this work. All we're looking for is enough to live on, which is what we usually have left from our regular zoo salaries after we finish paying expenses for this work. What we're trying to do now is set up a nonprofit organization and get some donations to help us. But even if we do go south we plan to keep up our efforts in breeding, continue our work with the Muhlenberg turtle, and push on with behavioral studies."

What about exhibiting, that is, setting up a public zoo for the reptile collection as it grows larger and more comprehensive?

"Maybe," said Anthony. "Could be that we'll go public ourselves. Or maybe we might integrate our collection into an already existing zoo that needs a good reptile collection. But it'll have to be run on an animal-oriented basis. Exhibiting will be only a minor role. Until people learn to respect *all* of the animal kingdom, education and conservation are more important than exhibition. Here's an example of why that's true. Last year when we were down in Florida we were riding along a highway and saw a southeastern gopher turtle about to walk across the highway. Bob jumped out to catch it before it got out on the road, where it could easily be hit. Just as he was about twenty feet from it, a car shot in ahead of him and deliberately ran over it. Do you know why? Because some people think it great fun to hear the shell pop when they crush a turtle!"

Perhaps one day, they say, all people will come to have that "reverence for life" of which Albert Schweitzer spoke. Then the private zoo, or at least the 900 South Kenwood Avenue variety, will no longer be the kind of institution to which one must be specially invited.

4 The San Diego Zoo

Anyone familiar with the genus *Taxi driver,* especially the urban variety that roars through American citics dispensing unsolicited opinions, knows how low on the scale of reliability his pronunciamentos often turn out to be. In San Diego, California, a city of 700,000 that acts as a giant USO for sailors stationed at the Naval facilities, the local taxi driver is no exception. Or at least so it seemed initially to a visitor headed in a taxi for a first visit to the San Diego Zoo.

"Finest zoo in the world, that's for sure," pronounced Mack, the San Diego taxi driver as he whizzed the visitor down a somewhat garishly appointed boulevard.

"Finest zoo in the world, buddy, no question about it," he insisted, turning his head around to glare the visitor down. "The Metropolitan Opera's the finest opera in the world, right? Anybody knows that without ever leaving New York, right? Well, I'm telling you San Diego Zoo's the finest anywhere."

Mark one up for Mack, for long before the visitor had sat down to talk with Director Emeritus Dr. Charles R. Schroeder, the "grand old man" of zoos and one of the individuals who gave San Diego Zoo its worldwide fame, he was willing to concede that at least in this instance the taxi driver had been absolutely right. A cursory stroll through the hundred acres of exotic flowers, shrubs and trees that run riot over a Garden-of-Eden panorama of mesas and canyons where wild animals are visible at every turn of the head is enough to convince a visitor that if San Diego's Zoo is not the finest zoo in the world, it is doubtless the most attractive.

"Yes, San Diego's physical attractiveness is one of its outstanding assets," agreed Dr. Schroeder, the seventy-three-year-old veterinarian who served as the zoo's director from 1953 to 1972. "We've got the largest collection of wild animals in captivity on these grounds —that is, if you exclude insects and fish, which would make West Berlin's the largest. And as valuable as the animal inventory is, it doesn't even begin to match the worth of the botanical collection in which it is housed. The trees, plants and flowers in that Garden of Eden you just walked through, not one of which is indigenous, have been appraised at $38 million, about nineteen times the value of the animal collection and they bloom in 330 days of sunshine. So you see we are a real animal Garden of Eden, as you call it. But physical beauty and financial worth are not necessarily the most exciting parts of the San Diego story."

The big story, explained Dr. Schroeder, who is himself part of the legend, was the way this Louvre of zoological gardens was put together. It all grew out of a visit that a physician named Harry M. Wegeforth made to the Panama–California International Exposition in San Diego in 1916. Dr. Wegeforth, an ardent animal-lover ever since as a boy he rescued a small garden snake from a pugnacious dog, was outraged by the plaintive cries of the beasts he saw penned in the tiny cages of the Exposition's second-rate menageries. He vowed to himself that he would build in San Diego an animal garden that, dollar-for-dollar invested, would outdo any zoo in the world. Starting in 1916 with a few scruffy monkeys, coyotes and bears abandoned when the Exposition pulled up stakes, 330 days of free sunshine, and a flair for promotion second only to P. T. Barnum's, that was precisely what the Doctor did—right there at the edge of the very park where the Exposition had displayed its miserable collection.

"Dr. Wegeforth got together three other doctors to form a zoological society," said Dr. Schroeder. "He talked the City into giving him a charter and the use of public land on the pretext of making zoo animals available for the study of medicine. He prevailed upon Ellen Scripps of the newspaper family to drop a few coins into the coffer, and, presto, the Zoological Society of San Diego was in business."

"In business" was about the size of it; "*no* business" would have been a more accurate description of the state of affairs. Not only were there no capital funds to back up Wegeforth's dreams of a great zoo, neither was there public support in San Diego for even a mediocre zoo. Moreover, to many influential citizens the idea of so relatively small and isolated a city as San Diego aspiring to a zoo that would surpass those in the great cities of the world, particularly when set down in a scrubby tangle of mesas and canyons, seemed the product of an unhinged mind.

Dr. Harry's mind could in no way be likened to that of the ordinary influential citizen. His was the vision of the maverick, the eccentric, the walker-where-angels-fear-to-tread. Laying out the zoo on horseback, he went about making plans to combine his scrubby mesas and canyons with moats, and thereby eliminate caging many large animals—a revolutionary advance in American zoo design. Buildings also would be largely dispensed with because San Diego's sub-tropical climate eliminated the need for general heating. In addition, the climate made possible the kind of landscaping that would reproduce the natural environment of many animal species in addition to providing the kind of vegetation on which they fed in the wild. These, and other great potentials, Dr. Wegeforth saw in the very things his critics viewed as insurmountable negatives.

It was a one-man crusade from the very start. The Scripps family, particularly Ellen Scripps, continued to support the project, not only with much of their time and energy, but also with contributions for an animal hospital, and donations for the importation of Mbongo and Ngagi, the first mountain gorillas to go into captivity anywhere. And there was Belle J. Benchley . . . if Wegeforth can be said to have fathered the San Diego Zoo, Mrs. Benchley can be said to have mothered it. Dr. Harry knew what he was doing when, as president of the Zoological Society, he hired the dynamic little schoolteacher, gave her the title of executive secretary and maneuvered her, against much opposition from his Board of Trustees, into active direction of the zoo. Belle Benchley was the first woman ever to run a zoological garden in this country, and without her the San Diego Zoo might never have survived. Without Harry Wegeforth it might never have been born.

"What he went through nobody in his right mind would go through," said Dr. Schroeder. "He was trying to run a zoo in hard times with no money, practically no staff and little if any support from the City government. He had his own money, of course, and lots of that went into it, but he was always short. This fantastic botanical garden you see here—this $38 million paradise—know how much of it got here? Wegeforth got into his Lincoln Zephyr, made trips to Florida, came back loaded to the roof with cuttings of tropical plants. He personally greened the scrubby mesas of Balboa Park with his own hands. 'If only a fourth of what I've planted grows, we'll have a great show,' he told his critics. And it did grow, as you can see. He made a trip to Sumatra, established good relations there and came back with two orangutans, something of a coup in those days. He brought in many exotic birds, one of which still sits on a tree just inside the entrance to the zoo, the oldest inhabitant of the place. He did the same thing in Singapore. He sent a man, at his own expense, to Africa, who came back with a boatload of exhibits for his zoo. I met them myself at the dock in New York. But that's only part of it. For example, he was very concerned about blackhead, a disease of domestic turkeys caused by protozoan organisms—a very serious malady. One day a woman called him in to look at home of her turkeys that had died, and while he was outside busily post-morteming them the woman said, 'You don't mind, do you, but I have to take my husband to a doctor,' and left him out there posting turkeys! Here was a distinguished physician whose medical reputation had so faded away in the service of zoo animals that the public hardly thought of him as a medical doctor anymore."

If, however, *Dr.* Harry's medical practice was beginning to fade out, *Mr.* Harry's zoological reputation was on the rise. Zoo professionals were beginning to take notice of the imaginative way in which Wegeforth was displaying his animals, particularly the way he had reversed the plan used in the East. There animals were generally exhibited indoors in cages along the walls, but at San Diego he made the cages—wherever he was still using cages—part of the outside wall and built sleeping quarters behind them. Thus both people and animals were *outdoors* viewing each other.

"But here's where the really crazy part comes in," explained Dr. Schroeder. "As the zoo expanded, its needs, particularly for money, increased enormously. It was always on the verge, in those early days, of going bankrupt. That didn't stop Dr. Harry. If there were no fish for the seals—and that's all seals will eat—he went out and begged fish on the waterfront. And he could put on a real act, believe me. Another thing he used to do was steal water for the zoo. That's right, actually steal it—rip it off, as the kids say. One day he told the plumber to dig a hole in the street, connect a T-joint to the City's water main and run water into the zoo. 'But that's against the law!' the plumber complained. 'I don't give a damn,' replied Wegeforth. 'The animals need water. You go out and tap that line in.' The City eventually caught up with him, but not before he had tapped the gas and electric lines too."

A combination Robin Hood and Don Quixote, he acquired white pine lumber from a Works Progress Administration project, unused steel rails from railroad yards to reinforce his concrete structures and quantities of poles (Dr. Harry would never dream of cutting down those lovely, exotic trees the people of San Diego were now beginning to love so much) from the unintentionally philanthropic utility company.

"He'd bamboozle the local merchants," Dr. Schroeder said, "into kicking in on the promise of putting up some kind of exhibit that might promote their product. Dr. Harry was a pioneer in that kind of barter publicity. Add P. T. Barnum to the Robin Hood characterization. He took from the rich company to give to the poor zoo, and when he couldn't manage that he used his circus showmanship."

Indeed, he wangled zebras, tigers and camels whenever the circus came to town, not from Barnum, who was dead by Wegeforth's time, but from Barnum's successor, John Ringling. Typical of Dr. Harry's technique was the way he paid off a loan on the first two elephants the zoo acquired. One day he collared John D. Spreckels, one of California's richest men, and asked him why he did not help with the zoo's elephants. "I will help you, provided you can get whiter elephants than some I have now," replied Spreckels, hoping that by referring to some of his less fortunate business deals he could brush Wegeforth off. That was one joke Dr. Harry was determined to boomerang on its maker. He bought a large keg of white powder and four of the biggest powder puffs he could find and turned them over to the elephant keepers with pertinent instructions. Then he embarked on a sustained campaign of telling Spreckels about fantastic fights between king snakes and rattlesnakes until at last the millionaire asked to see one. "Never had a snake fight drag on so maddeningly," Wegeforth wrote in his diary. "An hour and a half crawled by before we could call the king snake victor and rush Mr. Spreckels over to the elephant compound, where the men had been busy wielding powderpuffs. There stood the two snowy white beasts—looking like nothing ever seen before, their black eyes and pink mouths the only spots of color in the large white expanse. The keepers carried out the white color scheme—they too were covered with powder from head to foot. Mr. Spreckels laughed heartily at the fantastic picture and promised to pay not only for the elephant loan but for the compound as well, and, sure enough, in the first mail we received his check for $7,500."

And in that manner the great American institution known as the San Diego Zoo began. It was a combination of "Hey Rube! Here Comes the Sheriff!" and "The Show Must Go On!" Once the Zoo was actually put up for auction for taxes by the city assessor, but none of the attending animal dealers or zookeepers would buy anything because of their high regard for Wegeforth. This, and the resultant public pressure, caused the city fathers to reverse the situation. Instead of demanding tax money from the Zoological Society, they *granted* it tax money: two cents on every $100 collected by the city in property taxes, a provision which was written permanently into the charter.

"I was the only one who got a regular salary," said Dr. Schroeder, "which was because I was paid by the County as a veterinarian to test for salmonella (a bacteria which causes food poisoning), innoculate rabbits, check for rabies and do other county work. And I did it at the Zoo because it had a good laboratory. I had to check for parasites, do post-mortems and all the surgery as well. With

Wegeforth behind you, you put the show on the road, no matter how. Mrs. Benchley, too. She worked harder than any of us, saving nickels and dimes. And when she'd accumulate a few dollars, Dr. Harry would dip into it to buy turtles or something. 'Why, Dr. Wegeforth,' she would complain, 'what have you done to me! You've taken out of my payroll. How will I pay these people?' And he'd say, 'Oh, for pity's sake, how much do you need?' And he'd reach into his pocket, but there was never any money there, and poor Mrs. Benchley would have to scrounge around and find it somewhere. I can tell you, they were really on their uppers!"

Today the San Diego Zoo has a gross budget of approximately $12 million, over which it shows earnings of some $1 million, all of which, since it is a nonprofit institution, is plowed back into its operation. Its annual attendance is around nearly 3 million, half of which is paid at a top of $2.00 for adults, the other half being free to children and those in military service. Some 40 per cent of these vistors come from outside California. Had Dr. Harry M. Wegeforth lived six years longer to attend a zookeepers' convention in San Diego in 1947 he would have heard his creation described by no less a zoo personage than Lee Crandall, general curator of the Bronx Zoo, as "Unbelievable! I've seen things I don't believe, animals almost running loose—specimens of nature I have never seen outside a museum."

Belle Benchley, who died in 1973 at age ninety-one, although never granted official recognition as director of a zoo, which she in fact directed, was nevertheless eventually credited as director emeritus. And seventy-three-year-old Charles R. Schroeder, D.V.M., who raised the Zoo to first rank as director in the years 1953–1972, now is the grand old man of the zoo world, enjoying a retirement. What then of the creation of those people—considered by many to be the world's finest zoo.

The visitor usually arrives by bus, car or cab awash in the brilliance of Southern California sunshine. Even before he reaches the admissions gate his eyes are startled by the intense colors of the tropical plants and shrubs which, together with the swirling flags and pennants that line the approachways, create a dazzling kaleidoscope. Early in the morning when the wind is right, the fragrance of the flora wafts from the other side of the turnstiles, adding to the visitor's sensual delight. Once past the uniformed ex-Marines who practically "pipe you aboard" through the turnstile (San Diego is a mariner's town) the eye is again met with a blaze of color. This time it comes from dozens of shrimp-pink flamingos, quarreling and jabbering, which streak back and forth over the green turf and blue waters of the moated Dryer Lagoon, just inside the entrance. A regal peacock with feathers displayed in full panoply moves through the crowd of flamingos like a king among his courtiers, while red-and-gold Indian jungle cocks peck about his feet like jesters catching at royal crumbs. Up in a tree at the far end of the lagoon sits the oldest inhabitant of the Zoo—the cockatoo who has been there for 49 years. It is a fitting entry into a zoo which, as Dr. Schroeder has said, "even if there were no animals inside, would still be one of the most spectacular botanical gardens in the world."

The old cockatoo's hoarse cries are drowned out by an enormous sound that suddenly booms out from an unseen place, mounts to a huge crescendo, fades just as suddenly and then immediately repeats itself. Sonic boom, a visitor speculates. Navy jets have broken the sound barrier somewhere to the west over the San Diego Naval Base. Or else the Zoo's public relations department—known for its initiative in providing unusual media copy—has installed the San Diego Symphony in the 3000-seat Wegeforth Amphitheater and overamplified the orchestra's brass section trumpeting out a horn passage from Handel's *Water Music*. The weird sounds, one discovers, are actually the cries of gibbons in their open enclosure beyond the tall trees, trumpeting perhaps how good they feel about being gibbons in the open sunlight and open space of the San Diego Zoo. This uniquely zoo music, which can be heard at a distance of two miles, together with the ballets of the long-stemmed birds in the Dryer Flamingo Lagoon—these are the sights and sounds with which a visitor on foot opens a day at the San Diego Zoo in Balboa Park.

There is also the San Diego Zoo guided bus tour. "We were the first in the country to provide guided bus tours around a zoo for the public patrons," Dr. Schroeder had said. "It began in 1926 with two Model-T Ford buses and worked up to a fleet of eighteen modern vehicles from which 45 percent of our visitors get their first view of the zoo. No zoo in the world has quite as popular a guided tour as ours. The passenger is seated up high enough in the bus to see over the heads of the people standing in front of the enclosures. You are close to the animals, you can easily photograph them, even read the exhibit signs. And the drivers know how to relate their commentary to the animal the passenger sees. 'If you want a cut-rate looksee at the animal kingdom, get yourself a seat on the bus . . . adults, $1.25; under sixteen, 75 cents,' is his advice.

"Ladies and gentlemen, a word of advice at the start," announces the bus driver at the takeoff of his open, windowless vehicle. "Keep your arms and other parts of the body inside at all times. The Zoo's charms include winding roads and deep canyons and your own closeness to the exhibits. Let's all come back from this tour in one piece." Thus Richard Knowles, one of the dozen or so drivers who pilot the tour buses around the Zoo, begins his act. And the San Diego Zoo guided tour is just that, a charming, witty show—in the tradition of San Diego's longtime theatricality—in which the animals become characters in a panoramic, informative revue. Knowles brings to his performance a pleasant midwestern tone, livened by its resemblance to the twang of Jimmy Stewart.

"Okay, let's take a look on down this road and see the Monkey Mesa down there," he begins. "We have the gorillas down there way on out past the bougainvillea. Gorillas, orang-utans, chimpanzees and other great apes are in large, open, moated enclosures where they are extremely visible. You can go down there later and see them close up, completely out in the open." San Diego's subtropical climate permits the Zoo to show practically all of its animals out-of-doors all year round. People and animals view each other, almost eyeball to eyeball, across a moat or other natural barrier. All this in a center-city zoo.

Coming down past the Dryer Flamingo Lagoon the tour resumes: "Here we have four different kinds of flamingoes, two from Africa and two from North and South America. They're nesting on their eggs now—you see them on those volcano-shaped mounds. Here's a male peacock displaying his feathers (the regal monarch the visitor previously saw at the entrance) and a beautiful macaw, a parrotlike bird from the South American tropics. And on the tree is King Tut, a salmon-crested cockatoo from the Spice Islands given to us by the big-game hunter Frank Buck in 1925, which means he has been here forty-nine years. You can see he's in pretty good condition now even though we don't know how old he was when we got him. Up here through the windshield of the bus you see the Wegeforth Bowl, where the sea-lion show is held, and then the reptile house, the red-tiled building, and beyond it the Children's Zoo."

The Children's Zoo is an exhibit Dr. Schroeder claims is perhaps San Diego Zoo's best. The winding, one-way traffic pattern and the numerous exhibits are designed for child-size viewers. Children ride atop a slow-gaited tortoise; rub noses with a baby antelope; stroke a baby leopard's spotted fur; peer at seals through underwater windows; hold a baby chick in their hands; delight when a baby elephant tickles an outstretched hand with its trunk in search of peanuts.

As for the sea-lion show, "Yes, I am against putting zoo animals through theatrical performances on general principle," said Dr. Schroeder. "That's not the way to educate people about the real life of the animal world. But seals are an exception. They are a sport-loving animal, and they like the shows as much as we do. They come to it naturally."

Now the driver comes to the entrance to the Skyfari Ride which, he explains, is a cable-car excursion that carries visitors 1850 feet from a starting point near the entrance to the Children's Zoo up to the Deer Mesa. The Skyfari, opened in 1969, was the first in America and provides a breathtaking view of the Zoo from six stories above the ground.

"We are entering Cascade Canyon now, the site of the Zoo's major exhibit changes. And here we have a vanishing species . . . a Malayan tapir, a very distant relative of the horse and the rhinoceros. They were found quite commonly over the face of the earth thirty-five million years ago, but now are restricted to the Malayan Peninsula and the Amazon rain forests in another two species.

"Here we have the upper falls of Cascade Canyon. There are 1600 gallons per minute coming over that falls, all man-made. It took eight million pounds of rock to build these waterfalls.

Harry Wegeforth, M.D.—the physician who founded the San Diego Zoo. *(Photo credit: San Diego Zoo)*

Dr. Charles Schroeder, Director Emeritus of the San Diego Zoo, and Arthur Godfrey. *(Photo credit: San Diego Zoo)*

Mrs. Belle J. Benchley, former director of the San Diego Zoo, with leopard cubs. Mrs. Benchley was the first woman director of a major zoo in America. *(Photo credit: San Diego Zoo)*

The chubby gray Koala is the living counterpart of the Teddy Bear. A tailless marsupial from Australia it devotes most of its life to eating and sitting in a tree. Only San Diego and San Francisco zoos are permitted by the Australian Government to import specimens because those zoos grow the eucalyptus tree on whose leaves the Koala feeds. (*Photo credit: San Diego Zoo*)

"Queen Victoria" sits be-shawled on her throne as visitors pass on the San Diego Zoo guided bus tour.

Giraffes "at liberty" in the open spaces of the San Diego Wild Animal Park. No auto-mobile (except a service ve-hicle) ever enters the park. The animals are viewed from an electric monorail, in a natural non-polluted environ-ment.

Arabian Oryx at the eighteen-hundred-acre San Diego Wild Animal Park, thirty-five miles outside the city. Note how the horns of the pair at the right look as though they are one instead of two. This illusion is thought to have given rise to unicorn legend. *(Photo credit: Ron Garrison, San Diego Zoo)*

A giraffe is easily seen closeup in a cageless, moated enclosure as the zoo bus carries visitors around the San Diego Zoo.

Now we're going under a hanging bridge modeled after bridges in Africa . . . There's what we call a yellow-backed duiker over there in the palm trees. This whole place has African animals and plants in it, a simulation of the mountains of Africa.

"Over on this side is the largest of the pig family—Lotus Blossom, the hippo, and her son Duffy. Duffy's mother was born in this zoo. . . . Here's his grandfather and grandmother now, Rube and Ruby. Hippos can walk underwater, which is just what grandma's doing now. Even with their lungs full of air they don't rise to the top. They can stay sound asleep under water because of an automatic reflex which makes them rise to the surface for air and go back down without waking up.

"Over on the other side is the Australian emu, the third largest bird. The emu lays a very interesting egg: the size, shape and color of an avocado. The female lays all her eggs in the same nest and then goes galavanting off to the woods, leaving the male to incubate, hatch and raise the young.

"And here's the second largest bird, the cassowary from New Guinea. A very powerful bird; its feathers have no quills, they're more like long hair or fur. Cassowaries are flightless birds but they can run thirty-five miles per hour, and they can kick like mules. Like the emu, the females also go off and leave the males to raise the young."

As the bus careened around the bend, a clutch of the red-and-gold Indian Jungle cocks that had been crowing and strutting by the hundreds all over the place grudgingly yielded the road. Two free-roaming baby rabbits continued to munch calmly on shrubs. Even the least exotic of creatures seemed secure and at-home on the grounds of the animal-oriented San Diego Zoo.

Now the bus passed the long-legged South American maned wolf, the so-called "fox on stilts." Next came a baby mountain lion asleep on a rock, an aardwolf—a member of the hyena family that burrows and sprays a skunklike odor—and a beautiful little golden cat of Asia, which drew "ohs" and "ahs" from the passengers.

Dick Knowles nodded toward the porcupine enclosure. "He's not all that bad, you know. Porcupines don't shoot their quills at people, as so many may think. You must touch them first. Then the quills stick to you better than they do to the porcupine.

"Look over here now, behind the box. That's a fennec, a tiny fox and the smallest member of the dog family. They only reach a weight of two pounds, and those large ears, which are characteristic of desert animals, are not for hearing. You can hear very well in the desert. The large flat surface of those ears help them to lose excess body heat. Next to him is the serval, the spotted cat from Africa. That little fellow can jump ten feet straight up to catch birds in flight. Now here's the striped hyena asleep and there's the laughing hyena, largest of the species. He has the strongest jaws of any animal in the world. Been known to crush the forelimb of an ox with a single bite. And that nifty little fellow coming up is the African hunting dog. They hunt in large packs, killing everything they come to, hungry or not. Even lions make way for these fellows."

Now there was a short stretch of road unoccupied on either side as the bus proceeded from one canyon to another. Over to the left, beyond the peripheral fence of the Zoo's grounds, the passengers could get a glimpse of the California freeway traffic pouring north and south over Interstate 163. Knowles pointed out the difference between the "freedom" of the motorists competing for space on the crowded freeway and that of the animals "imprisoned" in the spacious enclosures of the Zoo.

"Over on your right," he pointed out, "you have the highest fence of the San Diego Zoo, designed to contain the most dangerous, active and aggressive of all wild animals—the North American road hog. They're still quite common at this time, as you can see down there on the freeway, but they may soon be in danger of extinction due to shortages of their favorite food.

"Now look up here, those are red kangaroos from Australia. Kangaroos are marsupials, which means that their new-born are only half-developed and are fed and carried in their mother's pouch. A kangaroo, which can weigh as much as two hundred pounds at maturity, is no bigger than the tip of your little finger when born. He has two arduous tasks to complete before he has any success at all. First he has to find his way to that pouch all by himself and second he has to find the snack bar [mother's teat] once he gets there."

Now the African Plains exhibit came into view. Here there were

Thomson's gazelles, Grant's zebras, impalas and other hoofed and horned animals, including the oryx, an African animal which when seen in profile looks as though he has one horn and is thought to have given rise to the unicorn legend. The scimitar-horned oryx is now almost extinct in the wild, partly due to oil-company employees in Africa who use their high-powered rifles to slaughter them for "sport." Some zoos, however, particularly San Diego, have managed to save and breed enough individuals to keep the species going.

"There's Archy, the tallest animal in the zoo, seventeen feet high," announced the guide. "Notice how giraffes walk with both feet off the ground on one side and then both off the ground on the other. That's called pacing—takes a long time to teach a racehorse that but giraffes do it naturally. They also have seven vertebrae in that long neck, same as you and I. And a powerful kick, most powerful in the animal world. Been known to kick the head off a full-grown lion with a single blow. See the hole in that metal gate in the giraffe enclosure? Looks suspiciously like the shape of a hoof, doesn't it?

"Humpless camels, over on your right. We have four kinds. That one with the white coat is a llama, a breed used by the Inca Indians to carry loads over the Andes mountain trails. The one with the brown coat is an alpaca—she's got twelve pounds of wool growing on her. Over there, that's the guanaco, wild ancestor of those two. And the fourth one is the vicuna, another wild camel. His wool is the finest in the world, costs $3,000 for an overcoat. You may remember he almost caused a Watergate in the Eisenhower administration with all those White House people walking around with gifts of vicuna overcoats."

Back down the road to another exhibit the bus meandered slowly, working its way through the strings of spectators walking from one exhibit to another. As the big vehicle threaded its way over horseshoe turns and figure-eight roadways, the visitor could imagine some of the problems Dr. Harry must have confronted when on horseback he laid out his zoo in the thick tangle of mesas and canyons. And yet a single turn of the head reveals how successfully he worked out his imaginative plan of utilizing the natural topography of the park. In every direction there is something to see. Down in a grotto a group of chimpanzees chase each other across a log; behind, in another canyon, bears are fishing in a pool; up on a hill sable antelope graze—birds and aquatic and land mammals provide an amazing panorama, a giant multimedia show.

Now the bus arrives in the area occupied by many animal species which have been reduced by man to near or total extinction in nature. The blackbuck, a beautiful antelope from India totally extinct in the wild for over a hundred years, is now extant only in zoos. Przewalski's wild horse, the only true wild horse in the world today, ancestor of our domestic horse, is practically nonexistent outside of zoos—San Diego has twelve of them. This is the small, swift Mongol steed whose stamina and speed helped Genghis Khan carve out his vast empire. And there's the American plains bison, the largest land animal in the western hemisphere, sixty million of which existed when Columbus arrived, reduced by unchecked slaughter to about fifty individuals. Now, as a result of measures by zoos and other conservationists, they number about twenty-five thousand and at least are no longer in danger of extinction. Finally the bus moves past the wallowing ground of the African Cape buffalo, perhaps the most savage and dangerous of all big-game animals, even though he's a vegetarian. The tour was now on the farther side of the Zoo, abreast of the western terminus of the Skyfari.

"Speaking of sky," said Dick Knowles, "here are some animals that live as close to the sky as you can get. See those wild yaks from the high mountains of Tibet? Without them the people who live up there would not be able to survive. The yak provides meat for the table and its heavy fur is used to line the walls of the mountain-top houses as insulation against the bitter cold. And here are some Tahr goats who live at a higher point than any animal in the world—15,000 feet up in the Himalayan Mountains.

"Now let me tell about some of our birds. We missed the ostriches as we went by their enclosure, but you can stop by and see them after you get off the bus, which is what you of course should do with other exhibits that interest you. The ostrich is the largest bird, flightless, weighs up to three hundred pounds and has two toes on each foot. One of the toes is getting smaller and will probably disappear eventually. But his toenail is getting larger and may very likely become like the hoof of a horse, so that one day, if anybody's still around, he may well be seen running at Santa Anita racetrack with the thoroughbreds. An ostrich can run at thirty miles an hour now, with two toes. And its egg is the equivalent of three dozen hen's eggs and would make an omelet a yard wide if you were able to get hold of one.

"We also have one of the most magnificent of all creatures, over in the hummingbird walk-through aviary, which is something you should make a point to visit. The hummingbird is the smallest of birds, the tiniest being only about two inches long. Yet this tiny creature requires the greatest input of energy of all living things. That's because its wing-beat is so fantastically rapid that it can hover in mid-air or execute sharp turns from a stationary position. The humming sound comes from the speed of its wing-beat. In addition to thousands of other birds—we have some 3000 of them —San Diego has the largest collection of parrot species in the world, some two hundred. They're also over on the bird side. Eagle owls, storks, crested cranes, hornbills, birds of paradise, condors, toucans, secretary birds—you name it, we've got it—and you owe it to yourself to go over to the bird section and have a close look at them."

Now the bus was swinging up the canyon again to complete the final and what is no doubt the most popular part of the forty-minute guided tour—the exhibit of lions, tigers, bears and elephants.

"Take a look at that handsome fellow up there on the shelf. That is the Bengal tiger, favorite of maharajahs and big-game hunters—not many left thanks to the hunters. These fellows have a reputation for being man-eaters. Actually, they're not. Only one out of five hundred gets around to dining on *homo sapiens,* and that's usually an old, tired and wounded cat who can catch nothing else. Once they taste human flesh, however, they develop a preference for it because we have salt in our blood and they like salt. . . . There's the Siberian tiger, the largest cat in the world; biggest one ever shot weighed 847 pounds. And down there are the African lions, a male, a female and three cubs. That's the male off to the right, the three cubs are up on the sleeping platform, and the tail of the female is sticking out from behind that big rock. The lion is the only big cat allowed to remain with the female after the cubs are born because the male is so gentle he will not harm the babies. As you can see, all these big mammals are in open enclosures surrounded by moats instead of caged. Considering this is an urban zoo with only a hundred acres to house thousands of animals, each individual has plenty of space.

"There are our polar bears, but they're taking a siesta so let's not bother them. Now what do we have here? Yogi and BooBoo, our North American grizzly bears. They just finished their siesta."

"What're you doing?" says Dick, throwing a piece of food at the bears. "Cleaning your teeth or blowing us a kiss?" The bear responds by catching a piece of Zu Preem, a processed zoo animal feed, in his mouth and waving his paw in greeting.

"And here's Chester, our most talented bear. Chester is an Alaskan Peninsula brown bear, the same bear as the Kodiak, which is the largest bear in the world. They get up to seventeen hundred pounds. You going to do your sliding-into-the-pool-with-your-tongue-hanging-out trick? [which Chester does and catches the Zu Preem flung from the bus]. Good, now wave. Okay, here's our dancing bear, Mark. Mark, will you give us a big salute, a really sharp salute? That's not a sharp salute, ah, *that's* a sharp salute. These little spectacled bears do really good work, don't they?

"Here are the sun bears, the smallest of the bears, from the Malayan Peninsula. This is Straw Bear. She's going to show you the tooth she had extracted—lower right canine. And Razz Bear, and Boysen Bear. Boysen Bear, back by the tree, is going to wave to you, and Razz Bear, coming up on the side here, has the longest tongue in the Zoo."

"How do they get them to do that?" asks a passenger.

Here one sees a zoo functioning in its best tradition of entertainment, a far remove from the dressed-up chimpanzee acts and the bear-boxing-a-kangaroo shows. None of the bears was doing anything that was not natural to him. None was performing an act that had been forced on him. How they got them to do that was simply a matter of intelligent, humane training. Every bear sticks out its tongue, waves a paw as if in salute, slides backward into water, does dancelike turns and many other "human" movements naturally. What the zoo people do is observe and reward the young animal when he performs one of these actions spontaneously. With successive rewards the "trick" becomes established and is executed on demand.

Dick Knowles now brought his bus down past the few remaining exhibits on the tour, which still did not cover the total population of the zoo. Important places such as the reptile house, the great-apes enclosures, and the flight cage for birds were left to the visitor to see on foot, because of readier accessibility that way. What remained of the tour was mostly the elephants. Off on one side near the end of the ride was visible a small rabbit-sized furry animal named the hyrax (popularly called the coney, as mentioned earlier), the only living relative of—unbelievable!—the elephant.

"And over here on the other side," said Dick, in a reverse of ordinary perspective, "is the only living relative of the hyrax—the Asian elephant. The Asians are the ones in the circus, the ones that haul out the teakwood logs, the ones in all the trained elephant acts. They are the work-and-performing variety. Notice that they have large heads, small ears, a high rounded back and a shape like a blimp.

"The African bush elephant, on the other hand, these down here, have a high sway back, small head and large ears . . . before we go, take a look at that blimp over there—that's the African black rhino, the hostile and dangerous animal that you see in the movies knocking over Land Rovers. And they're really fast-moving—they have a policy of charge first and ask questions later. They can only see about ten feet ahead, which leaves them very little time to make decisions. Not that they make good ones anyway. They have a brain the size of a tennis ball and have been known to charge full-bore into a speeding locomotive.

"And now we'll get *this* locomotive off the road and close the tour with a look at the koala "teddy" bear—that is, if we can find him. The koala was one of San Diego's greatest acquisitions. Comes from Australia and feeds on eucalyptus leaves, which we grow right here on the zoo grounds. There are only five of them on exhibit outside of Australia and they are all right here in San Diego. That's because this little marsupial was once nearly extinct, and before the Australian Government would allow any to be exported it made sure the animals would have a good supply of their basic food—fresh eucalyptus leaves. San Diego got the koala because it has eucalyptus trees growing here on its grounds. Well, it looks as if we won't see them from the bus, . . . they spend most of their time in the trees. . . ."

Richard Knowles is representative of that new breed of person now becoming associated with zoos, although, having been around animal gardens for some ten years, it must be said that he is already something of an oldtimer.

Like so many other zoo people, particularly the younger generation, he is college-educated, animal-oriented, and responsive to what might be called the new nonreligious spirituality. Dick does not wear his hair long (San Diego, for unstated reasons, does not permit hair to "exceed two inches in height from the crown of the head nor cover any portion of the ear nor touch or extend over the collar; beards also are not allowed nor may mustaches extend beyond the corners of the mouth"). But length of hair would be no clue to the character of this man's inner lifestyle in any case. That would be evidenced by his actions, not appearance.

Knowles majored in zoology at college and taught school in San Diego for fourteen years. During that time he also periodically drove a zoo bus, in addition to giving lectures on the whale when the great schools came through off Port Loma. He eventually became disenchanted with the way young people were being educated in the public-school system and "just kinda blew out." He joined a commune, traveled the United States with his comrades for a while, and then went into the Mojave Desert, built a cabin and lived by himself for four years. After that he roamed northern California for a year and then moved back to San Diego and took up driving the zoo bus again.

"I'm now with the Arica Foundation," he said. "Arica is a kind of self-discovery organization. I just finished a forty-day intensive training program. I'm really worn down now. What I'm trying to do is get enough money together to go to New York and take the advanced Arica course. Then I'll probably go to Hawaii and work in Arica House there.

"The big thing in life is ego-reduction. Just living is one long, hard road and a big help in making it is to trim the ego's demands. But I'll always be around animals, I guess, no matter where I am.

Because another way of finding yourself is to relate to the whole of life. We're all part of one big animal family."

For years San Diego Zoo officials had been brainstorming the idea of a truly *natural* zoological garden located well beyond the steel and concrete of center city, where "one big family" of exotic species could live together in surroundings similar to their native homelands. "Lion Country Safaris" and "Jungle Habitats," so-called drive-through zoos where animals roam "free," had already come into existence in the United States, but although many of these latter were a considerable advance over the city-based zoo, they were essentially what their name implied—drive-through affairs where the "free-roaming" animals were confronted by long lines of exhaust-spewing automobiles cutting through their habitats. San Diego, on the other hand, wanted a true wild-animal park, a type of zoological preserve that would be unencumbered as far as possible by human intrusion within the animals' territory, a place where the occupants, especially the endangered species, were free to breed and reproduce their kind and otherwise live according to natural behavior patterns and still be available for observation by zoo-goers.

In 1964 the San Diego Zoological Society got what it was looking for. The City Fathers cooperated with the wild animal park idea by including a provision for such an installation in its master plan for the 11,000 acres of land which the municipality owned in the San Pasqual Valley. Eight years later, in an 1800-acre tract of virgin chaparral flanked on all sides by the primitive hills of the California coast range—thirty miles north of San Diego but still within city limits—the nation's first nongovernmental, noncommercial wild-animal park came into being.

The ride by bus from the Downtown Zoo to the Wild Animal Park is an important part of a visitor's program. In spanning the distance from urban squeeze to rural space as it does, the trip parallels those recent changes in zoo philosophy that have seen the removal of the zoo animal from steel cage to open preserve. Moreover, it is conducted in the usual San Diego tradition—authenticity spiced over but not drowned with a pleasant layer of theatricality. Bus driver Bob Cowan, as does Dick Knowles, gives a running commentary based on a script of his own contrivance (San Diego Zoo bus drivers all seem to be amateur actors). Bob Cowan, however, stresses history over zoology.

He hooks his audience with a typical showbiz ploy—a comic bit for starters—in this instance pointing out the spot on the highway where the "first Indian streaker, Chief Running Bear, once lived." A few miles farther out of the urban part of the "cleanest city in the world," however, the script takes a more serious but still historical turn. There the passengers see the real thing (no Disneyland reconstructions here)—a little mountain called Mule Hill where a famous battle took place in the American struggle to take the West from its original owners. Up on top of the hill, Bob recounts, 150 Federal troops were cut off by a large band of Mexican Indians and reduced finally to eating their own mules. But Kit Carson, a kind of one-man CIA of the period who was operating in the area, managed to slip through the lines with intelligence of enemy dispositions. A large United States force was rushed from the main base to route the Chicanos and soon the Federals were dining not on mule but on juicy bison steaks, while yet another chunk of California fell to the Stars and Stripes.

Bob next began ticking off the names of more Sans and Santas than a visitor could keep up with—San Diego, San Pasqual, Santa Maria, Santa Clara . . . puzzling to a tourist until he learned that another conquering force also had left its mark on the virgin West. The early Spanish padres had erected missions to nearly every patron saint, spreading them one day's journey apart, or every thirty miles, up the entire length of the California coast. And so there was virtually no place along the whole of "El Camino Real" (the main highway) where the itinerant Indian, or the Spanish colonist for that matter, could evade the clerical influence—if in name only.

Outside the window could be seen the least attractive consequences of this zeal when misplaced and abused. Former royal Spanish land grants, now broken up into squat housing developments, featured "all modern conveniences." And side-by-side with these were farmlands mechanized to a point of human disappearance and serviced by immense movable irrigation pipes on wheels.

Soon the bus leaves behind this modernity and is careening over country roads through virgin land ripe with grape, alfalfa and avocado. Finally it is in an area more compatible with what it is headed for—wild, bare terrain, with the scarred hills of the coastal range beyond. Not so bare, however, that, as Bob warned, "the land-developers wouldn't like to get their hands on it and mutilate it. But that won't ever happen here because we're now in the San Pasqual Agricultural Reserve, which is where the Wild Animal Park is located."

As the bus enters the Park over a wood-plank bridge that buckles by deliberate design, the feeling of a return to nature is intensified. "The bridge was intentionally constructed that way," explains the Wild Animal Park's official designer, Charles R. Faust. "We based it on the scare-safe principle. The purpose of this kind of entrance-way to the Park was to provide for the visitor a psychological break between the secure world of modern civilization that he has just left and the unpredictable world of nature that he is now entering."

Inside the Park, this unpredictable world of nature is represented chiefly by the 1800 acres of veldt and hill, among which some 1500 wild birds and beasts live. These can be observed, from an unin-truding monorail, eating, sleeping, fighting and mating in the field according to their natural inclination. There are, however, a number of other exhibits of a more artificial character, such as an Elephant Bath where the big animals are washed, chiefly, it seems, for the benefit of hordes of tourist photographers. There are also a Kraal [corral] in which docile animals can be petted, a simulated Congo River fishing camp, and synthetic grottos that house gorillas. Not-withstanding their artificiality, these primate enclosures are immense departures even from the already revolutionary primate enclosures at Downtown San Diego—the Gorilla Grotto, for instance, a 300-foot moated enclosure with a floor of grass instead of the usual concrete. And the Giant Aviary, although really a giant cage, is enclosed with a net which permits the entrance of natural light and air, and is the largest free-flight cage in the world. Moreover, there are structures of a commercial nature, such as the Nairobi Village complex of shops and exhibits, a Mombasa Cooker where one can eat and drink, and a performing animal show. But these too are essential compromises with the Zoo's need for revenue and the human taste for a bit of light diversion.

The latter is provided by San Diego Zoo's official ambassador to the world of entertainment, the attractive Joan Embery who, when

she is not chaperoning animals on Johnny Carson's Tonight show
and making other appearances, serves as ringmistress in the Wild
Animal Park's amphitheater. Ms. Embery puts elephants, pumas
and other wild beasts through their paces at regular intervals in
exhibitions at which many visitors make their first stop after leaving
the Giant Free-Flight Aviary. A former keeper in the Downtown
Children's Zoo, and notable in the zoo world, Joan Embery is not,
as her beauty might suggest, a Hollywood starlet turned animal trainer
but rather the reverse—a zookeeper who functions as occasional TV
performer. Children love her, animals love her and, without doubt,
the audience loves her.

The biggest attraction at the Wild Animal Park is the five-mile,
fifty-minute monorail ride around the animal preserves. These preserves are divided into six ecological sections separated by natural
barriers—the savannas of East Africa; the Asian plains; the mountains of North Africa; the Asian swamps; the Australian plains; and
the veldt of South Africa. Lions and other predators are of course
segregated from their prey but they are visible close up as the monorail pauses at their territory. And, as the electric train, silent and
unpolluting, proceeds around the other ecological sections, groups
of compatible animals—such as the rhinos, waterbucks and ostriches
in the South African veldt—can often be seen challenging each other
for territoriality. On one spot an ostrich is observed threatening another as the intruder passes too close to the mound of sand where
it is incubating its eggs; while in another place a big waterbuck
lowers its horns at a white rhino in a gesture of defiance over possession of a waterhole. Giraffes go bounding across the savanna,
seemingly in slow motion, as they do in animal movies—for the immense spaces allow wild animals to indulge in natural behavior.
Barbary sheep are perched all about the craggy rocks, as they are
in North Africa; Cape buffalo low and moan in the muddy swamps;
and two wild Golden eagles, uninvited but welcome guests, swoop in
to the nests they built for themselves on a mountaintop.

These are the natural features that foster instinctual behavior—
and make the San Diego Wild Animal Park the enormously important sanctuary that it really is. And in this respect the Wild Animal
Park is different from practically all other zoos in the country.

The "flight-distance" behavioral reaction, for example, is an instinctual reflex that almost every animal has and rarely has an opportunity to express in conventional zoos. Flight distance is the space a wild animal keeps between itself and a potential enemy. If a man or other enemy approaches within, say, one hundred feet (there are fixed distances for each species) the animal will put another hundred feet between itself and the enemy or will attack. It will stand there and stare at the intruder, and if the intruder again pierces that barrier, it will once more take flight and so *ad infinitum*. The animal seesaws between two instinctual drives—to remain in its own territory and to keep itself at a distance from which it can escape the enemy. Even the drive-through zoos short-circuit the expression of this instinct, for in most cases the best of them corral their animals in cleverly concealed enclosures that lack sufficient space for many animals to maintain their natural flight distance. The result of this instinctual frustration is often an animal that is seriously disoriented.

San Diego Wild Animal Park, however, provides ample space, free of restricting barriers, for the full play of the flight-distance reflex. In the main this is because it is structured to be a wild-animal sanctuary with incidental public sightseeing, while most drive-throughs operate on the opposite principle. Consequently it has had an enormously successful breeding program, particularly among some of the endangered species. The cheetah, for instance; at last count twenty of these increasingly rare cats, notorious for their poor breeding record in captivity, were born at the Wild Animal Park—an astounding performance.

Or the white rhino, another rare animal. "We had a breeding pair at the Downtown Zoo," said Dr. Schroeder. "We gave them a big exhibit, lots of room, but instead of breeding they lived together as brother and sister. We then bought twenty white rhinos from Ian Player in South Africa, most of them females. We sent them up to the Wild Animal Park and after they were established there we sent the big Downtown Zoo bull up there as well. Why, that fellow didn't waste a minute in breeding all those females, one right after another so that we had nine born and seven raised. We also sent the old downtown cow up there—the gal he'd only looked at all those years—and he promptly bred her too. I guess he didn't know what he was missing until he got to the Wild Animal Park. It was such a phenomenal breeding achievement that the behaviorists descended on us in droves to study scenting, mating, feeding, territorializing, the whole bit."

The man who assembled the Wild Animal Park's enormous collection, at thirty-seven, a rather young man, considering the magnitude of the job, is Dr. James M. Dolan Jr., the Park's General Curator. A tall slender Irish-American, Jim Dolan looks more like the male star of a romantic Broadway musical than like the man who at one time tracked down the world's largest collection of parrots—some 200 species for San Diego Downtown—and later, nearly a thousand animals for the Park. Perhaps Dr. Dolan's ability to ferret out hard-to-find individuals could be said to come naturally, for his father was a detective in the New York City Police Department and there is still a hint of the Irish brogue in his lilting voice. As a boy in New York Jim Dolan was already preparing himself for his future assignment with his job of keeping an eye on the denizens of Roland Lindemann's Catskill Game Farm, "the typical syndrome of an urban kid going nuts over animals."

The job of collecting the specimens for the Wild Animal Park goes down as perhaps the all-time biggest one-shot gathering of zoo animals in history, if Ptolemy II or William Randolph Hearst is excluded. Jim Dolan prepared for this enormous project by obtaining a doctorate in Zoology in zoo-conscious Europe at the Christian Albrecht University in Germany. "Actually I'm a mammalogist, a taxonomist—somebody who works on the relationship of mammals to each other—although I put in a stint as assistant curator of birds at Downtown before I came up here. The type of thing I'm trained for is natural-history museum work—teaching."

To round out this background, Dolan visited every important zoo in Western Europe as part of his education, and by the time he got around to the job of bringing together the Park's collection, he was one of the most knowledgeable zoo men in the country. Collecting so vast an assemblage is not only an undertaking in logistics, it is equally a job in politics, wheeling-dealing and detective work, to say nothing of zoology. One does not simply pick up the phone and order twenty addaxes, or put on his pith helmet and run down a pair of tigers in India. First of all, tigers from India are not available anymore, due to export/import restrictions. Nor can animals classified as endangered species be purchased even from another

zoo in the United States, as a result of recent Federal regulations
—at least not without filing unbelievably complex applications
which, for voluminosity, as Dolan says, "are second only to the
New Testament."

Then there are the dealers who, sensing the interest in so vast
an acquisition, often manage to corner the market in some species.
Moreover, since import restrictions mandate that most of the collection come from domestic zoos, a consummate knowledge of animals
is required, in addition to knowing what specimens are available
where. Perhaps most important, an extraordinary sense of balance
is necessary to establish and maintain the kind of collection desired
for the Wild Animal Park. For all this, Dolan's varied background,
particularly his taxonomist's knowledge of the interrelationships of
mammals, ideally prepared him. In less than two years, the young
Bronxite-turned-San Diegan had the hills and plains of the Park
filled with one of the most outstanding collections of rare and endangered wild animals, the great majority of which came from other
zoos, including of course San Diego Downtown. And in less than
four years this achievement has provided not only a first-rate exhibit
zoo but also an unmatched breeding success, together with immense
advances in reproductive behavioral science.

"We've solved the cheetah reproductive problem now," said
Dolan. "The twenty we have had born here since 1970 is the most
any zoo has ever had. And we've also had the largest cheetah litter
ever born in captivity, eight of them, and that's a fantastic thing.
We're over the top now with cheetahs. Dr. Griner, our pathologist,
came up with the answer to cheetah reproduction. The thing is not
to keep them together. They're naturally solitary animals and the
mistake was in keeping them together. Now the male is introduced
only when the female is in estrus. Everybody's agreed on that.
Initially, our first couple of litters were produced by one female,
and there was great concern that maybe we were just lucky in
simply having one oddball female that was going to reproduce for
us. But now we have three females with youngsters, so it's all
firmed up that this is the way you must do it. Because in the wild—
often people who are professionally trained miss this—in the wild
these animals don't appear in groups. If you see more than one it's
either a female with its litter almost full grown, or a female in estrus

with a few males hanging around. With the tiger it is a little different. The male will tolerate the presence of the female in his territory in a kind of loose on-going association, but—for the cheetah—no sir, total separation except when receptive. These are some of the things we've learned here and that is why we expect to be a factor in saving endangered animals from extinction. That, after all, is the Wild Animal Park's main objective—not exhibiting animals. Eventually we hope to be able to reintroduce some of these zoo-born species into their native habitats, that is, if the habitats are still there."

Despite the preeminence of the San Diego Wild Animal Park in the world of zoos, life there is not all perfection, as Dr. Schroeder is quick to admit. Occasionally a weaker animal dies under the onslaught of a more-powerful neighbor. Not too long ago the corpse of an infant impala was discovered in a section also occupied by Cape buffalo and zebra. Presumably it was killed by one of the buffalo since, as investigation revealed, there were no zebra tracks around the scene. Still, that sort of thing also happens in the wild, Dr. Schroeder pointed out.

"What we are more concerned with are things like the scarification of the land at the Park. We may have too many animals in too small a space to allow the plants to survive. The animals of course don't live off the land—they are fed rations of conventional zoo feed—but they do go at the grass and shrubs and that's good for them. So right now the land is almost totally scarred, shrubs all pulled out. The Barbary sheep make certain there's not a root left on those rocks. We've put poles around the plants, shock wires in other areas, stone walls. Now, young Charlie Bieler, who succeeded me as director, is heading up a program to try to find shrubs that the animals don't like, if that's possible. They're using a special grass with deep roots that makes a solid turf. We've got to watch out that in saving the fauna we don't kill the flora."

Also in the works is a walkway that will go over but not into the preserves and permit closer observation of the animals without intruding on them. The next move, according to Dr. Schroeder, is the installation of a cable-car system over the Park for those who prefer to see without walking. In addition, there are more than 1200 acres to expand into. Conscious of this, of all he had seen, and all the new projects being planned, the visitor, as he rumbled back out over the buckling wooden bridge, remembered the words of Mack the cab driver: "You don't ever have to leave New York to know the Met's the finest opera in the world, right? The same with the San Diego Zoo—I know it's the finest anywhere."

5 The Safari Zoo

"BUGS BUNNY AND THE LOONEY TUNES ARE ALIVE AND WELL IN JUNGLE JUNCTION" (the amusement section of Jungle Habitat) declares a huge billboard planted in a stretch of wooded New Jersey hillside just forty miles outside of New York City. To a visitor just returned from the tasteful quiet of San Diego's Wild Animal Park, the circuslike ballyhoo of the first wild-animal park in the Northeast comes as something of a shock.

But then, Jungle Habitat, the thousand-acre safari or "drive-through" zoo that opened on the outskirts of West Milford in 1972, is owned by Warner Brothers of Hollywood and not by a nonprofit zoological society such as the one that operates the San Diego Zoo. Jungle Habitat is one of the rash of commercial, privately owned animal parks that have cropped up over America in the last eight years, often with an eye to the profit to be made on the enormous upsurge of public interest in ecology and conservation.

Like Jungle Habitat, many of the existing drive-through zoos are owned by movie and television producers—with auto dealers, real-estate developers, pub owners and other animal lovers on the trail for promising new locations. Taft Broadcasting Company, a producer of Saturday-morning TV cartoons, is readying a new Lion Country Safari that will be incorporated into a Cincinnati amusement park, and American Broadcasting Company is coming up with its own version of the African jungle down in Maryland. With more than a dozen new "animal kingdoms" in the works it would not be surprising to see drive-through zoos soon stretched out across the entire republic like a chain of McDonald hamburger heavens.

"The money men took over the virgin wild-animal preserve that was once America for 26 bucks in beads," remarked one oldtime zoo professional (who refused to be named for fear he may one day have to work for the new zoo-tycoons). "They wiped out the forests, the natives and the animals. Now it looks like they're going to put it all together again and give it back at maybe an even-greater profit—this time with a bit of entertainment thrown in for teasers."

This is not to imply that there is anything wrong with either making a profit or providing entertainment. Even the purist Zoological Society of San Diego uses a pirouette or two from its bears and elephants to amuse its patrons. As for turning a profit, there are any number of items and services that conventional zoos sell at a considerable markup from cost. But in the main, entertainments at most conventional zoos have some relation to ecological reality and to good taste. Joan Embery, the attractive young lady who puts the elephants through their paces at San Diego Wild Animal Park, is a serious zoo professional. She obviously makes more sense at a wildlife preserve than does Bugs Bunny. And infinitely more fun, too. Further, "profits" from a zoo such as San Diego Wild Animal Park are plowed back into operations that are designed only for the interest of the animals and the visiting public.

With the new conglomerate-owned wild-animal park, however, there are stockholders' interests that take precedence, as they must in any publicly held business corporation, over other interests. Shares in Lion Country Safari, for instance, are currently traded over the counter under the symbol of GRRR. Once, when their price retreated momentarily from a peak of fifty times earnings, there were angry growls to be heard from insiders other than the lions. Profit-and-loss statements, financial reports, Securities Exchange regulations, marketing surveys, *Wall Street Journal* quotes are all introduced into the world of ecology and if the bottom line is too often red, a collection of rare wild animals can wake up one morning and discover that they are parties to a bankruptcy proceeding. This is what happened recently when Animal Kingdom, Inc., in Clermont, Florida, folded because of insolvency. More than fifty wild animals—lions, jaguars, addax, greater kudu, elephants and others—wound up in the possession of a "zoological" organization called HNC Mortgage and Realty Investors of Westport, Connecticut, as a result of a foreclosure action.

What, then, is this new phenomenon that in 1973 mesmerized millions of Americans into parting with as much as $7.50 each for a drive through a hot animalarium, just as Donald Duck once pulled them into steaming summer movie houses?

Bearing such names as Lion Country Safari, Jungle Habitat, Great Adventure, Wild Animal Kingdom and the like, the new safari zoos generally describe themselves as "authentic wildlife preserves where animals roam free in their natural habitats." The public generally drives through the zoo parks in automobiles and views, with auto windows rolled up, wild beasts "behaving," in the language of the promotional literature, "as they do in the wild." This—the back-to-nature syndrome that is an ever-growing symptom of our machine-sick civilization—is one of the big attractions of the new animal parks. But the main attraction is the opportunity, when it occasionally presents itself, of ogling a full-grown lion or bear "eyeball to eyeball" from behind the safety of the car window. No contact that can be made with the animal at a conventional zoo can equal the drama of meeting it face to face in the open.

"In a car you are on the animal's level," says Colonel G. D. Dailley of African Lion Safari and Game Farm in Ontario. "There is something really exciting about having to put your foot on the brake to stop because there is an antelope or lion in front of you."

Undoubtedly this is what prompts the more show-biz-oriented drive-through operators to heat up their promotional literature with such as, "experience the hot breath of a full-grown lion clouding up your windshield" or "enjoy the thrill of being marooned in your car by a curious herd of camels."

And indeed it is man that, for a change, finds himself caged instead of the animal. Confined to the enclosure of his car, *homo sapiens* stares back at the wild beast as it moves unconfined about its territory. In the conventional zoo the sign reads: DON'T FEED THE ANIMALS; but in the safari zoo, considering the mobility of the animals and the occasional visitor who neglects to roll up his window, it might well read DON'T FEED [ON] THE PEOPLE. There is no doubt that an additional excitement in the drive-through experience derives from just this simple reversal.

The history of the wild-animal park, in a sense, goes back to Egyptian Queen Hatshepsut, except that, in her establishment, the more dangerous animals must have been caged or pitted. And the only vehicles that drove through her zoo were most likely Her Majesty's royal litter and the accompanying conveyances of invited noble guests. In modern times the San Simeon zoo of William Randolph Hearst could also be considered a kind of drive-through —patronized, interestingly enough, mostly by the Hollywood community that later would furnish impresarios to turn the drive-through technique into another highly profitable entertainment medium. But San Simeon, too, like Queen Hatshepsut's zoo, was essentially a closed-to-the-public affair.

It was Lord Bath, a debt-plagued British nobleman, who opened the first commercial drive-through zoo in history. That was in 1966, in Wiltshire, England. The hard-pressed aristocrat, also the first to open his castle to a paying public, got together with a circus fellow by the name of Jimmy Chipperfield who had a stableful of unemployed lions. Together they laid plans for exhibiting the big cats to whomsoever was willing to lay down the price for driving through the ancient grounds of Longleat, Lord Bath's hereditary estate in Wiltshire. The idea horrified His Lordship's neighbors, and particularly *The London Times,* which pilloried the idea as ". . . one of the most fantastically unsuitable uses of a stretch of England's green and pleasant land that can ever have entered the head of a noble proprietor . . . a lion in Wiltshire is as out of place as a Wodehousian Empress of Blandings would be in Kruger Park. . . . " But Lord Bath needed money, and besides, the public disagreed. They came by the thousands from all over the British Isles to stare at the Lions of Longleat from inside their Austins and their Bentleys. Soon the idea of the drive-through wild-animal park spread to other parts of Europe and the British Empire. In 1967 Jimmy Chipperfield, now associated with Harry Shuster, a South African attorney, opened the first one in the United States: Lion Country Safari, in West Palm Beach, Florida.

There the new idea was blessed by climate and terrain. Lions indeed were "out of place" in the temperate clime of Wiltshire, England, as *The London Times* had complained, but in the semi-tropical region of Florida they were as authentic a creature as any local specimen. The same applied to the hippos, rhinos, ostriches and other exotic African animals in the collection. To this extent the first commercial wild-animal park in America was not resorting to artifice when its guidebook claimed that, "This is nature in the raw. This is Africa transplanted to America."

As to claims that its animals were "free," that is quite another matter. They were more free, perhaps, than animals caged in conventional zoos, but certainly not free. True freedom exists only in the real wilderness. Lion Country Safari animals are also still confined to specific areas, as they are in any zoo, by fences, moats and barriers, no matter how cleverly some of these are concealed.

The first drive-through zoo in the United States was also blessed by another peculiarly American phenomenon: the combined promotion techniques of Madison Avenue and Hollywood. Catchy titles enliven the show, such as the one at the entrance that playfully warns that "Trespassers Will Be Eaten." Girls in fetching safari uniforms sell tickets in as coy a style as Follies girls once sold charity kisses. And once inside, the visitor is supplied with a cassette player that describes the unfolding panorama with voices that sound like Arthur Treacher and Buddy Hackett playing Dr. Livingstone and Rudyard Kipling respectively. In the background, drums and tom-toms underscore the warning to drive at no more than five miles per hour with windows closed. Farther on, as the scene changes from species to species, appropriate music is introduced to set the mood for the varied cast of characters: sinister, threatening tones in lion country; dulcet, Bambi-music for the antelopes. It brings to mind the production techniques that MGM used in its latest all-star extravaganza, *That's Entertainment!*

This odd mix of near-authenticity and show-biz razzmatazz,

combined, as it was, at the first Lion Country Safari, with a truly interesting parade of wild beasts that are visible in a way in which Americans had never seen zoo animals displayed, produced an immediate sensation at the box office. By its third year the Florida Lion Country Safari was already drawing a million visitors; in five years, on an initial investment of $500,000, the parent company owned additional parks in Texas and Georgia and had built its net worth to $35 million.

Other native entrepreneurs—entertainment moguls in the American Broadcasting Company and Taft Broadcasting Company; New York real-estate tycoons Herbert and Stuart Sheftel; movie pashas in the Warner Brothers organization—saw a new leisure-time bonanza in the making and jumped on the bandwagon. Presently ten to fifteen thousand denizens of the wild are strutting their stuff to choreography devised by the new fang-and-claw ballet masters in ten make-believe wildernesses throughout the land. Jungle Habitat in New Jersey, World Wildlife Safari in Oregon, ABC's Wild Animal World in Maryland, World of Animals in Texas and others have recently opened, with more—ten additional Lion Country Safaris, for instance—in the planning stage. Within four hours of New York City alone, there are or soon will be five wild-animal parks. Even the staid old Bronx Zoo is thinking about some kind of joint enterprise with Lion Country Safari. But the biggest news of all: that penultimate ringmaster, the arch-guru of animal make-believe, the creator of Mickey Mouse, Donald Duck and Pluto is himself (or at least via his current representatives on earth) going to step into the picture. A Walt Disney Wild Animal Kingdom is about to be born on a thousand acres of Disney World in Orlando, Florida. There, in addition to enlarging his world from plastic-animal to real-animal, the Disney master magicians are planning to add real Masai, Zulu, Watusi and Bedouin tribesmen to the wildlife exhibits in his drive-through zoo. Although the idea of displaying people as "cultural exhibits" is not exactly new (Cardinal Ippolito, some 400 years earlier, exhibited humans in his Florence zoo), at least it will be the visiting tourist and not the native tribesmen who will be confined to cages—in this case motels on wheels—as once they were in the Cardinal's zoo.

African lions stop "safari" traffic as they cross the road in front of motorists at Jungle Habitat in West Milford, New Jersey.

Ostriches are the pedestrians at Jungle Habitat. Human beings are not permitted (nor would most of them want) to go through the drive-through zoo in automobiles with windows tightly closed.

In between sessions of driving through the "jungle" at Jungle Habitat, visitors can sit by a pool and watch the dolphins perform.

One of the major problems of the safari zoos has in fact arisen from this reversal of roles. Even though rules require people to stay inside their cars with windows shut, policing humans often seems to be more difficult than policing animals. In Kruger Park, South Africa, the first "free-roaming" (but noncommercial) wild-animal drive-through in the world, a young man was foolhardy enough to ride a bicycle along a short stretch of the public road. A lioness spotted him, charged out of the bush, and killed and devoured him only fifty yards from a rest-area gate. In another instance, in the same park, a European couple in a small car pulled up to an elephant standing in the road. The elephant refused to budge. This annoyed the driver, who first honked his horn to no avail, and then decided to prod the beast from behind. The big pachyderm responded by sitting on the front end of the car and reducing it to a pancake. Luckily the couple lived to tell the story.

Despite the display of signs everywhere warning visitors to keep car windows shut, some people insist on opening them. Baboons, particularly, are not averse to joining the occupants inside the car; in one case, one of these fierce creatures, unable to get out of the automobile, went berserk and severely mauled the passengers. In another instance, a group of riders rolled the window down and allowed a lion to stick his head inside. Fortunately for them, when they tried to roll the window up, the animal became frightened and, instead of tearing the occupants apart, withdrew his head and only tore the window out.

To a large extent such flirtings with death and mayhem come from the misguided sense of security that derives from seeing wild animals peacefully wandering about with no obvious intent of mauling anything. That nice bear wouldn't harm a fly, one thinks—why should he?—he's living in an authentic, normal habitat, well-fed and walking around free, so to speak, as a bird. In a cage he might well be angry, but here, why should he be at all dangerous?

In 1972, at Jungle Habitat in West Milford, New Jersey, this attitude was responsible for a severe mauling of an Israeli tourist by a lion. In this instance the passenger leaned out of the car window and beckoned to the lion, who moved so fast that its head was in the window before the passenger could close it. "When you first enter Jungle Habitat, it is not dangerous," a member of the injured man's party said. "There are ducks and elephants and everybody leaves the windows open. We approached the area that is supposed to be dangerous, and we went through a gate, but we didn't feel it was a dangerous place." Dangerous delusion.

If the paying customer at the drive-through zoo is sometimes treated badly by the animal that is supposed to entertain him, what about the animal itself? What is the real story behind this fast-growing phenomenon of American big business? Are the drive-throughs nothing more than "blue-chip" concentration camps for animals, as some critics have branded them? Or do they at least succeed in giving the zoo animal an authentic reproduction of his natural habitat, where he is free to move about as he likes? Does the stocking of all these new make-believe wildernesses require such a vast amount of wildlife that, like other resources that Americans consume to excess, soon there will be none of certain species remaining in the real wilderness? Or are the parks an improved breeding environment that may well mean survival for the endangered species? Propaganda, advertising, good intentions aside, how does the animal really fare in the new safari zoo?

A telling evaluation of a safari zoo is given in the following description of a visit to Jungle Habitat by Edward R. Ricciuti, former curator of publications for the New York Zoological Society and ex-editor of its *Animal Kingdom* magazine. Mr. Ricciuti has observed the wild-animal scene as both a traditional zoo professional and an outside reporter of new developments. "The strongest impressions I have of my visits to Jungle Habitat," writes Mr. Ricciuti in the November 1973 *Audubon* magazine, "are not of animals but of rock, mud, and dust, a clutter of construction equipment, torn and battered trees and brush, and piles of earthen spoil heaped at the roadside. Cages may be absent from this 'non-zoo' but seldom was I out of sight of fencing, much of it apparently new.

"Visitors to Jungle Habitat may follow two 'safari trails,' each about two miles long, which lead through an area roamed by white rhinoceroses, zebras, deer and other hoofed animals. The animals have stripped· and barked many of the trees (some of which appear to have been felled and left on the ground) and have trampled the underbrush so that they live in mud or dust, depending on the weather. The trails also lead through compounds that contain predators and such problem animals as baboons and baby elephants; one features some of Jungle Habitat's forty-three lions, the other holds thirteen tigers—one Bengal and twelve Siberian.

"If a visitor has a car radio he can tune to a special low-power radio system that broadcasts static and, occasionally, the voice of author-naturalist Roger Caras, whose narrative happily sticks to facts about the animals and does not attempt to convince visitors they are in the wilderness.

"Among the sights and sounds of Jungle Habitat:

"Just within the gate of 'Baboon Hill' a driver snoozes in a pickup truck emblazoned with the name Consolidated Fence Company. The chain-link fence surrounding the compound is being covered with shiny sheets of metal that shimmer in the sun. Fence-piping lies in piles, and a young Arabian camel picks its way through a pile of broken rock. High above the road a party of baboons clambers up a small wall of boulders.

"The roadside on Baboon Hill is littered with orange peels and greens, obviously the remains of a primate meal. A large Alaskan malamute chained at the gate guards against baboon escapees.

"Domestic cattle, zebras, rhinos, and American bison gather around a feed trough next to the road. A llama approaches a galvanized water pail whose brown paint is peeling.

"The driver of an automobile with steam boiling from under its hood honks the horn monotonously for aid. Nearby, within the fenced-in boundaries of Elephant Camp, two very young African elephants demolish a sapling.

"A guard at a gate watches without comment as the driver of a car opens a window—disregarding advice that windows are to be closed for safety reasons while touring the park—and tosses a cracker in front of an ostrich.

"Within sight of the driver of one of Jungle Habitat's official 'safari buses,' an elk begs from the occupants of cars which are lined up waiting for the animal as it makes its rounds. The driver of the first car opens a window and reaches out to grab the elk as it peers at him. Another hand reaches out and pets the animal on the nose, then feeds it something. At the next car, a hand offers the creature a tidbit, which it refuses. The hand drops the piece of whatever-it-was on the ground.

"An emu wanders along the road, stops at a car, and gobbles up a pretzel that is proffered.

"Blinking but otherwise unmoving, a large eland sits in the mud of a deep ditch along the road. The ground for several yards around is bare.

"Twenty feet up a tree, a large black bear sleeps sprawled in the branches. Several other bears group around a ditch full of muddy water. Dust and dirt cling to their fur. Another bear strips the leaves from a beech and stuffs them into its mouth.

"At the side of the road, on the bare earth, someone has left a rusted automobile battery.

"Atop a huge pile of wet earth, barely covered with straw, a lion watches several other members of the pride dozing in the mud below. The mud is crisscrossed by tire tracks.

"The tigers are stretched out in the grass of their nine-acre compound. Two keepers drive their vehicles back and forth along the road that loops through the enclosure, and at the gate a young attendant waves his arms frantically, hustling the traffic along.

"Eventually, Jungle Habitat visitors encounter a large green-and-black sign that reads, 'There are no animals from here to Jungle Junction.' The sign is unnecessary. The thick green foliage and absence of fences testify that the animal compounds are behind. After a drive of a few minutes, past signs pushing—in Burma Shave fashion—African dancers, Bugs Bunny, and the other delights of Jungle Junction, visitors reach the parking lot.

"No corner of Jungle Junction lacks concessions: pizza, hot-dog and ice-cream stands are scattered among the entertainment area's small-animal exhibits, amusement rides, theaters for dancers, porpoise show and 'fully costumed Looney Tunes characters.'

" 'Bugs Bunny is the hit of the whole place,' says Jungle Habitat's young publicist, Kerry Smith.

"Jungle Junction has a petting zoo where an attendant sells a prepared mixture that youngsters can feed to the goats and miscellaneous small creatures. A food dispenser also perches on a bridge over pits that hold young lions, black bear cubs, and crowned cranes. Visitors lining the railing pelt the bear cubs with a rain of the straw-colored food mixture. More than twenty of the cranes, gorgeous birds with a spray of golden feathers about their heads, are jammed into a rocky pit roughly the size of a handball court.

"In one Jungle Junction pen, African and Indian elephant calves mix with five Aldabra tortoises, which, according to an attendant dressed as a white hunter, 'don't need much water.' He knew they were tortoises but was not sure what kind. Jungle Junction abounds with young men and girls clad in safari garb, most of whom appear to work at the various shops and stands. I questioned some of them. None was an animal keeper, nor did any know where to find an animal keeper."

Evidently the claim "natural habitat" for the animal population in the drive-throughs is somewhat exaggerated. The natural habitat of a wild lion of course is in the tall grasses of the African savannas. A patch of New Jersey woods or an even stretch of Florida glades that has a stream of automobiles pouring out carbon monoxide fumes as they roll over macadam roads that lead through the middle of the lion's territory can not properly be termed "natural habitat." Rather the reverse: it more resembles the habitat in which the animal caged inside the car has become accustomed to living. It is surely going too far to call drive-throughs "concentration camps"; it may not be unfair to compare them to "Long Island Expressways that have wild animal exhibits instead of Howard Johnsons along the way."

This is an environment that is not present at a noncommercial wild-animal park, such as San Diego's. There, as Dr. Schroeder pointed out, no automobile goes into the animals' territory except the occasional truck that delivers feed. "The million or so visitors that viewed our wild animals in the first year of operation did so from *outside* the animals' territory," he said. "Automobiles aren't allowed anywhere in the Park, not even on the periphery of the animals' territory. But that didn't discourage a million people from coming forty miles or more to see the animals. An electric, silent, nonpolluting monorail takes you around the peripheral fence of the exhibits. Animal and auto are kept well separated. There's no such thing as blowing a cloud of gas exhaust into a wild animal's face."

This of course means that binoculars are required at San Diego for "eyeball-to-eyeball" confrontation, except in those cases where an animal voluntarily comes up close to the peripheral fence, which some often do and entirely on their own. But the feeling of being in Africa rather than on the Los Angeles Freeway is certainly much stronger at San Diego Wild Animal Park than at the commercial drive-through. And the behavior of the animal is much closer to his natural behavior.

"This is something that is better for the animal in the long run," says Charles Faust, designer of the San Diego Wild Animal Park. "Granted you don't see some of the animals up as close as in the drive-through—and in many cases you don't see them so close there, either—but the public has just got to accept this if it is going to be at all concerned about the future of the world's wildlife. At San Diego the animal comes first."

As far as "freedom" is concerned, that also is a considerably over-used word in the lexicon of the commercial drive-throughs. Some animals, as earlier pointed out, are much freer in a safari zoo than they would be in a conventional zoo, others no more so. The crested cranes that Edward Ricciuti saw at Jungle Habitat were "jammed into a rocky pit roughly the size of a handball court." In other safari zoos some species are also deliberately confined to small spaces so that they may be visible close up to the paying patron as he drives by. Else why a safari zoo at all? In such cases the inadequate space does not permit the "free" animal to have the natural flight distance that is built into him, and often results in a disorientation of his instinctual mechanisms. With other animals, such as lions (which like to sleep about twenty hours a day), "rangers" or "game wardens" herd the lethargic animals up to the roadside where they may be photographed or stared at by the safarist. Electric fences and trained dogs, on the other hand, are used by some parks to keep more active animals, such as baboons, confined to their compounds, all of which methods substantially qualify the claim of "free." The safari zoos were not even the innovators of the idea of displaying zoo animals roaming free, as many of them assert. The Bronx Zoo as long ago as 1941 had exhibited lions in the open on its Lion Island, the only difference being that the viewer does not drive through the animals' territory with an exhaust-spewing automobile.

Also, perhaps in an even more critical sense the animal in the commercial wild-animal park is not free. Whereas the public zoo and the quasi-public institution such as the Zoological Society-operated Bronx and San Diego Zoos are assured of a certain continuity of existence and its animals the status of public property, the commercial safari zoo is a private business corporation and its animals commercial commodities. The animal's home is always under the threat of foreclosure, liquidation and auction, and the animal himself subject to an unknown fate in the event of business failure. With the proliferation of commercial wild-animal parks, should tastes change or economic conditions worsen, many of these trendy emporia will go down the drain and their excess of animals become a drug on the market. (One such case has already been noted in the failure of the Clairmont, Florida, drive-through and the subsequent seizure of its animal population by a mortgage company.)

As for the charge of consuming wild animals to the point of near-extinction, the drive-throughs, despite the huge inventory their stocking requires, cannot be considered guilty. The major part of their inventory of endangered species comes not from the wild but from the surplus of other zoos. This is necessarily so because of the Endangered Species Act passed by the United States Congress in 1970, which scrupulously controls importation of endangered species to this country, requiring permits in each case. Moreover, the produce of their own breeding stock furnishes the drive-throughs with additional exhibit specimens and with animals that can be traded to other zoos.

In the instance of certain hoofed animals, such as antelope and giraffes, no wild-animal park may import any of these animals because of the danger of spreading hoof-and-mouth disease to domestic animals. Only a few traditional zoos meet the strict requirements of fencing, distance from domestic livestock, and other controls specified by law. "But there are ways of getting around these hurdles," explained one zoo professional. "You can make deals with those zoos that can legally import wild animals and buy the offspring of both the endangered species and the hoofed animals they bring in." Such an arrangement has indeed already been made between Lion Country Safari and Columbia Zoo of South Carolina under which the drive-through zoo is financing Columbia's purchase of wild-caught hoofed animals whose offspring will go to Lion Safari.

The drive-throughs, however, have generally relied on local purchase and on their own breeding potential to fill their need for
inventory. And in breeding, their record is excellent, even when
compared to the great public zoos. For despite their rather over-
blown claims of freedom and natural habitat for their animals, the
drive-throughs do provide enough measure of these stimulants to
reproduction to come off very well in newborn.

"We have just begun to explore the role of private enterprise in
animal conservation and research," asserts Jay Emmett, Warner
Brothers vice-president, "but we know it is enormous. Almost overnight we have accomplished more with animals, with greater success
and less red tape, than most zoos in their entire histories. More
important, we have forced zoos to take a hard look at themselves."

This assertion is backed up to a large extent by the breeding
results in many of the drive-throughs, even in such cases as the
cheetah, a notoriously difficult breeder in captivity. Lion Country
Safari in California and World Wildlife Safari in Oregon, particularly, have had notable success with this endangered animal.

Yet none of the commercial wild-animal parks can approach the
breeding success of San Diego Wild Animal Park, especially with
difficult species. San Diego's record of twenty cheetah births since
1970 is unmatched. In addition, during the first fifteen months of
its operation, it had 258 successful births of all kinds, with 93 percent of its seventy-nine species procreating, including ten of the
eighteen endangered species in its collection.

Nevertheless, the safari zoos have also made a notable contribution to conservation, at least in terms of their combined overall
record of breeding results. They certainly cannot fairly be indicted
for depopulating the wild-animal kingdom for the sake of profit.

On the whole, their animal care and maintenance programs are
excellent too. It can be said they are, over all, no better than the
best, or no worse than the worst of the traditional zoos. Some have
indeed been known to put forest-dwelling apes on a bare, treeless
island, but that is no worse than caging a lion in a 10 x 10 iron
cage. One drive-through entrepreneur installed his wild-animal
"park" on a baseball lot beautified by artificial trees—but is this

any more deplorable than some of the miserable housing in which even some large municipal zoos still keep their collections? When such deficits are compared with assets such as the deep stream at Lion Country Safari, where elephants come to bathe and hippos rise suddenly to the surface and long-legged waterfowl stalk fish and toads, the drive-throughs indeed have little to apologize for when compared with many traditional zoos.

"Animals kept in cages or in small enclosures have a higher incidence of disease and suffer from limited physical activity and increased psycho-stress factors," Dr. Randall Eaton, director of Oregon's World Wildlife Safari, has said. "You never see a truly representative pride of lions in a [conventional] zoo, and no zoo has more than one pride. The competition among prides, the social interaction, the hunting, stalking, demarcation of territories are all impossible in a zoo."

Where the drive-through zoos do suffer in comparison with the traditional zoo, however, is in the area of trained personnel. The rapid explosion of the commercial wild-animal parks across the country has created a great demand for professional animal keepers. Apart from the fact that much of the curatorial fraternity has tenure with stable and prestigious public zoos and is unwilling to sacrifice it, even for the often better financial rewards offered by the drive-throughs, there are just not enough experienced zoo people on every level to fill the demand. This has led, in some cases, to the employment of inexperienced people to care for the animals. Unfortunately, many instances of devastating mortality among the wildlife population have been reported where human professionalism has been lacking. One park, indeed, closed only months after it had opened, largely because it could not keep its animals alive.

What is perhaps most to be feared is the faddism that occasionally sweeps over America. Wild-animal parks are, as of this writing, "in." If there is going to be a great overextension, as can very likely happen where a new trend looks like a "good thing," the avowed purpose of the wild-animal park movement—conservation and education—can be severely compromised. If parks open and fold haphazardly, the obvious casualties are the animals and our sense of concern for them. If, on the other hand, drive-throughs are visible at every turn of the road, they may be taken for granted and tuned out, much as a space flight is hardly noted today due to massive overexposure.

Of the five commercial safari zoos within driving distance of New York City, vigorously competing for the consumer's dollar, one will be a part of Great Adventure—an amusement conglomerate that will use 1500 acres of New Jersey's Pine Barrens, a precious part of America's vanishing wilderness. Great Adventure is the dream of Warner LeRoy, a young man who comes by his name as the result of his blood relationship to two oldtime Hollywood personalities, Harry M. Warner and Mervyn LeRoy. Among Warner LeRoy's other connections with the animal world are the fine steaks he serves at Maxwell's Plum, an elegant pub on the East Side of New York, of which he is an owner. In addition to having a "Dream Street" shopping area, an "Enchanted Forest," and a Western emporium shaped like a revolver, Great Adventure will, according to its prospectus, have the "largest assortment of wild animals in the world outside of Africa." As Charles Faust, designer of the San Diego Wild Animal Park has noted, "In a wild-animal park there's a tricky balance between the public and the animals. The public brings in the dollars. But in some cases the animal population suffers because they are drawn from other areas that could use them better." It is hoped that Mr. LeRoy's animals at Great Adventure will not be caught up and dragged down in that treacherous country that stretches between the dollar and conservation.

6 *Carl Hagenbeck*

One of the strangest paradoxes in the story of zoos is that a man who was the world's leading dealer in wild animals—a profession often considered an instrument for enslavement of wildlife—was at the same time their foremost liberator. It was Carl Hagenbeck, second-generation member of a German dynasty of animal dealers that consigned countless numbers of wild beasts to zoos and circuses, who created the cageless zoo and a method of training wild animals without cruelty. All moated, open-enclosure zoos, all modern drive-through wild-animal parks, all the free-roaming concepts for exhibiting captive wildlife, in addition to many of the techniques for training animals by simple reward-and-punishment instead of by fear-and-torture methods, derive from the vision of a man whose life was spent in the unsentimental world of the animal trade.

It was in his role of wild-animal dealer—first in the act of capturing specimens in the field, second in the process of maintaining them in "holding areas" while awaiting sale—that Carl Hagenbeck acquired the vast knowledge of animal behavior which nourished his

137

revolutionary ideas. It was Hagenbeck the animal dealer who made possible the pursuit of happiness by zoo animals and freed the circus beast from cruel and unusual punishment.

Carl Hagenbeck was born on the 10th of June, 1844, in a suburb of Hamburg, Germany, one of six children of a fishmonger. One day when Carl was four years old, his father, Gottfried Claas Hagenbeck, received six seals from some fishermen under the terms of a contract that gave him the right to everything they caught. Gottfried Claas Hagenbeck, besides being an animal lover, was also a shrewd businessman. He decided to share his interest in natural history with those of his fellow citizens who could pay one Hamburg shilling each for a look at the six strange animals which he had installed in his wife's washtubs in his back yard. The response was so overwhelming that Gottfried decided to add animal trading to his main occupation of fishmongering. Soon he had a sizable menageries consisting of goats, monkeys, talking parrots, waterfowl, polar bears, hyenas and other mammals, including, yes, more seals. For a look at this expanded collection he now charged four Hamburg shillings.

This was the least of it; the major part of his income from animals did not come from the showing but rather from the sale of his acquisitions. Seals, particularly, were good business. These he disposed of to owners of itinerant menageries and circuses which exhibited them to a gullible public as *mermaids.* And so began the House of Hagenbeck, a dynastic business that eventually reigned over the wild-animal world as purveyors extraordinaire to zoos, circuses and private menageries for over a century. In the process it also picked up its own circus, the world-famous Hagenbeck's, and a zoo of its own—the renowned open-enclosure Stellingen Animal Park.

"From my earliest childhood," Carl Hagenbeck wrote in his memoirs, *Men and Beasts,* "I was accustomed to dealing with living animals. My early education was somewhat meagre, for I only went to school when I could spare time from my work with the fish and live beasts, and this did not amount to more than three months in the year. It was not that my father failed to appreciate the benefits of a good education . . . But he was eminently a practical man, and whilst he impressed upon us the urgency of learning well the 'Three R's,' he used to tell us that we 'were not expected to become parsons.' "

This kind of no-foolishness upbringing—hard work by day to further a growing family business together with catching up on a rudimentary education by night fitted Carl Hagenbeck for the role of traditional nose-to-the-grindstone dynasty builder. After his father had invested in his first large collection of wild animals—five lions, several leopards and cheetahs, a number of hyenas, antelopes, gazelles and monkeys—the question was firmly put to Carl: "Would I choose as my future calling to be a fishmonger or an animal dealer, and, after placing all the pros and cons before me, my father finally advised me to take up fishmongering as being the less speculative trade. I am sure, however, that he did this with a heavy heart, for we all loved our menagerie; and when I decided in favor of the animal business he showed no displeasure, but immediately gave his consent to this course of action. I left school before I turned fifteen and from that day to this I have devoted all my energies to the care and development of the business which my father founded."

Carl Hagenbeck's choice suited the times. During the latter half of the nineteenth century, Africa was being explored and colonized by the great European powers. At the same time the public zoological garden was becoming fashionable both in Europe and America, creating an enormous demand for wild animals. Now in his late twenties and in full charge of Hagenbeck's Animal Dealers, Carl established a network of agents—adventurous men who often explored regions where no white man had ever been. They sent back shiploads of exotic animals, many of which had never been seen in Europe, at least not in modern times. Even with these vast resources Carl was frequently unable to meet all the demands for captive wildlife. P. T. Barnum, for instance, placed enormous orders for circus animals, particularly the racing elephants of India and ostriches, which he used as saddle animals. Other circuses, traveling menageries, zoos, private collectors all over the world, even armies in search of camels and other pack animals, all contributed to making Hagenbeck's the greatest wild-animal emporium in the world. It was a little like the old British East India Company that dispatched adventurers to the four corners of the earth in search of spices, jewels and other exotic treasures.

One of these adventurers in Hagenbeck's employ was "the African traveler," Lorenzo Cassanova, who had brought into Europe the first African elephant the continent had ever seen. In 1870 Cassanova brought back perhaps the largest consignment of African mammals ever to reach Europe in modern times, certainly the largest that Hagenbeck's had ever imported.

"On Whit-Monday of that year," Carl Hagenbeck reported, "I heard from Cassanova and from another of my travelers, by name of Migoletti, that they were both making their way out of the interior of Nubia with huge caravans of captured animals, and expected to arrive together at Suez. Cassanova stated that he was dangerously ill, and that it was therefore imperative that I should come to Suez, in order to take charge of the animals on the journey to Europe. Under the circumstances this appeared to be unavoidable; and so, the next day, accompanied by my youngest brother, I departed for Egypt. We traveled via Trieste, and arrived at our destination after an uneventful journey lasting eight days. On entering the station at Suez we were greeted by some of our prospective pets, for in another train opposite we saw several elephants and giraffes, who pushed out their heads to welcome us. This, however, scarcely prepared us for what met our gaze when we reached the Suez Hotel. I shall never forget the sight which the courtyard presented. Elephants, giraffes, antelopes and buffalo were tethered to the palms; sixteen great ostriches were strolling about loose; and in addition there were no fewer than sixty large cages containing a rhinoceros, lions, panthers, cheetahs, hyaenas, jackals, civets, caracals, monkeys, and many kinds of birds."

Naturally, it was a gargantuan undertaking to transport this immense living cargo to Europe. Apart from the fact that in those days the trip had to be made by sea, the problem of feeding this huge collection was enormous. Grains, fruit, hay by the ton (one elephant requires about 200 pounds of food daily), vegetables and meat were needed in vast amounts. And there was no such thing as modern refrigeration to keep the milk which orphaned young animals need. Hagenbeck solved this problem by bringing along with him a hundred nanny-goats to provide the young giraffes and other animals with milk. When the goats were no longer able to supply milk they were slaughtered and given to the carnivores as food.

"The journey to Alexandria, where we were to embark for Trieste, was by no means uneventful," reported Hagenbeck. "On the way to the station the ostriches escaped, and were only recovered after considerable delay. Then one of the railway trucks caught fire, endangering the entire menagerie; and finally we were furnished for the last part of the journey with a drunken engine driver who nearly burst his boiler. Moreover, the poor creatures were so closely packed together that it was impossible to feed them. We travelled all through the night and arrived in Alexandria at 6 A.M. Here we joined forces with Migoletti's caravan. The whole of the next day was occupied in feeding and in general attendance upon my unfortunate beasts, which had suffered considerably from their long train journey. . . . It will be readily believed that I suffered no little anxiety when I saw my valuable animals, cumbrous elephants and long-legged giraffes, hanging from the crane betwixt sky and sea. However, at last they were all safely deposited on deck and the passage to Trieste was accomplished without serious mishap."

The entire population of Trieste turned out to witness the massive unloading. Each time a giraffe or elephant came dangling across the pier in a crane a roar of delight would go up from the crowd on shore. Before they were through, the stevedores had unloaded, in addition to hundreds of smaller animals, five elephants, fourteen giraffes, four Nubian buffaloes, a rhinoceros, twelve antelope and gazelles, two wart hogs, four aardvarks, and sixty carnivores, including seven lions, eight leopards and cheetahs and thirty hyenas. There were also twenty-six ostriches, one of them so tall it could reach a cabbage which Hagenbeck placed eleven feet above the ground.

Although there undoubtedly must have been some animal fatalities, the irony is that the chief casualty was Lorenzo Cassanova himself, the collector of this great horde, who died in the middle of the unloading. But such occurrences were hardly unusual. The life of the animal dealer in those days, particularly those who involved themselves directly in the capture and transport of wild beasts from distant places, was a precarious one.

By the middle of the 1870s the jungles of Africa and Asia had been fairly well penetrated by animal dealers and the supply of wild beasts began to exceed the demand. Profits from the trade declined substantially, and Hagenbeck looked about for other ways to increase his dollar volume. Zoologist Hagenbeck now became anthropologist Hagenbeck. To his exotic *animal* business he now added an exotic *people* business: pageants of primitive humans that he called his "ethnographic exhibitions."

The first of these presentations featured a group of Laplanders, nomadic tribes indigenous to the remote regions of northern Russia, Sweden and Norway, going through a typical day in their lives while a paying public observed them.

Exhibiting the short, brachycephalic Laplanders would not of course have been the first time that human beings were on public display in the centers of civilization. Cardinal Ippolito had a "people zoo" in Florence during the height of the Renaissance; Hernando Cortez had seen retarded men and women in the cages of Montezuma's menagerie in Mexico; even into the twentieth century, "freaks" were still being exhibited in circuses as the result of P. T. Barnum's popularization of tent sideshows.

But Carl Hagenbeck's ethnographic exhibitions were nothing like this. Admittedly they must have had considerable appeal for the curious, but they also had educational impact, which was what he had in mind with these shows—living travelogs about "exotic" peoples. Relatively few individuals in those days could afford to travel the world to observe foreign cultures. Moreover, if they could there was no such thing as air transport to speed them there. What Hagenbeck did was to bring a bit of an unfamiliar culture to people who could never hope to get much farther than their own doorsteps.

"The first glance (at the Laplanders as they arrived for the Hamburg exhibit) sufficed to convince me that the experiment would prove a success," said Hagenbeck. "Here was a truly interesting sight. On deck three little men dressed in skins were walking about among the deer, and down below we found to our great delight a mother with a tiny infant in her arms and a dainty little maiden about four years old, standing shyly by her side. Our guests, it is true, would not have shone in a beauty show, but they were so wholly unsophisticated and so totally unspoiled by civilization that they seemed like beings from another world.

Carl Hagenbeck, inventor of the moated, natural habitat, cageless zoo. This famous German naturalist was also the world's foremost animal dealers and creator of the "gentle" method for training wild animals. *(Courtesy of New York Public Library Picture Collection)*

Carl Hagenbeck's Zoo opened in Stellingen, Germany, in 1907. It was the first zoo in which animals were exhibited in mixed groups in simulated natural environments and without cages. *(Courtesy of New York Public Library Picture Collection)*

Carl Hagenbeck's Tierpark, Stellingen-Hamburg
Heufressergehege

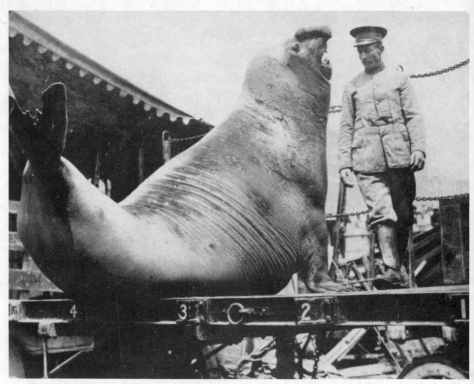

Zoos and circuses all around the world stocked their inventory with wild animals obtained from Hagenbeck's. This huge sea elephant was purchased by Ringling Brothers and Barnum & Bailey from the Hagenbeck Zoo in Hamburg. It was exhibited on a wagon drawn by six horses around the circus floor. Below, circus poster advertising the Goliath. *(Courtesy of New York Public Library Picture Collection)*

"This first of my ethnographic exhibitions was from every point of view a huge success. I attribute this mainly to the simplicity with which the whole thing was organized, and to the complete absence of all vulgar accessories. There was nothing in the way of a performance. The Laplanders themselves had no conception of the commercial side of the venture, and knew nothing of exhibitions. They were merely paying a short visit to the hustling civilization which they saw around them, and it never occurred to them to alter their own primitive habits of life. The result was that they behaved just as though they were in their native land, and the interest and value of the exhibition were therefore greatly enhanced. They took up their abode in the grounds behind my house at Neuer Pferdemarkt, and lived entirely out of doors. All Hamburg came to see this 'Lapland in miniature.' "

Hagenbeck (a sort of outrageous innocent—as indicated above) lost no time in following up his Laplander success with ethnographic exhibitions of other "wild" peoples. Nubians were brought in from the Sudan, together with their families, domestic animals and, a special object of interest, a pack of their great black dromedaries. These were succeeded by a group of Eskimos, people who were then much in the public mind because of the polar expeditions but who had never before been seen in the heart of Europe. Ukubak, a wide-smiling Greenlander from way up around latitude 69° came into Hamburg, not only with his wife and two little daughters but also with the totality of his worldly goods, including dogs, tents, sledges, household implements, canoes—even his arsenal of Iron Age weapons. After Ukubak and his family had been exhibited in Hamburg, Hagenbeck took them to Paris, Dresden and Berlin. In these places Ukubak performed aquatic feats in his kayak, the Eskimo's traditional skin canoe. On one occasion he stayed under water so long that German Emperor William I, a visitor, nearly ordered the exhibit closed for fear of the small man's safety. But Hagenbeck assured the monarch that such stamina was typical for Eskimos—after *all*, they knew nothing of tobacco and alcohol—and so the show went on. Ukubak and his family completed their tour and, in a year's time, returned to latitude 69° none the worse for their contact with the heartland of Western civilization.

After the Laplanders, Nubians and Eskimos came Somalis, Indians, Kalmucks, Sengalese, Patagonians and Hottentots, until the races of "wild" men seen in Hagenbeck's exhibition areas almost began to match the numbers of species of wild animals in his holding areas. But after the largest of his ethnographic exhibitions—the great Sengalese Show of 1884, which caused a sensation in Europe with its caravan of sixty-seven people, twenty-five elephants and a multitude of cattle of various breeds—Hagenback felt that "the public might, perhaps, have had enough of ethnology for the time being. I therefore set to work to devise some new form of entertainment. The result of my meditations was a revolution in the methods of training wild beasts for the circus. For many years, indeed ever since I could remember, I had been greatly distressed by the cruel methods of teaching animals to perform, which were then in vogue. My enthusiasm for my own calling originated more, if I may say so, in a love for all living creatures than in any mere commercial instincts. I had no doubt inherited this passion from my father, and under the circumstances in which I found myself there was, of course, every opportunity for cultivating the taste. I do not intend to imply that I have not also had an eye to the main chance; but I can, I think, say with perfect truth that I am, and always have been, a naturalist first and a trader afterwards. This being the case, it was only natural that I, in common I am sure with all other lovers of animals, should be greatly distressed at the wicked ill-treatment to which 'tamed' beasts were in those days subjected."

In 1887 Hagenbeck opened in Hamburg a circus that incorporated his new technique for training performing animals, which he called the "gentle" method. Up to this time the prevailing technique for getting a lion or tiger to execute certain desired actions, such as jumping over obstacles, was to fill it with fear. Whips and red-hot irons were used to terrify the animals so that at the very sight of these instruments of torture the beasts would race through the cage and leap over any hurdle placed in their path. Hagenbeck had seen innumerable old performing lions whose whiskers had been scorched off and who were frightfully burned and lacerated around the mouth and head.

Hagenbeck, however, was convinced that even the most dangerous species of carnivore is susceptible to acts of kindness. Animals soon perceive whether they are being treated sympathetically or otherwise, and quickly attach themselves to those who use them with kindness and consideration. Their memories, too, are usually retentive, a fact important to the trainer's method. Most carnivores in captivity are not so dangerous as the people who know nothing about them suppose. Indeed, the majority of them are by nature of a peaceful and even affectionate disposition. It was this one simple insight into animal personality that enabled Hagenbeck to substitute for the whip and the red-hot iron a humane method of rewards-and-punishments which completely revolutionized the age-old methods for "training" wild animals.

Basic to his system was his recognition of the fact that each animal has its own personality over and above the general psychological traits which it shares with all members of its species.

"This is a discovery I had to make for myself," he said. "It is a cardinal principle of the new school to expel from the troupe any animals which do not possess sufficient intelligence, or are too clumsy to become successful performers. Each beast must be carefully selected in accordance with its aptitude for the work it is wanted to perform. To recruit beasts indiscriminately is to court failure."

After making his initial selections, the first stage in Hagenbeck's gentle method of training was to accustom the young, unsophisticated animals to each other. All the cubs were placed in a row of single cages so that they could see each other and "converse together in their own language." During this period the trainer spends much time visiting and petting each animal individually, so that they all become acquainted with each other and with their master.

Then comes the first lesson in which, as in a kindergarten, there is no real work done. The cubs are simply let loose to play in a large arena, where they can get to know one another and their master more intimately. Despite the fact that there is no real work at this point it is nevertheless a crucial time. All young animals are fond of play but some are apt to lose their tempers and misunderstand each other's actions. A bear, for instance, may lumber toward a lion and playfully tug at his mane, but the king of beasts may not get the point of the joke and give his playmate a heavy box on the ear. Here is where permanent bad habits might be formed, so the trainer is quickly on the spot and, by a kindly blow on the ribs, intimates to the lion that civility is expected during lessons. Or a tiger, an animal which is by nature somewhat of a hooligan, may decide to take a poke at a leopard as it trots peacefully by, whereupon the leopard responds in kind. But here again the trainer rushes into the fray and soon separates the two young combatants. These are most important sessions for the trainer, for they enable him to get an idea of which animals are peaceful and obedient, and which pugnacious and obstinate.

In the second stage all the paraphenalia necessary for advanced training is brought into the arena. Wooden blocks are piled up in the form of a staircase and there is a barrel on which an animal, say a tiger, must learn to balance itself. The animals are now brought in and they stare curiously at the new objects in their playpen. But they are not permitted to nose around too long. This stage involves their first work, and it is only through his observation of work habits that the trainer can decide which animals are good prospects as performers and which must be discarded as inept and backward. At this point the trainer carries a whip, but far more important than this is the leather pocket attached to his belt, for it is there that he holds the keystone of Hagenbeck's system: the little pieces of meat with which he rewards the animals for their obedience.

On the top step of the pyramid of wooden blocks a lion must now learn to sit; on the step below, two tigers, then two leopards, and in front, on two blocks, the bears must learn to sit, while the dogs must learn to jump over the backs of the leopards. This is work that requires infinite patience on the part of the trainer and must be done over and over until the animals understand what is required of them. Some must be made to realize that they are expected to stay quietly in place until ordered to move, others to grasp the idea that they must maintain grotesque positions as, for instance, the tiger does when he mounts the rolling barrel.

As soon as the animals composing a troupe have been selected, each is given its own name to which, inasmuch as it always hears that name shouted when anything is required of it, it soon becomes accustomed. Next, each gets its own place—a kind of individual territory—generally one of a number of small wood blocks placed around the arena near the wall. The first thing that the animal has to learn here is to stay put on its own block until called, and to trot back to it as a matter of course after each trick it performs. To teach this the trainer walks up to a lion and holds out a piece of meat with which he tries to lead the young animal to a block. Sometimes he has to use rougher methods, such as pulling it over to the block by its hair. Having arrived at the block, however, the lion is not given the meat; it is only when he climbs up on the block that he gets his reward. But then, having eaten the meat, he generally jumps off the block and proceeds to enjoy himself around the arena. The trainer must then lead him back to his block and make him stand on it again, for it takes a long time for a young animal to understand its master's wishes. Every member of the troupe must be put through these paces innumerable times before they are ready for advanced training. This of course is the first and easiest stage of their education; but even as early as this many have to be re-placed because of viciousness or other faults. Extreme punishment, as Hagenbeck saw it, was of no use in these cases. It would only make the animal more stubborn and, if kept in the troupe, set a bad example to the others.

Now comes the teaching of individual tricks. The living pyramid of animals has to be constructed over and over again. The tiger needs countless lessons before he can stand on his rolling barrel. And, most important, the trainer, despite the great strain on his patience, must make sure to restrain his anger, for the slightest loss of self-control could easily ruin everything.

"But while he is careful to keep his temper," warned Hagenbeck, "the trainer must at the same time maintain the strictest discipline. As he leads the animals upward step by step in their difficult task, he must imbue them with the feeling that disobedience is an im-possibility. I need hardly say that the arduous labor involved in training wild animals can only be successfully carried out by one who is really fond of them. A genuine affection is needful for the establishment of mutual confidence between teacher and pupils. Courage too is most essential, for it must never be forgotten that however domesticated they may appear to be, they are yet at heart wild animals, and in all wild beasts there remains—deep down, perhaps, but there all the same—some remnant of their primitive ferocity. And this liability to outbreaks of temper increases with advancing age. If, however, the few cardinal principles which I have mentioned are carefully followed out, the danger ought to be very slight."

This final statement may sound to modern ears like the cliché of the century. The "cardinal principles" to which Hagenbeck referred, that is, the patient, gentle system of rewards and punishments instead of the whip and iron, has now been in use by animal trainers for so long a time that one can hardly imagine that there was ever a different method. But it is also just as difficult to conceive that not too long ago human beings were burned at the stake as witches. For animals it was Carl Hagenbeck who made the difference.

Besides being the world's leading animal dealer, Carl Hagenbeck was also its most revolutionary zookeeper. Like his ethnographic activity and his animal-training career, his zoo grew out of his activity as a dealer. As an animal trader dealing in large volume, it was important for Hagenbeck to "acclimatize"—to condition huge numbers of exotic animals to living in alien environments. Otherwise, mortality rates could be devastating. It was therefore necessary to acquire space that would be sufficient both for a proper holding area for large inventories and for the conduct of his experiments in acclimatization and breeding. He found this in Stellingen, a place in Prussia not far from Hamburg.

"Now at last I was in a position to carry out my long-nursed project of founding a zoological park of a totally different kind from anything that had been before attempted," wrote Hagenbeck. "I desired, above all things, to give the animals the maximum of liberty. I wished to exhibit them not as captives, confined to narrow spaces, and looked at between bars, but as free to wander from place to place within as large limits as possible, and with no bars to obstruct the view and serve as a reminder of the captivity. I wished also to show what could be accomplished in the way of acclimatization. I desired to refute the prevailing notion that luxurious and expensive houses with complicated heating apparatus were necessary for keeping wild animals alive and healthy. I hoped to show that far better results could be obtained when they were kept in the fresh air and allowed to grow accustomed to the climate. I wished my new park to be a great and enduring example of the benefits that can be wrought by giving the animals as much freedom and placing them in as natural an environment as possible. A certain point must be fixed in the garden from which might be seen every kind of animal moving about in apparent freedom and in an environment which bore a close resemblance to its own native haunts."

The Magna Carta for captive wild animals for all time to come! In that one statement were drawn the guidelines for every zoo, every wild-animal park, every wildlife preserve that, in the three-quarters of a century since its proclamation, has boasted of a revolutionary approach to animal exhibition. Every one of them—including the San Diego and Bronx zoos, all the drive-throughs, even the most modern of moated, cageless zoos in Europe—date back to that vision of Carl Hagenbeck.

More than a vision, it was a living, tangible accomplishment. When the Hagenbeck Stellingen Zoo opened to the public on May 7, 1907, it incorporated most of the goals that he had set down in his proclamation. For the wild sheep and the ibex, both rock-climbing animals, artificial mountains had been thrown up; for plains-dwelling species, such as giraffes and zebra, wide, open meadows were set apart. Ravines were cut out for the big cats, not surrounded by rails or fences but separated from the public only by deep moats, just large enough to prevent the animals from escaping. In the center of all this was a large arena for performing purposes, while close by were spacious areas for "holding" animals which were in transit to Hagenbeck's customers, one of these, for example, being the German Army, to which he once supplied 2,000 dromedaries.

All of them—the traded animals housed in spacious accommodations, the exhibited animals lodged in cageless, open enclosures, the performing animals no longer threatened by hot iron and whip—were freer than captive animals had ever been. More important, at the Stellingen Zoo Hagenbeck came through on his claim that many African animals could thrive in the temperate zones of northern Europe. His lions and monkeys did beautifully in the open winter of Stellingen, having, as they did, closed protected quarters to retreat into when the weather became too severe. His "simulated habitat" arrangement for his wildlife also proved a catalyst to their breeding activity and this, in turn, supported his theories about the interrelationship of an animal's habitat and its reproduction. Perhaps most significant was that the public, including kings, emperors, zoologists, environmentalists, scientists, statesmen, menagerie keepers and just plain common folk, flocked in droves to see the most revolutionary advance in wild-animal exhibition since man set up his first zoo.

Carl Hagenbeck died in 1913 at the age of sixty-nine. His work was carried on by his sons and today is continued by his grandsons, Carl-Heinrich and Dietrich Hagenbeck, the fourth generation of the world's most distinguished dynasty of animal men—zookeepers, trainers, and dealers.

The Stellingen Zoo is now the Hamburg Zoo in the sense that the smaller village has since been incorporated into the larger city. Thus the six seals that old Gottfried Claas Hagenbeck exhibited in Hamburg in his wife's washtubs 125 years ago are now part of that great city's zoo traditions. Rebuilt in 1948, five years after air raids destroyed much of the Zoo and Hagenbeck's Circus winter quarters—including eight people and 450 animals—the Zoo is still owned by the Hagenbecks, with Carl-Heinrich and Dietrich directing it under contract to the city of Hamburg. It is still operated on the principles laid down by its originator and is still visited by animal lovers from around the world as the very model of an ideal urban zoo. Animals still move about in simulated natural habitats separated from the public and each other, as they were in the original park, by obstacles so cleverly concealed that they seem non-existent. Even the old Wizard of Menlo Park, Thomas Alva Edison, was once fooled by Hagenbeck's optical illusions. Touring the zoo back in 1911, Edison walked around a group of trees to suddenly confront a lion face-to-face, with nothing, apparently, to separate them. It scared the daylights out of the old inventor, but he was so fascinated by Hagenbeck's own inventive genius that he insisted on continuing his tour of the zoo.

Hagenbeck's Circus, which had toured the world until the 1950s presenting shows based on Carl's "gentle" training system, no longer exists. It folded its tents forever when Heinrich Hagenbeck, who ran it, died. But animal performances still take place at the Hamburg Zoo, and other circuses everywhere still train their animals according to his principles. As for the animal-trading business, the family has also retired from that, except to the extent that zoos trade their surplus stock with each other. Dealing in animals is not what it was in the days when Carl Hagenbeck could turn over 2,000 dromedaries to the German Government or 67 elephants to P. T. Barnum as casually as another man might ship a gross of soap. The supply of wild animals to stock a business on the scale of the old Hagenbecks', the family says, has dwindled too much to justify so complex an operation. Expeditions to capture specimens are financially unfeasible today. Besides, there are import-and-export restrictions, quarantine requirements, and bureaucratic red tape in today's animal-dealing business that make it altogether too wacky a business for the conservative descendants of a fishmonger who got his start with six seals in his wife's washtubs.

7 *Animal Traders*

In the days when Africa and Asia were still colonial lands, "white hunters" could come in and, almost in the style of the old slave-traders, buy, trade, capture, steal or shanghai a boatload of native wild animals and sell them into bondage to zoos back home. The animal-trading business was then indeed a "wild" affair, full of crazy adventure, storybook romance and, not the least, a most gratifying profit.

Sometimes zoos themselves would organize their own collecting expeditions, sidestepping the commercial dealer and thereby considerably cutting the cost of obtaining new animals. This was often the case with zoos such as the National Zoo in Washington, which is subject to the whims of federal appropriations. Dr. William M. Mann, National's director, had to stay awake nights dreaming up gimmicks to prod the Office of the United States Budget, which approves the National Zoo's budget, into moving along with zoo appropriations. On one occasion he pressed into service one of the zoo's mynah birds which had an extraordinary facility for imitating human speech, one of its pet phrases being, "So's your old man!"

Dr. Mann trained the bird to say, "What about the appropriation?" and, hoping to charm stuffy old General Lord, Director of the U.S. Budget, into expediting a long-delayed appropriation, placed the bird on display at an annual exhibition for Government brass put on by the Smithsonian Institution, which runs the National Zoo for the Federal Government. When General Lord came up to the mynah bird, it cocked an unimpressed eye at him and said: "What about the appropriation?" Everybody in the room burst into laughter, but not General Lord. He squinted his eyes and angrily exclaimed, "Why, Dr. Mann, I think's that's impertinent!" To which the mynah bird replied, "So's your old man!"

The National Zoo did not go out of business because of Dr. Mann's impertinence, nor did Dr. Mann. Years later after he had almost singlehandedly built the zoo into a major institution, but still in need of new animals, he was still up to his old tricks trying to get money to buy them. President Franklin D. Roosevelt was touring the zoo one day. The mynah bird story had by then been a kind of legend in official Washington for years and, bearing this in mind, Dr. Mann craftily detoured the President's car to the Bird House. As expected, after viewing a number of exhibits, FDR asked, "What about that mynah bird, Dr. Mann, the one that requested the appropriation? Is he still here?"

"Oh, that fellow?" replied the doctor. "He died, Mr. President, he died of old age waiting for the appropriation."

In 1937 Dr. Mann pulled off one of his most ambitious enterprises for acquiring new specimens for the National Zoo. He headed one of the largest animal-collecting expeditions of modern times, acting in effect as his own dealer, under the sponsorship of the National Geographic Society and the Smithsonian Institution. Accompanied by his wife Lucile, he departed for Sumatra, then part of the Netherlands East Indies, his base camp for a journey that would stretch nine months and 30,000 miles to collecting points throughout the world.

Since he expected to make trades as he went along, Dr. Mann assembled a collection of domestic fauna, such as opossums and racoons, which he hoped to exchange for exotic creatures of the Far East. To a Chinese, a raccoon is as strange a sight as a pangolin is to an American. In all he took along twenty-six of these "zoological ambassadors" as he called them—two mountain lions, ten alligators, three opossums, two raccoons, two black bears, two South American jaguars, and five hellbenders, or large salamanders, found in Ohio Valley streams. As exchange animals he hoped to get such exotic species as tapirs, wild cattle from India and Africa, mouse deer (a true deer only 12 inches high), rare Oriental birds, tree kangaroos, tree shrews, Komodo dragon lizards and the most beautiful of all cats—the rare, clouded leopard.

At Shanghai, where there was still a foreign Concession with zoos in it, the expedition began to acquire some of his prizes, particularly a pair of blue sheep and a Chinese alligator. In Hong Kong, he picked up several rare giant salamanders, largest of amphibians; in the snake stores, which are really drug stores since the Chinese eat reptiles to cure various ailments, he and his party shuddered as they watched the merchants calmly grope among tangled clusters of snakes, including cobras, to reach the desired ones. Four days at sea brought them to Singapore, where they found crowded into the tiny shops on just one street enough specimens, many of them rare, to stock a sizable zoo. As their ship sailed for Sumatra, they caught sight of something perhaps not so rare for that time and area: a K.M.P. boat, one of the Dutch colonial merchantmen that served the entire Malayan Archipelago, carrying coolies to various labor bases.

"Our purser asked us to guess how many passengers were aboard," reported Dr. Mann in the *National Geographic* of June, 1938. "We guessed forty. He said there were more than 1,400—coolies coming from Java to work on tea or rubber plantations in Sumatra, where they stay for at least two years.

In Sumatra, on the outskirts of Pematang Siantar, the expedition, consisting of the Manns, two keepers from the National Zoo, a senior writer from the *National Geographic* magazine and two other colleagues, had, in effect, their own plantation, the Roemah Sakit ("Sick House"), an abandoned hospital for plantation workers that they rented from the manager of the plantation. Along with this "simple little hut in the jungle," as Dr. Mann called it, went a corps of five native gardeners who manicured twelve acres of lawn surrounded by a dog-proof fence made even more secure by a Sikh night watchman. The whole arrangement, including electricity and an icebox, rented for less than a penny a day, $16.00 a month in U.S. currency.

"The first thing one does on such an expedition," Mrs. Mann told a recent visitor to her apartment not far from the National Zoo, "is to interest the natives. When they know that there are foreigners in the vicinity who will actually pay money for what they consider vermin, animals come in faster than expedition members could catch them. As soon as they heard about us all kinds of things started coming in: chromatic pythons, alligators which we had to keep in the bathtub, Siamese gibbons, Monitor lizards, wild dogs—an endless supply of fine specimens. One of them came in with a baby tiger and I got the job of bottle-raising the little thing."

That was thirty-seven years ago and Mrs. Mann, now a widowed grande dame of the zoo world, recalled the incident with a twinkle in her deep brown eyes. Nursemaiding wild animals in the jungles of Sumatra was a far cry from the sheltered life of a proper young lady from Massachusetts who had been an associate editor of *Woman's Home Companion* before she met and married "Wild Bill" Mann.

"We hired a local native there, a young man who had once been a taxidermist for the American Museum of Natural History, a very competent fellow. We spread the word around further into the villages and soon more animals started pouring in—hornbills, cockatoos, orangs, everything. We even found a 12-foot king cobra in our backyard. We traveled by car through the villages and all along the way the natives would bring us the most unusual specimens. And we also gave away some of our own specimens to small village zoos, the animals Bill called zoological goodwill ambassadors. One day a messenger brought us word of a very rare animal which a native had trapped—something nobody in the area had ever seen before. We went to have a look at it. It was one of our goodwill ambassadors: one of the common opossums which had escaped from a village zoo we had given it to!"

In five months, through trapping, buying, exchanging and receiving, the expedition acquired an immense and quite representative East Asian collection from the island of Sumatra alone. Meantime its collectors in other parts of the Archipelago were busy. In Makassar on the island of Celebes, for instance, Captain J. W. F. U.

Diedrich got them three pigmy buffaloes (anoas) and a wild pig, both carefully protected animals which were first seized and then released by the police. Other catches included a couple of 18-foot pythons, and dozens of crested lizards, collared loris, racket-tailed parakeets and cockatoos. "We were using 700 bananas a day in getting this catch from Celebes to Sumatra," wrote Dr. Mann, "in addition to potatoes, apples and greens, with, of course, grass for the anoas. At Soerabaja we had to transfer to another K.P.M. steamer, always an anxiety when cages of delicate birds and animals have to be moved. However, they were well handled there, and stowed between decks along with 2,000 coolies going to Sumatra . . ."

At Bangkok, in Siam, the expedition acquired six gibbons and a collection of poisonous snakes given to them by the Pasteur Institute of Siam. This gift, housed in five teakwood boxes, contained king cobras, kraits, Siamese cobras and Russell's vipers—enough venom, literally, to kill an army.

Finally, the day for the prize: a Siamese clouded leopard, most beautiful of the cats. It was now August; with some six or seven weeks on the high seas ahead of them there would be a hint of chill in the air by the time this delicate tropical animal reached its destination in New York. It was time to lift anchor for home.

The expedition departed from Bangkok on a little Danish freighter bound for Singapore, where they transferred to the motor vessel *Silverash*, which was to be their home for the next seven weeks. With them on the ship was the clouded leopard and the Komodo dragons they had wanted so badly, in addition to their Siamese, Malayan and Batavian collections. At Belawan they found their huge Sumatran collection stacked in freight cars on the wharf waiting to be loaded aboard.

Among the stores on the ship were more than a ton of bananas— which were to be the staple of vegetarians on the voyage—plus 250 pounds of string beans, 1,250 pounds of sweet potatoes, 100 dozen eggs, 75 pounds of peanuts, 90 pounds of papaya, 900 pounds of fresh grass, 600 pounds of frozen beef, 100 pounds of frozen fish, and several crates each of evaporated milk and strained honey. Added to these would be fresh supplies taken on board at frequent stops on the way home.

In Bombay they picked up a pair of gaur, the largest and most ferocious of jungle cattle. At Karachi the ship took on some cobras, four Indian pythons, a cage of finches, along with a quantity of bad drinking water, which set off an epidemic of dysentery among the officers and killed their big orangutan.

Which was the least of it. There was mutiny, nearly unbelievable heat, fierce Atlantic storms, and seasickness—all with nearly 1,000 wild beasts of every variety stowed in the holds below.

"At Port Sudan we took aboard four giraffes, two African buffaloes and two shoebill storks," Mrs. Mann recalled. "The giraffes and buffaloes were in padded cages too large to go below, so the cages were lashed to the rail. For three days in the Red Sea we suffered through the most unthinkable heat. Our senior author and a Himalayan bear went down with heat stroke, and our gibbon, 'Decline and Fall,' died from it. Every one of the animals was exhausted by it."

During all this, the "delicate" little lady from the *Woman's Home Companion* was down below chopping away at mountains of bananas and pumpkins. She had assumed responsibility for feeding the collection on the long voyage. "That gave me a little idea of what poor Noah and his daughters must have gone through," she told her visitor. "Every once in a while I had to scoot up to the deck for a breath of that fresh hot Red Sea air."

By the time the *Silverash* reached Port Said on the Mediterranean coast of Egypt the crew was ready for mutiny.

"We had just come through that terrible Red Sea ordeal. Everybody was dried out from the heat, including the sailors. Now here we were in the blue Mediterranean and a chance for the crew to have a break. Port Said, too—a classical sailor's town. But the Captain wouldn't give them shore leave despite the fact that sailors from other ships were getting time on the town. Before we knew it fighting broke out below. We could see the scuffling from above. Guns, threats, yelling and fists flying. I don't know how he did it but the Captain put the mutiny down and some of the sailors were hustled off in irons to jail. We actually were more in danger from humans than from animals."

In the Mediterranean the ship dodged a floating mine, and passed under the scrutiny of an unidentified warship on the prowl for pirates. (In 1937 there were still pirates on the high seas. In fact, at the very time their ship was passing through the Mediterranean the Lyon Conference on Piracy was taking place and the *Silverash* passengers gathered around the radio every night to learn whether another cargo ship had been sunk.)

The climax of the journey came in the Atlantic Ocean, two days out of Halifax, Nova Scotia, their first stop in the Western Hemisphere. That evening the ship ran into a gale that made animal-collecting a nightmare. About midnight the giraffe cages which had been lashed to the rail on deck, broke loose and started to slide back and forth. Huge waves washed across the eleven-foot-high cages as the ship dived and rose. It was pandemonium. Finally the Captain managed to heave to, called all hands on deck and the crates were made secure again.

After this the remainder of the voyage was relatively calm. The ship docked at Halifax to take on a new supply of bananas, of which they had only six left. It stopped at Boston for a day and, on September 27, 1937, fifty days after leaving Singapore, reached New York, the end of the sea voyage, where the cargo was unloaded. Hoofed stock went to quarantine at the United States Department of Agriculture Station at Athenia, New Jersey, and the rest was shipped by express train to Washington.

"The following morning the joy of taking the animals (nearly 900, of 172 species, some never seen in America before) out of their shipping crates and putting them in their comfortable cages in the Zoo more than made up for the work and worry we had on the voyage," wrote Dr. Mann.

"And my husband might have added another fringe benefit which I'll tell you about now," Mrs. Mann informed her visitor with that merry gleam in her eyes. "Old Gilbert Grosvenor, president of the National Geographic Society and editor of the magazine, didn't like snakes and never allowed photographs of them in the magazine. Well, he was so impressed by the expedition and its results that he finally broke down. That picture on page 695 of the *National Geographic* of June 1938 is historic—it's the first photograph of snakes ever to appear in the magazine. It was taken at the Pasteur Institute in Bangkok."

The National Geographic–Smithsonian expedition of 1937 was one of the last of the great wild-animal-collecting expeditions. Hagenbeck's did send their "travelers" into the jungles in 1950 and they returned to Europe with a large booty, but it was not nearly so ambitious a project as the Geographic–Smithsonian and it was also Hagenbeck's last expedition.

Since then the world has changed. So-called Third-World countries —the animal-supplying countries—have taken over management of their own affairs. The Frank Bucks, Trader Horns and assorted "bring-'em-back-alivers" who plundered native wildernesses under the guise of zoological research have, for the most part, been booted out of Africa together with the colonial administrators who issued export permits and native safari boys at ten cents a day. In the Far East, Holland's Queen Juliana's birthday is no longer a national holiday in wildlife-rich colonies such as Sumatra, nor are thousands of coolies packed with animals below decks as labor-cargo for foreign plantations. Even a prestigious, government-supported zoo would today find it politically impossible, as well as financially unfeasible in the face of soaring costs, to mount a large-scale collecting expedition.

Moreover, the commercial dealers who might be equipped for large-scale collecting have found themselves buried in mountains of import restrictions and red tape in the animal-demand countries. Piled on top of this are new laws that ban trading in animals such as those protected by the Endangered Species Acts of many nations, which is to say, much of the kind of wildlife in which zoos are interested. The "romance" and most of the profit have gone out of large-scale wild-animal collecting, which has led to the retirement from the animal-dealer business of many of the oldtime adventurous individuals and even of reputable conservative companies such as Hagenbeck's.

What's left? How do zoos go about replenishing their stock of wild animals in today's rigidly controlled trading environment? How does a zoo director, for example, go about obtaining a giraffe for his collections?

The answer is, first of all, by breeding. Most United States zoos now have productive breeding programs, due in large measure to an increased knowledge of animal behavior. A zoo's own giraffe breeding pairs may deliver a new giraffe to the zoo gratis, except for the overhead. The newborn may then be considered surplus stock and be sold or traded, either directly or through a dealer, to another zoo—a good piece of business for both zoos; for the seller because a giraffe, at $15–$18,000, is one of the most expensive of animals; and for the receiver, because he would obtain his giraffe without the need to go through import red tape, quarantine, unexamined purchase and all the accompanying rigamarole. Multiply the single giraffe surplus in one of 100-plus United States zoos in addition to all other surplus animals in any year, and it is obvious that there is considerable interdealing in animals by American zoo directors. The American Association of Zoological Parks and Aquariums in fact sets aside time at its annual national meeting, and also at regional meetings, to allow the assembled zoo people to do their individual wheeling-and-dealing.

Among these is Dr. Ted Roth, one of the most colorful and knowledgeable individuals in the zoo world. In addition to his former careers as a doctor of veterinary medicine and General Curator at the National Zoo, Dr. Roth fought with the French Partisans in World War II, in the aftermath of which, as part of the staff of Vienna's Schönbrunn Zoo, he wound up hassling with the Russian occupiers of that city.

He has also chased down considerable numbers of giraffes and other animals in jungles all over the world, both on his own account as a freelance collector and for Ruhe, Inc., a large commercial European dealer. In between he operated his own research farm in Virginia, offering services in primate supply and logistics—that is, bringing African green monkeys from the wild into laboratories for medical research. Currently, as assistant director of the Baltimore Zoo, he is daily involved in the buying and selling of zoo animals.

"Actually, only about one-fifth of the new stock acquired by United States zoos today is wild-caught," explained Dr. Roth. "That compares with one-half to three-quarters twenty-five years ago. And that one-fifth is mostly in the rare-animal category. Practically all rare animals we get come from dealers now. Plus those that the traditional zoo is too ineffectual in breeding, such as rhinos, elephants and certain antelope that are special feeders. They would be the most expensive and would generally be imported. A rhino, for example, might run to $20,000, whereas a large python, of which there are plenty, would cost only $500-$600. Or take the cheetah. Its importation is banned at present. Those that are brought in are smuggled, but they still cost only $1,200-$1,500 because they are now being successfully bred by zoos. Soon even cheetahs will be a drag on the market.

"What's true of the cheetah also applies to the other big cats," explained Dr. Roth. "The lion may be the King of Beasts, but he breeds so well in zoos today that his sale price is not kingly but beastly. I can get a top price of only maybe three to four hundred dollars for a good lion, that is, even if I could move him. That's getting more impossible each day with the enormous red tape and restrictions. Soon the big cats will be coming out of our ears. I'm stuck now with two jaguars, two leopards and two puma cubs because I can't move them. And that's only since last year."

What about the other categories of wild animals—birds, aquatic mammals, others?

"Flamingoes that used to sell for $38-$40, depending on species, are now up to $2,500 each—that's where you should have invested your money—flamingoes, not Polaroid. They come from Chile, Cuba, Guinea, and must go through quarantine at the dealer's expense. If just one bird doesn't pass quarantine, all the others must be killed off because they might be carriers. You have to start all over again. All this sends the price sky high."

The reasons for such rigid quarantine restrictions are of course mainly related to health. Newcastle's disease in birds, for instance, can wipe out poultry populations in epidemic proportions. Any bird can carry the disease. So, despite the hardship imposed on zoos, even those that are engaged in saving endangered species, the protection of domestic poultry would seem to have more of a claim on government watchfulness than does zoo stock. To keep America's hens safe from foreign contamination, the United States Department of Agriculture decrees that all birds must now be quarantined—which is a bother to the zoo people but for the rest of the population seems a useful precaution.

"And of course we've had the Lacey Act since 1901 which bans import of most hoofed stock," said Dr. Roth. "That's to protect our cattle and horses against hoof-and-mouth disease. You will see no wart hogs here, only American swine. Banned totally. Even if you wanted an exotic hoofed animal such as the giraffe you mentioned, it must go through ninety-day quarantine outside the United States in one of the four American stations around the world. Then it must come to the Port of New York, where it is sent to additional quarantine at Clifton, New Jersey. It might be eight months before you get your very tired giraffe. As you can see, the cattlemen's lobby knows how to protect its interests.

"Also the procedure has been immensely complicated in the last years by regulations requiring bleeding of import stock at regular intervals in foreign quarantine stations. Each blood sample must be sent to the United States for examination. If one animal is not up to specifications the whole station is wiped out. Theoretically the animals go back to their original owners. But it is too expensive to reship, so they're destroyed and wind up in the meat market.

"Seals, dolphins, walruses, too. They may be imported only under permit, the piled applications for which would dwarf *War and Peace*. They are endless and though their objective is to protect endangered species—which is, of course, good—in some cases the protected animal is not even endangered and would be better off in a good zoo. Some Washington gentlemen don't know the difference. They lump all marine mammals together.

"Then there is another thing called the Injurious Animal Act now in the works. It would prohibit importation of any animal except those specifically exempted on its list. And do you know what those exceptions are? There are about four or five: the guinea pig, Norway rat—both of which are reasonably injurious if let loose—the gerbil . . . others . . . On the bird list, there are also four or five exempted: the canary, the society finch . . . why the society finch was exempted nobody knows. It is no more or less injurious than the Bengal finch or the African grass finch. The bill must have been written by some fish lobbyist because there's a whole long list of exempted fish. In other words, fish may be brought in but only four of five mammals and four or five birds. That bill might well finish zoos off unless we can get changes made to permit us to import a much wider range of species. But that's going to be tough because as a pressure group we're small and not nearly as well financed as, say, the livestock industry. Perhaps now you can understand why Hagenbeck's retired from the dealer business."

What is left, then, of the fabled old animal-trading business, that legendary profession filled with the exploits of "bring-'em-back-aliver's" like Frank Buck, round-the-world expeditions such as Dr. Mann's, and the vast caravans Lorenzo Cassanova pushed through the African jungles? What has happened even to the adventurous freelance trapper of lone giraffe, as Roth himself once was?

"Me? I guess I just got too old for that kind of action," said Dr. Roth. "I was one of the last few freelancers who worked the bush collecting for zoos and big dealers. Unfortunately the whole business has just gotten too complex, especially for the freelancer. Out of a total of about forty dealers worldwide there are few that are really qualified and reputable. Say three or four in the United States and a couple in Europe that a good zoo would feel confident in dealing with."

In Europe one of those would be Ruhe, Inc., an old firm, something on the order of Hagenbeck's, whose founders as far back as 1846 were street-peddling canaries to housewives out of wooden containers strapped to their backs. They finally wound up with not only a worldwide trade in canaries and wild animals, but also with their own zoos in Germany, Spain and Denmark, which they used as holding areas for their trade animals. Ruhe, Inc., for whom Dr. Roth worked, also had an American operation but closed that down and appointed a representative here in 1960 when the trading business began to get so complicated. The other major European dealer is the Holland-based firm of Franz M. Van Dan Brink, which operates along classical dealer lines.

In the United States the field, as Dr. Roth stated, is now left chiefly to three or four major dealers, each of whom approaches the business from an essentially different angle. The one with perhaps the greatest volume is the International Animal Exchange, Ferndale, Michigan, owned by the four Hunt brothers. International Animal Exchange tends to use a good deal of showbiz schmaltz. Its president, Don Hunt, comes to work in the firm's office in Nanyuki, Kenya, attired in elegant bush jackets, often accompanied by actor William Holden, with whom he is a partner in the plush Mt. Kenya Safari Club. Holden is also an associate of Hunt's in the Mt. Kenya Game Preserve, which breeds a number of exotic species, and occasionally joins in the hunt for the wild animals. (It's either an interesting coincidence or a more deliberate affectation that so many of the animal dealers have names that describe their profession—for example, Don Hunt.) Originally Don Hunt came out of the pet-shop business in Detroit, where International Animal Exchange still maintains two thriving pet stores called "Bwana Don." The name derives from the syndicated children's TV show called "Bwana Don in Jungle-La," which earned Hunt enough money to put him in the worldwide animal-trading business. (Bwana, incidentally, means "master" or "boss.") In addition, Hunt's animal conglomerate organizes "zoofaris" to East Africa under the banner of Hunt's International Travel Organization. One of his brothers, Brian, is also president of New Jersey's Jungle Habitat.

Despite its Madison Avenue overlay, International Animal Exchange has some of the oldtime animal-dealer characteristics. Practically all of its animals are caught to order in the wild, never on speculation, although a good part of its trading involves buying and selling zoo surplus. Don Hunt personally captures many of the specimens himself, working out of his base in Kenya. If the previously mentioned hypothetical order for a giraffe is placed with International Animal Exchange, the requisition goes to the Ferndale office, whence it is forwarded to Africa and Don Hunt, who, unfazed by the mountainous red tape that has liquidated so many other dealers, goes into action. First, he gets his capture permit from the Kenya Ministry of Wildlife (for giraffes at a fee of around $400). "Then," says Hunt, "we select our terrain, set up a camp and build a *boma*, or corral, to keep the animals in after we catch them. Giraffes have to be lassoed. It has to be done quickly because of their delicate structure. If you chase a giraffe more than a hundred yards you can badly damage it."

Once captured, the giraffe is kept in the *boma* to "acclimatize" it to captivity, and give it a chance to quiet down and become used to the kind of food it will receive in a zoo. After this it goes through a sixty-day quarantine in Africa, after which it is ready for the month-long voyage to the United States and another thirty-day quarantine in the USDA station in New Jersey. Some seven months after the order was placed at Ferndale, if the giraffe has survived (and International Animal Exchange has an excellent record for live delivery), the animal will be delighting visitors in some American zoo. About one-half of Hunt's trade in exotic animals is conducted with zoos in this fashion. The rest is in monkeys and other primates for research needs of government institutes of health and for pharmaceutical firms, with about one per cent going to circuses and private collectors. Among zoos, International Animal Exchange's reputation ranks as the highest.

Another dealer of good reputation is Charles P. Chase, Co., of Miami, Florida, whose president, C. P. (Bill) Chase—like Don Hunt—was seemingly named after the fact of his trade. Bill Chase chases down mammals, birds and reptiles for zoos, exhibits and research laboratories, but his company concentrates mostly on South America, especially on ring-tailed monkeys and snakes.

Frank M. Thompson and Associates, of Bradenton, Florida, might be considered the third of the triumvirate of leading United States wild-animal dealers. He also operates somewhat along the lines of the traditional trader, with his own acclimatization farm and breeding facilities. (Thompson seems the exception in the linkage of name to profession.)

Somewhere between this type of wild-animal dealer and the kind who will supply anything "from a hamster to an elephant" is Henry Trefflich, who for years has operated out of a pet shop in New York's lower Manhattan. Trefflich, whose Yellow Pages advertisement notes that in addition to hamsters and elephants he will also supply "chimpanzees, monkeys, parrots and birds," has not yet fulfilled his dream of a "monkey in every house." But he has put lots of them in the streets. Once known as the "Monkey King of America," he has on occasion had hordes of his primates escape at high noon and run wild in the areas just off Wall Street. Despite the heavy emphasis on monkeys and monkey haberdashery (you can buy clothes to fit your monkey) Trefflich does a considerable business with zoos. His emporium is a kind of Hammacher Schlemmer of wild animals. A zoo director might obtain a rhino from Trefflich for $25,000, and a child might pick up a hamster for $2.50.

If an individual named Leon Leopard who runs Viva Animales in Waco, Texas, is taken into account, plus the other twenty-four dealers listed in the 1973 Directory of the American Association of Zoological Parks and Aquariums (AAZPA), the roster of acceptable people dealing in wild animals in the United States is about complete.

One maverick among them is especially notable. Like Hunt, Chase and the others, F. J. Zeehandelaar bears an appropriate name— Zeehandelaar in Dutch, which is F.J.Z.'s national background, means "Sea Trader," and he is a trader in wild animals that come from overseas.

Like many dealers, F.J.Z. fancies the word "bongo" (as in bongo drum) for his cablegram code, his being embroidered with the prefix "Zee" (ZEEBONGO). This personalizes his own brand of drum-beating almost to the point of trademark. And in speculation about his name and cablegram code is perhaps the essence of the story of one of the most unusual people in the world of zoos.

F. J. Zeehandelaar can't be found in the Yellow Pages under Animal Dealer, or under any other category for that matter. But any zoo director in the United States, and indeed in any part of the world, knows that if he contacts ZEEBONGO, NEWROCHELLE-USA to buy a giraffe, F.J.Z. will start one on the way almost as fast as he can move his fingers across the keys of any of the several teletype machines in his two-by-four cubicle office next to the New Rochelle railroad station in Westchester County, New York. Also the other way around: if somebody wishes to dispose of a giraffe or other zoo animal, F.J.Z. will set in motion his worldwide electronic communications hookup and, *Bongo!*, said animal will be as good as en route to willing receivers in Copenhagen, Majorca, Honolulu or San Diego.

Despite all this traffic to and from distant points, F. J. Zeehandelaar does not, as do other major dealers, stock a single animal. No wild beast is ever unloaded at his location, even temporarily, despite the fact that it is right next to the New Rochelle railroad station; F.J.Z. does not have room enough to stock a marmoset. Neither does he catch wild animals; as one of his zoo-director clients has said, "Zeehandelaar has had so little personal contact with wild animals he wouldn't dare to try catching an arthritic doe antelope that has lost all her teeth. But he certainly does have something else."

That "something" is a continuously updated file in his head of who is thinking what about which wild animal at any moment nearly anywhere on earth. The result of this extraordinary talent for cross-indexing has been a meteoric rise in an animal-trading career that over the past twenty-two years has grown from part-time dabbling while employed by a spice trader to a full-time business that deals with just about every zoo in the world. And all from an office that, for identification, has nothing more than an ordinary mailing label pasted on the door.

"I don't care what they say about me—how I have no personal contact with animals and all that," Mr. Zeehandelaar told his visitor. "Does Rockefeller drill oil? The business of wild animals is not a business of animals, it's a business of people. I know the quality and condition of every animal I export or import because I know who I'm dealing with. In twenty-two years I know who to buy from or sell to and who not to. Besides," he emphasized, putting aside a Schimmelpennick cigar to light a Camel cigarette, "I've *seen* more animals in my life than many of those who make such remarks. Ninety-five percent of the animals I handle personally I personally see. No shipment goes on the road without my seeing it. If anything goes wrong with the animal the cause is not zoological, it's anthropological."

"You mean the problems in your business are caused by people and not animals?"

"Exactly right. When I send an animal out, it's in sound condition because, as I said, I know who I buy from. Whatever happens to it after, it's the fault of people—in the handling, crating, shipping and feeding. That's the first anthropological problem. The second is the over-regulation, particularly in the United States. It all starts in the name of conservation and then goes haywire. People who can't make it in private life become public officials. They get power-drunk and take out grudges against little zoos. You have a great bureaucracy that knows too much about ecology and too little about animals. One department's regulations contradict those of another. In five years we will see plenty of empty cages in which they can exhibit their regulations instead of animals. They would like that, but what about the wild animals that only zoos can save . . . but wait—there's the teletype!"

In an alcove of his tiny cubicle a machine starts clicking and F.J.Z. rises from his desk to check it. As the visitor looks around the two-by-four workspace hung with testimonials from leading zoos and zoological organizations around the world, he gets the feeling of being in the presence of one of those "park-bench" entrepreneurs —some Billy Rose or Barney Baruch—whose entire armory of tools is in his head and who will forthwith close some farflung deal without so much as a line of secretarial dictation. It becomes even more unlikely when one considers the setting for this particular operation: an office on the second floor of a beige-brick monstrosity with a roof of loosened Spanish terra-cotta tiles shaded by a mangy old tree on Route One in a small suburban town. You walk up a flight of creaky stairs to go down a hallway dimly lit by a single gasping fluorescent tube, past an office door boarded over with plywood, past the Clarendon Detective Agency, Rothstein Furs, Renaissance Garden Projects—cubicles all—and you come to a door on which the only identification is a casually pasted three-inch mailing label reading, "F. J. Zeehandelaar," 405 North Ave., New Rochelle, N.Y. 10801. POSTMASTER: This parcel may be opened for inspection if necessary."

Inside, international messages are clicking back and forth through the teletypes. F.J.Z. picks up one. It is a telex from Alberta Game Farm, Edmonton, Canada. "No quarantine space available at present," the telex reads "Possible in week or ten days." With that F.J.Z. goes to another machine and taps a cablegram. "To Honolulu Zoo," it reads. "Make sure animals are released upon arrival even if check not arrived." That apparently is good enough for the Honolulu Zoo, considering F.J.Z.'s excellent financial reputation. The transaction involved a giraffe born in Honolulu and imported by F.J.Z. for the Indianapolis Zoo. In between these communications he was sending out a mailgram to the Oakland, California, Zoo to urge dispatch of the health certificates for some baboons he had just purchased from them. So he goes, day in, day out, keeping check on the traffic of his animals around the world like the keeper of a one-man Aerospace Center in a one-room office in a creaky building athwart a one-horse railroad station.

"Maybe I don't handle animals so much, as they say," observed F. J. Zeehandelaar. "Maybe I don't even catch them. But, as I said before, does Rockefeller drill oil? The point is that nobody operates the way I do. You want a wild animal, you've got it, if it is at all available and the conditions are right. That's because I do my spade work and I know every detail of my operation personally. I brought in the first okapi and takin, now at the Bronx Zoo. I've brought in many rare animals: sea elephants, snow leopards, mountain gorillas

—they're in all the best zoos. What difference does it make if, as they say, I never leave this office—which, of course, is not true. Or if I don't personally catch them? My job is to buy and sell, import and export."

F. J. Zeehandelaar, the one-man, exotic-animal stock exchange from New Rochelle, is indeed a phenomenon with a reputation and crustiness that seem especially welcome in a time of too much slick-and-easy virtue.

William G. Conway, general director of the New York Zoological Society (Bronx Zoo) with the first zoo-exhibited James's flamingo which he captured in South America. *(Photo credit: New York Zoological Society)*

Frank Buck, the famous "bring-em-back-alive" animal dealer of the 1930s, at the circus in Madison Square Garden, New York City. *(Courtesy of New York Public Library Picture Collection)*

Mrs. Martin Johnson, big game hunter and collector of the 1920s. Mrs. Johnson and her husband presented captive, live specimens to many zoos. *(Courtesy of New York Public Library Picture Collection)*

Don Hunt and the Mount Kenya Game Ranch Capture Unit, with a newly captured reticulated giraffe on the Laikipia Plateau, Kenya. *(Photo credit: l. Breidenbend, Mt. Kenya Game Ranch)*

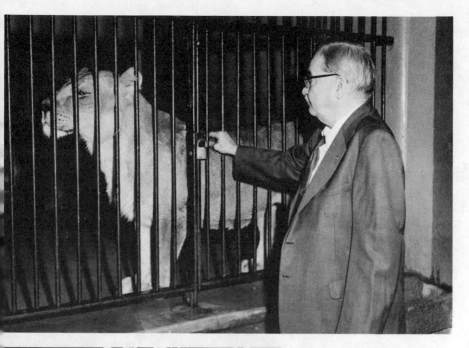

Mrs. Lucile Mann and her husband, Dr. William Mann —one time director of the National Zoo in Washington. The Manns led the 1937 National Geographic–Smithsonian Institution expedition that brought back to the U.S. nearly one thousand wild animals for the National Zoo. *(Photo credits: Smithsonian Institution)*

Don Hunt and Captive Unit with a newly captured White Zebra. There are only two White Zebras in Africa, both now at the Mount Kenya Game Ranch. *(Photo credit: Breidenbend, Mt. Kenya Game Ranch)*

Dr. Ted Roth, assistant director of the Baltimore Zoo with two rare Snow Leopards. One of the last few free lance trappers of wild animals, Dr. Roth's collecting exploits have taken him through the wilds of India, Ethiopia and other parts of Africa and the Far East. Before he came to the U.S. he worked at the world's oldest zoo, Schöenbrunn, in Vienna, then occupied by the Russians. (Photo credit: *Baltimore Zoo)*

8 Capturing Wild Animals—From Queen Hatshepsut to Frank Buck

An oddity happened to Doctor and Mrs. Mann in Sumatra when civets and cobras wandered uninvited into their backyard, remained, and eventually became tenants of the Washington National Zoo. Clearly most other creatures from the wild are less cooperative. Even those nonmammalian species which wind up in a zoo through the incubation of an egg taken from the wild, such as the ostrich or crocodile, come by their new home through capture—often at considerable danger to the captor from an enraged parent.

The basic capture technique has persisted since the time of Egyptian Queen Hatshepsut: taking the young by trapping the adult with net, snare, pit, rope or box; also, chasing groups of animals with young at their sides until the smaller ones fall with exhaustion and are taken in that fashion from the adult. The recently perfected dart- or capture-gun immobilizes the adult by firing a drug into it at a distance. In some cases, of course, adult wild animals are themselves also taken capture for confinement in zoos and other arenas. Adult lions, bears and other fierce beasts were brought from the wild to Rome in ancient times for use in the bloody amphitheater games, and even in modern times some wild-caught adult animals have been placed in zoos both for exhibit and breeding purposes.

Whatever the age of the animal seized—adult or young—the old-time "bring-'em-back-aliver's" organized groups of natives to go into the bush and capture animals by methods that were essentially nothing more than refinements of age-old tribal techniques. The catching of young animals by chasing the herd on horseback until the little ones were exhausted was first used on giraffes in Ethiopia during the eighteeenth century. Today the animals are chased by white hunters' Land Rovers and Jeeps. Techniques for immobilizing large adult animals and then seizing their young were also practiced for centuries by castes of primitive African sword hunters, who, for example, paralyzed elephants by rupturing their Achilles tendons with their swords. This was done by using a group of riders all mounted on dark ponies except one, who rode a gray. The elephant, whose eyesight is poor, was attracted by the gray and made an assault on it, thereby freeing the other riders to come in from behind and deliver a blow to its left hind leg, slashing the Achilles tendon and laming the beast. When this happened, the elephant turned to meet his new attackers; whereupon another rider came from a different direction to deal the same kind of blow at the right hind leg, which totally disabled it. The rifle has, of course, long since replaced the sword as a weapon for attacking animals, but nevertheless mechanical dispatch of the adult still remains the staple for capture of the young. Today many types of large adults are also immobilized, as mentioned, by the drug dart or capture gun.

Young animals can also be captured by trap, a method particularly successful with the hippopotamus; the pitfall is a common variety. The hippo mother has a habit of letting her young trot along in front of her instead of behind so that she can keep an eye on it. The pit is built on a path the animal habitually uses, and one day the little animal simply vanishes into the camouflaged hole in front of its mother, who is generally so terrified she turns and runs off, leaving her offspring.

Snakes have also traditionally been among the easier to catch in the wild. The natives of India generally do their snake-catching before dawn, when the reptiles are so benumbed by cold that they can easily be trapped. This is done by means of a net fixed to the end of a long pole, or by a long, forked stick that can be applied to the reptile's neck and pressed to the ground. During dry season, heat rather than cold is often used as aid to capture. Nets are laid around a reptile haunt and the area is then set on fire. In their hurry to escape, the reptiles, particularly the large ones, become entangled in the nets and are quickly caught and placed in bags.

In Ethiopia, driving animals was for years a favorite method of capturing them. An army of as many as 2000 men would encircle a large tract of country where, for example, zebras were known to be found. The locality picked would be one in the center of which was a dried-up riverbed, common to that country. The circle of men would then slowly contract, driving the zebras into the center. When the animals were corraled within the riverbed, a barbarous spectacle would take place. A thousand men would ride in and thrash the zebras with long whips until the animals were thoroughly exhausted and their spirits broken. They were then fastened by ropes attached to each of their four legs and tied to posts—in a few days, they became quiet and tame. Many men were often killed in the process (some might say poetic justice).

Even the great Carl Hagenbeck used natives and native techniques for capture. "The Takruris—Mohammedan Negroes who have emigrated from Darfur—are especially skillful in hunting and trapping," he wrote. "They are equally adept in catching hyenas, panthers, and baboons in carefully constructed traps, or in digging out porcupines, or in securing birds, such as secretary-birds, francolins, etc., in snares and nets of ingenious patterns. This versatility renders them invaluable to us as assistants."

So it was with much of wild-animal catching throughout the late nineteenth and early twentieth centuries, the period accompanying the great expansion of the urban zoo. With modern technology, especially the motion-picture film, another kind of wild-animal catcher came on the scene—the "bring-'em-back-aliver" who immortalized his exploits with movies of real-life scenes of life and death struggles in the jungle. Martin and Osa Johnson, Carl Akeley and others brought back "thrilling film documentaries of wildlife in the rapidly vanishing wilderness, in addition to specimens of wildlife in the flesh. The many Denis–Roosevelt expeditions also acquainted large movie audiences with some idea of what the jungles and rain forests and savannas were like.

But the man who dominated the scene was Mr. Bring-'Em-Back-Alive himself, Frank Buck. His name was a household word in America of the 1930s. Dozens of movies, books and lectures told in graphic detail how Frank Buck, natty and debonair in his pith helmet, boots and riding britches sauntered through the thick of the Dark Continent's most ferocious animal fights and, swinging only his swagger stick, brought 'em back alive with never a scratch inflicted. Hollywood—even Disney—had not yet gotten into the live wild-animal business until Frank Buck gave them a lead character to dramatize. Much of the so-called real-life drama—tiger versus python, lion versus Cape buffalo, leopard versus hyena—which was the main focus of these "jungle documentaries" was actually filmed in the jungles of Hollywood's back lots. And the public streamed by the millions to see the "Great White Hunter" bring-'em-back-alive to zoos and circuses throughout the land.

"Oh yes, we used to deal with Frank Buck," San Diego's Dr. Schroeder told a visitor. "We called him Frank Bunk. That's because he was a faker—all the way. He never went out to *any* forest to collect *any*thing. He was a desk man, and a great guy with the martinis. They used to say that the only thing Frank Buck ever brought back alive was a double martini from 30 Rockefeller Plaza. That's because no matter in what jungle his press agent said he was, you could always be sure of really finding him leaning on the Old English Bar in Radio City."

How then did Frank Buck collect all those animals that he was supposed to have personally brought back alive? Where did he get the animals that he sold as a dealer?

"Singapore, where else? He had an office over there. He would have local hunters get the animals for him. That's no trick. You have a depot and you're going to buy stuff, it comes right in the back door."

What about the pith helmet, the riding breeches, the boots and swagger stick? Frank Buck looked the very model of the Great White Hunter.

"Well, I knew another dealer," said Dr. Schroeder, smiling with the memory. "His name was Ellis Joseph. Mother was a Bombay Indian, father a Welshman, spent years in Australia collecting marsupials. In those days they had a thing in New York called the Circus Buffs Association. Bill Mann was one of the enthusiasts, both Bill and his wife Lucy. They'd all go to the Ritz for dinner on opening night and then to the circus. Ellis Joseph took me to the last one with him. Frank Buck was already a household name and so the circus employed him to ride the elephants around, and widely publicized the fact. 'That's what I came to see,' said Ellis, 'Frank Buck riding an elephant. Why, that character was never on an elephant in his whole life.' And sure enough, when the elephants came out, where do you think Mr. Bring-'Em-Back-Alive was? *Walking* in front of the elephant, saluting the crowds with that pith helmet!"

Didn't he have an office, some kind of a place he operated from? After all he was an animal dealer.

"Oh, yes. Apart from his pew at the Old English Bar he had a place out in Amityville, Long Island. When the World's Fair went on he got together with Henry Trefflich. There was another one . . . we gave some of our business to Trefflich. But when things got slow Henry would let a few monkeys out of the back window of his pet store, and, with all the newspaper publicity, business would start booming again, especially in the pet department. Well these two got together. Trefflich would import the rhesus monkeys and they'd put them on Buck's place—called Frank Buck's Monkey Island on the Midway in Flushing Meadow. They'd let the public come and feed them. Then at night Henry could come and harvest as many as he needed for his shipments. They were all full of TB and many of them died, but it cost Frank and Henry nothing to maintain them; the public fed them."

It seems incredible, suggested the visitor, that, granted all this, such a man as Frank Buck could have dominated the wild-animal scene so completely and so long. How was this possible?

"Could be all those books he wrote and all those Hollywood movies. Hollywood could do anything in those days. But I do know that the U.S. Department of Agriculture thought the animal world began and ended with Frank Buck. Once we had Lebau Brothers bring in a shipment of animals for the Bronx Zoo by way of Mombasa. There were great restrictions on the import of wild animals then. Even the Bronx Zoo had trouble getting them in. Believe it or not, Frank Buck tried to kill the deal for the Lebaus. And we had a terrible time getting approval of these animals over his intervention. But Frank Buck couldn't get away with anything with Dr. Harry Wegeforth. Buck worked for a while as a keeper at San Diego before he became a big name. He kept oiling the elephants' hides despite Dr. Harry's warning that it would cause Bright's disease. Nevertheless Buck kept on oiling them and some of them did develop Bright's disease. Dr. Wegeforth fired him. Buck sued him and, of course, he lost. But that didn't stop him from going on to become Mr. Bring-'Em-Back-Alive even though he obviously didn't know how to keep even a zoo elephant alive."

Today the major change in the process of bringing an animal back alive to the zoo is not so much in the methods of capture as it is in the means of transport. Formerly, a shipment of newly captured animals was assembled more or less leisurely in the country of origin, where the animals could adapt more easily from natural food to captive food. Then there would be the long sea voyage which permitted them to adjust gradually to an alien climate. By the time the animals arrived, they were generally well acclimatized and the recipient had a fairly good chance of getting a sound healthy specimen.

Now, with the prevalence of air transport, wild animals are shipped mostly on planes, not only because it is more convenient but also, since almost any animal caught wild will survive a week or so without extreme care, it is less risky for the shipper. But this is often unfortunate both for the animal and for the zoo/dealer recipient. A wild animal may suffer from severe "jet lag" if shipped long distance by air, apart from the fact that it also often arrives stressed and debilitated because the acclimatization process has been cut off. When it arrives in the United States it is generally unloaded and reshipped to its final zoo destination, where, having incurred the additional stress, it often dies because its resistance has been shattered.

"There's really little that you can do to get around this," said Dr. Ted Roth. "The supplier is often a native of the origin country under direct orders from Achmed ben Buzzi or somebody and he just slaps the animal on the plane. If you're lucky you may get it alive. Of course there is insurance—the usual terms are 'safe delivery plus thirty extra days alive.' But you don't want the insurance, you want your animal."

According to Ted Roth, who has personally captured wild animals in India, Africa and the Far East, the greater problem begins once they are caught. How does one get them to feed? What feed, how much? How do you acclimatize them to captivity?

"Take a rare animal like the tapir, for instance. It's very easy to catch, but the average capturer usually loses it through rectal prolapse. If a tapir doesn't receive its natural food or some plant derivative thereof, its stool becomes so hard it presses out the animal's rectum, very often while in transport. One thing I discovered before I began making my field trips was that tapirs eat calmus extensively. This is a diuretic—a stool softener—but it is not allowed aboard ship in Aden or Singapore. But you can substitute calmus with huge amounts of rhubarb, which has essentially the same effect." (As with humans, animal medicine is not especially esthetic.)

Despite the great technological changes in the mode of wild-animal transport, however, there has been little technological change, as suggested, in capture methods except for the introduction of drugs for restraint and immobilization. These are administered by way of projectiles—darts or syringes containing the drugs—fired by an assortment of pistols, rifles and even crossbows. An early model of a firing mechanism, powered by carbon dioxide and employing a syringe containing the drug nicobine salicylate, was brought to Uganda for use on the Kob antelope by Dr. Helmut K. Buechner, now at the National Zoo. The drug proved unsuitable for this animal, but further research turned up suxamethonium, which did work. The latter drug, however, provided too small a safety margin for larger animals. This in turn led to the refinement of a *curare* compound (Flaxedil) for use on such animals as the black rhinos which had been stranded on the islands of Kariba Lake when a dam was built in Rhodesia. Even though the operation to remove these animals to safety marked the first successful large-scale use of immobilizing drugs, there were many fatalities—particularly among those animals that could not be found in time for the administration of antidotes.

In the 1960s, major breakthroughs in the use of drugs for the capture of large animals were made with the development of Themalon, a morphine mixture that increased the safety factor tenfold, and

M99, a synthetic morphinelike compound that has an analgesic activity up to 10,000 times that of morphine. These were used mostly on large ungulates such as the rhino.

In contrast to the immobilization of the large ungulates, the chemical capture of carnivores proved comparatively simple. A drug called Sernylan (phencyclidine hydrochlorine), which requires only a small dose and then an intravenous injection of a fast-acting barbiturate, has been used with good effect on lions in Africa's Kruger National Park. Another called Ketamine, a cyclohexamine derivative, has been suitable for other large cats. Immobilizing techniques for most large African mammals have been fairly well worked out.

Still, even though the capture guns have been greatly improved and proper dosages worked out for a great many species of animals, some zoo people say that chemical capture is not nearly as safe as its proponents claim. First, there is often the danger of regurgitation of recently eaten food and inhalation of liquids into the lungs with consequent pneumonia or even suffocation. This is especially true when immobilization is practiced by people with little experience.

There's also the problem of dosage. Generally the amount of drug to be injected into the animal is based on species and weight, but often it is an animal's particular characteristics that have been found to be more decisive. In one instance a basic dosage that had been worked out for an 800-pound elk was used on a four-ton elephant, which dropped like a stone. There simply are all manner of intangibles because of individual characteristics. Too little dosage for a particular animal means that it will run off and be lost to its would-be captor; too much can mean it will be dead.

There is the stress factor too. The popular conception about chemical immobilization is that the animal is shot with a drug dart, it goes down, one does what one wants with it, gives it an antidote and the animal is up again. Actually an enormous amount of shock can result from the psychological stress induced by alien chemicals, whereas the possibility of physical capture—either by man or by predators—is something that most wild animals live with every day and become more or less accustomed to.

Moreover, chemical capture is hardly of any use at all with forest-dwelling animals such as the arboreal primates. If a monkey is hit with a drug dart he takes off and drops somewhere in the deep forest. The chances of finding him are practically nil; under even optimum conditions predators will probably get to him first. So for purposes of capture in the wild, chemical immobilization is at present used chiefly on animals that live in the open, where they can be kept in sight after being hit with the drugs. As for drug use in zoos, it is employed extensively for medical and hygiene purposes such as care of animals' hooves, examination for injuries, treatment of sickness and vaccination. If an animal needs an antibiotic, for instance, the capture gun can be used to shoot the drug directly into the body without need for physical capture or restraint.

So by and large the old established methods are still the mainstay of the capture technique, and many of these are still terribly wasteful of wildlife. The only effective way to take young chimpanzees out of the wild, for instance, is to shoot the mother and bring the baby in. But for every young chimpanzee delivered live in this country there are ten destroyed in the wild—mothers that are shot and other babies that do not survive or are killed accidentally by hunters. "Right now there is just no better method," explained Ted Roth. "We can't send out the native poacher with drug darts because they have no tradition for that sort of thing. The mortality rate would jump from ten to one to a hundred to one."

There are, of course, other methods that have been tried for capturing chimpanzees and other primates with varying success. One of these was an adaptation of the rocket net developed in the past few years for catching water fowl such as cranes, which stand in water at some distance from shore. A rocket is attached to one end of a huge net, the other end of which is anchored to the shore, and the missile is fired out over the birds—generally at night when the light will blind them—to throw a cover over the terrified creatures. The director of the Warner Brothers' film *Hatari*, which starred John Wayne as a great white hunter, had seen Tony Parkinson, a British colonial, catch flamingoes with rocket nets. In the film, Wayne had a big order to round up research monkeys for a drug firm, so the director decided he would give a new twist to the Duke's usual hard-fisted, slam-bang roundup style. Instead of coming on with his trusty six-shooter, the defender of the Alamo would corral these primate varmints with one of the new-fangled rocket nets. Ted Roth was in the area and the director hired him to catch 150 African green monkeys for use in the movie.

"We put a very expensive ring of fire around a single acacia tree by pouring kerosene in a ditch out of range of the cameras," recalled Dr. Roth. "Then we released the 150 monkeys into that tree. The idea was to fire a rocket net over the tree and capture them all at once. Well, monkeys are very fast, you know. As soon as the rockets went off they scattered off the tree and, fire or no fire, escaped into the forest. So the director had another brilliant idea. He decided he would use dolls instead of monkeys. He brought in a couple of hundred rag dolls from Germany and pinned tails on them and tied them to the branches of the tree. And from a distance they did look just like monkeys. Then they shot a rocket net and after several tries—these monkeys didn't go anywhere—the net fell nicely over the tree. Here a bunch of natives were supposed to go through the action of chopping down the tree and collecting the phoney monkeys. They hacked away with axes as the cameras rolled and as the tree came toppling down 200 rag dolls sang out in unison: 'Mamma! Mamma!' The property men had neglected to cut off the Mamma mechanism. You never heard such a weird sound in any African forest in all your days!"

Duke was a little embarrassed that his *macho* had been reduced to the level of doing in helpless little things plaintively calling for their Mamma; *Hatari*, nevertheless, came off quite well. Happily the script did not call for sound recording of the cries and so the illusion of capturing real monkeys was convincing. . . .

Chief among the capture methods still practiced by collectors is running the animal down and lassoing it (remember Clark Gable and the wild horses in the movie, *The Misfits?*). However, today something called a fangstock, a long pole with a noose hanging loosely at the end, has supplanted the hand-thrown lariat. The noose is slipped over the neck of the animal as it gallops at the side of the pursuing vehicle. The pole then slips out of the noose and the pursuer has the rope in hand, a method that provides not only greater protection against strangulation than the hand-thrown lariat, but also better control. Once the animal is roped, the collector's "boys" jump off the truck and hang on to its ears and tail until it is subdued.

Running down an animal is a very exact science. The experienced collector knows exactly how long he can chase each species of animal without danger of harming it. A zebra, for instance, should be chased for no longer than eight minutes. If by that time the animal is not captured the collector should give up because the chances of the animal dying from stress are too great. The chasing time for giraffes, on the other hand, is about twelve minutes. Although it might strike forward with its feet for a bit when caught, the giraffe will soon give up and like a deer stand still and go quietly into the shipping crate. The same is true of camels and sheep, largely because they become ill when captured. The zebra, however, must be closely watched after being roped because of its tendency to kick violently and occasionally drag a handler across the savanna on his stomach.

With rhinos there is a double problem in the chase. The youngster has to be separated from the mother, which is highly protective of its offspring. A collector needs to use two vehicles, one to cut off the mother until she is driven far enough away to eliminate danger of attack on the other vehicle that is chasing the baby. If the young one is not caught in about eight minutes, there too the collector generally gives up because of the danger of losing it through stress. Some collectors, however, are turning more to the use of capture guns in taking the rhino because of that animal's uniquely good response to immobilizing drugs.

That other large pachyderm, the elephant, however, is still chased down for capture, the pursuing time for the young being about twenty-five minutes. Generally, because of the relatively high cost of capture, it is only the African elephant that is hunted down. The Asian elephant, the variety that is most used for work and performing, is usually bought from Indian lumber camps, where a young one can be purchased for one-fifth the cost required for capture of its African cousin. With the latter animal, trained packs of dogs are used to aid in the capture. The collector drives up to a herd and then releases the hounds to scatter it. Then he drives in and tries to cut off the youngster from the adult and make off with it in a hurry.

"Sometimes, in elephant chasing, things don't go according to plan," said Dr. Roth. "On one of my chases we managed to get the mother separated from the baby, but she got loose from the dogs. We already had the calf in our truck and it was screaming like mad. And here was mother charging at us full speed. My driver panicked and started screaming, 'We gotta get out! We gotta get out!' So we went off cross-country and not ten yards off plopped straight into an aardvark hole and got stuck. By that time mom caught up and leaned down on the hind end of our truck and the baby rolled off. We were lucky. She acted as a kind of hoist truck for us by lifting our front end up and so we were able to get out of the hole. While she was busy untying her baby, which she did with her trunk, we drove off. She had her baby and lucky for us we got out with our lives and only a badly bent truck. . . ."

So most hoofed animals are captured in the wild by techniques that disable, disarm, dispose of the adult and seize the baby. With large cats and bears it is generally the baited box, that is, the traditional container-type contrivance that lures the animal in with bait and then slams a door down on it.

Don Hunt of International Animal Exchange, however, has his own way of catching the cheetah. This is because the cheetah alone among the big cats refuses to be lured into a trap; it is also the fastest animal on earth, capable of seventy miles an hour. Hunt gets around these two problems by maneuvering the cheetah onto open ground, chasing it in a souped-up truck until it is within capture range and then reaching out and catching it by the tail. The trick then is to hold on until he can slow the animal down and toss it into a box. Where tail-grabbing does not work, Hunt goes for the traditional cowboy lasso. One way or the other his methods are obviously productive; despite the large number of scratches on his brawny arms, his company is the largest supplier of cheetahs.

Ted Roth too, although a traditionalist, often tries some rather personal ways of capturing wild animals. One of his methods for catching big cats, notably the leopard, was a new trick he learned from a Thai native.

"Usually you get word from villagers if they know you are after certain things," he explained. "If there's a killer leopard attacking the village they want to get rid of it anyway, so they're happy to help you. The way a leopard becomes a killer is that he starts first on the village dogs. The next stage is kids and then he graduates to adults. The standard bait for the trap is a pig or small goat—something that bleats a lot and makes its presence known to the killer. In this particular case the leopard was going after dogs, so one native said why not use a dog as bait. And he showed me this marvelous trap. Normally you check your trap every four or five hours. But this trap was constructed so that when the big gate fell on the leopard it simultaneously raised a little gate in the bait department and allowed the live bait to escape. So out comes this yelping little dog telling everybody the killer had been caught. This meant that we didn't have to get up in the middle of the night to check the traps and we also got our dog back.

"Of course at first we weren't sure it *was* a leopard in the trap. But we knew something was in there. We got to the trap late at night. We threw our flashlights on but we saw no shining eyes so then we knew there was no leopard. I lifted the big gate. It's very heavy and takes some time to raise, and while I was doing this I felt something slide by my feet. Immediately all my boys started yelling and rushed off leaving me there holding this gate up. Of course I then knew what it was—an immense python that had taken a fancy to our dog bait. I had no orders for pythons at the time so I just let it go."

Snakes of course are not generally caught in so offbeat a fashion as Ted Roth's double-gated dog-baited box trap. The methods are still mostly along traditional lines—catching with noose or forked instrument or net aided by fire or the natural torpidity of the snake, especially the big ones. Once trapped in the capture instrument the reptile is slipped into a bag and then placed into a shipping crate.

With birds, specimens get to the zoo by a variety of capture techniques, depending on the type of bird. Most gallinaceous (ground-nesting) birds such as pheasants or peacocks are box-trapped. Bait is placed inside a cage where a door is activated when the bird takes the food. It is as simple as that. The larger flightless ratites, such as the ostrich or cassowary, no one bothers to catch; it is much easier to take the eggs and hatch them.

Shore birds, such as ibises and spoonbills, are also caught with relatively little effort. These are captured mostly at night by driving a vehicle up close to the water line and turning on the headlights to blind them. It is then simply a matter of picking up all of the dazed birds one wants. The large waterfowl that feed some distance out from shore, however, present a different problem. Many of these are now trapped with the rocket net, as previously described in connection with John Wayne's misadventures.

With primates it is still mostly a matter of killing the mother and taking the helpless young, unless a collector wants to try his hand at what Duke Wayne was unable to bring off. Ted Roth often caught as many as ten African green monkeys with an inverted basket trap when he was collecting them in Ethiopia for use in vaccine production by drug companies.

"But that too, like most capture activities, involves employment of natives and consequently is subject to all kinds of hazard besides that coming from the animal," he said. "In Ethiopia many of the tribes hate each other like the devil. Tribal conflict can flare up in your camp on the slightest provocation. You live in constant fear that rival tribe members will sneak into each other's tent during the night and castrate each other. I guess that's one of the reasons Mussolini was able to take Ethiopia so easily." *Divisa et imperia.* It's an invader's slogan that fits the wild-animal capturer as well as Caesar.

9 *Breeding in the Zoo*

In the early afternoon of January 30, 1974—at 1:55 P.M. to be precise—an event transpired in the nation's capital that for many zoo people had a significance roughly comparable to Neil Armstrong's landing on the moon. On that day, after five and one-half years of intensive work by scientists, keepers and volunteer watchers, a one hundred-twenty-five-pound Indian rhinoceros (*Rhinoceros unicornus*) finally emerged newborn on the straw-covered floor of his mother's enclosure at the National Zoo in Rock Creek Park, Washington, D.C. No Indian rhino, a rare and highly endangered species, had ever been born live in the Western Hemisphere, despite a number of arduous tries.

Record-breaking events are a favorite preoccupation of zoos, as indeed of most Americans. *The International Zoo Yearbook* reveals, for example, that the Columbus, Ohio, zoo in 1956 bred the first captive gorilla born anywhere in the whole world. And, no doubt, this was a most considerable event for any zoo. The first captive-born chimpanzee occurred in a private zoo, that of Señora Rosalia

Abreu in Havana in 1915, five years ahead of the date when the prestigious Bronx Zoo was able to deliver its first chimp. The Indian elephant has been successfully bred by man for many centuries but not until 1943, when the Hellabrunn Zoo near Munich, Germany, produced one, could a zoo boast of the birth of an African elephant. And so it goes down the list of difficult-to-breed captive animals. As the possibility of Hank Aaron belting out his seven-hundred-fifteenth home run preoccupied baseball, so the zoo world was on edge with excitement at the imminence of a major new captive birth.

One reason for such concentrated attention to breeding is obviously a matter of pride in achievement. In addition, a significant success in breeding has enormous fringe benefits for a zoo. A zoo that can exhibit some special newborn can expect the public to flock in by the thousands, such as they did, and still do, at Central Park Zoo in New York to see Patty Cake, the first gorilla born there. And only heaven knows what millions will stream to Washington if Hsing-Hsing and Ling-Ling produce a baby panda.

But apart from its public relations value, breeding in zoos has a far more important meaning. Several species of wildlife would have totally disappeared from the face of the earth had they not been preserved in zoos. The Père David deer, the Przewalski's wild horse and the wisent (European bison) exist now only in zoos. The American bison was virtually saved from extinction by the Bronx Zoo. The beautiful scimitar-horned oryx owes the continuation of its species, for the most part, to its breeding in zoos. Additionally, as remaining areas of the wilderness give way to urban development, more animals will go on the extinct list. The next to go, for instance, will probably be the orangutan, the only redhaired ape and one of the most intelligent of all wild animals. Once a tropical forest is cut and cleared it can never come back, nor its animals with it.

"We're in a race against time," says Dr. Theodore H. Reed, director of the National Zoo. "As more and more animals in the world are threatened, the use of zoos as survival centers will take on increasing importance." And of at least equal importance is that, because of decreasing supply of animals from the wild, zoos are dependent on their own breeding activities for replenishment of stock.

"In ten years," says Dr. W. Peter Crowcroft, director of Chicago's Brookfield Zoo, "there won't be a single animal coming into zoos from outside this country. Maybe sooner. That's why we have to get better at breeding them. It's true we have a long way to go but I believe zoos are gradually becoming producets instead of consumers of wildlife. Every zoo director in the country is thinking of how he can breed rare animals."

So when a visitor puts to Dr. Helmut K. Buechner of the National Zoo the question: "With all the grave crises going on in the world for man, isn't it a little out of proportion for a corps of scientists, keepers and watchers to spend countless man-hours in a zoo taking notes on the birth of a ridiculous little Indian rhinoceros?" he gets a serious and considered answer.

"Man knows relatively little about the breeding behavior of wild animals," Dr. Beuchner, a slight, scholarly-looking man in his fifties, informs his visitor. "If zoos are to be successful in saving endangered species it is essential that we acquire a foundation knowledge of breeding behavior and the physiology of reproduction. Well, you might say: 'Look at all the success zoos have had in saving the Père David deer. They bred very well and you had no scientific foundation to go by.' My answer would be: 'That's fortunate. Perhaps we were lucky to have been successful without any scientific knowledge. But as insurance for those species that may be difficult to breed it's critical that we build up a body of scientific knowledge. From this knowledge we get clues as to what to look for in patterns of reproductive behavior—how, for instance, mating behavior may be related to territory. Territorial drives have a bearing on social organization, and we need to know about social organization in order to understand what's required in the way of habitat, management, so forth. Further, the more we know about the social organization of animals the better we will be able to understand man.' "

In this sense breeding in the zoo becomes perhaps its most important responsibility. If, as the professionals warn, there will soon be no more outside supply for zoos, there would eventually be no more animals to exhibit. Ergo, no more zoos.

Thus the captive birth of a Great Indian Rhino, that single-horned species of which only about six hundred now survive in sanctuaries in Nepal and India, is intimately related not only to the survival of its own species but also to the survival of man himself. The reams of newsprint that are daily devoted to detailing the titillative minutiae associated with human celebrities as they move across the jet lanes might well be spent more profitably, most zoo people feel, by focusing instead on efforts to save such marvels as the great beasts that once roamed over the larger part of Southern India.

Which is precisely what the National Zoo did in what was perhaps one of the more notable achievements of the Federal Government in 1974: the production of a baby *Rhinoceros unicornus*.

Like other members of the rhino family, the Indian rhinoceros is predominately nocturnal in habit, with poor eyesight but an excellent sense of smell. It is an unusually peaceable animal for its size and strength, and rarely attacks man unless taken by surprise or wounded. Living among the tall grasses and weeds in swampy areas, it eats leaves and twigs which it plucks with its prehensile upper lip, or roots which it digs out of the ground. But the rhino's tall grasses are now being replaced by turf grasses; its cherished swamps are giving way to the stone-and-steel of industry and its feeding areas taken over by domestic cattle. No longer does it have the cover, forage or wallowing areas which nature had provided. The rhino now dies of hoof-and-mouth disease contracted from domestic cattle; it is killed by poachers who covet the horn for its reputed aphrodisiacal qualities.

Tarun and Rajkumari (Raji) were two such beasts. But they were lucky. Tarun, a young male, had just been weaned when he was captured by the State Forestry Service and placed in the Gauhati Zoo in Assam. When he was about two and a half years old he was sent to President Kennedy as a gift from the people of India and placed in the National Zoo in Rock Creek Park. About three years later, on the sixteenth of December, 1963, just a few weeks after the President's death, Raji, an eight-month-old female born of a captured mother in the Gauhati Zoo, arrived in Washington with her parent. About two weeks after arrival, Raji's mother died and the youngster was fed by her keepers for about six months. As a consequence of being handled, Raji became very tractable, while Tarun, who was wild-caught, remained unpredictable and occasionally indulged in displays of intense aggression.

Safe in their new home in the Elephant House in the National Zoo, the two Indian expatriates lived a lazy carefree life with their every need and desire attended to by indulgent keepers. After all, the two animals were wards of the Government of the USA, consigned to the care of the Smithsonian Institution—as are all animals in the National Zoo—and, as such, looked after by a team of men responsible to nothing less than the U.S. Congress.

And so the days and months and years rolled by. Living each in its separate quarters at the Zoo, the two rhinos slowly matured into magnificent examples of their species. But Tarun was now ten, well past the time of sexual maturity which, in healthy male rhinos, is around six to seven years of age. Raji, too, although not so far advanced in sexual development, was over five, which for female Indian rhinos is the age when breeding becomes a possibility. The time had come to end the long years of separation. Rock Creek Park in the national's capital might well be the setting for a unique event in the history of zoos.

On July 1, 1968, Tarun and Raji were introduced to each other for the first time. Tarun lost no time in making his presence felt. He drove Raji intensively. But he made no attempt to mate. After a week of separation they were placed together again and stayed with each other daily for the rest of the summer from 8 A.M. to 3 P.M., which is feeding time. But still they did not engage in breeding activity; their summer-long liaison had produced nothing in the way of a get-together, which suggested that Raji, at the age of five, was not yet sexually mature.

All through the fall and the initial months of winter—from October 1968 until January 1, 1969—Tarun and Raji remained continuously apart from each other. On January 1st, and on six other occasions when the two met during the daytime only, there was still no attempt to mate. Even during the entire summer of 1969 and well into the summer of 1970, during which periods they were together almost daily, there was not the slightest sign of any interest in each other. Tarun was now 12½ and Raji almost 7½. After more than two years of close observation by a growing number of technicians, the promise of a zoo-born Indian rhino in the Western Hemisphere had not exactly the most encouraging of prospects.

"But on August 9, 1970, everybody received something of a lift," said Dr. Buechner, who as senior ecologist for the National Zoo heads the team of scientists concerned with Raji and Tarun's sexual activities. "For the first time Raji went into estrus. It began at about 10 A.M. and we immediately set up a continuous observation which lasted until 11:35 P.M., when the pair was separated for the remainder of the night. During this period the male mounted the female at least seven times, usually only momentarily and never longer than ten minutes. The female squirted urine horizontally at least six times, backed into the male four times, exhibited Flehmen (curling the upper lip to bring scent to an organ in the roof of the mouth known as Jacobson's organ) two times and had an intense discharge from her vagina—all of which are manifestations of strong estrus. She gave a two-toned whistle only during this estrus period; all subsequent whistling was one-toned. The male, too, was heard whistling at least four times, either when trying to mount, or when chasing the female. Once, during a 30-second period, Tarun actually 'danced,' that is, his forefeet left the ground as he jumped into the air, tossing and circling his head and snorting loudly. During an observational period on August 10, 1970, from 9 A.M. to 10:22 A.M., Raji whistled twice, Tarun drove her twice, circled her once and chased her twice. On November 5 and 6, 1970, there was no doubt that the female was clearly in estrus, but the male was placed with the female only toward the end of this estrus period and no mounting occurred."

The same kind of behavior occurred all during 1971. There were instances of mounting by the male and even ejaculations. But when this happened the ejaculation was always external. It was unsophisticated, aborted, almost-virgin sexual behavior right down the line. Could it be said, an interviewer inquired, that these primitive beasts, these end-products of eons of uninhibited sexual activity in the wild, really did not know too much about the nature of the sexual act itself?

"Yes indeed, such a statement could certainly be made," said Dr. Buechner. "That's what makes the story so interesting. Nature seems to bestow on all living things an innate capacity for performing the tasks necessary to their survival, but it often leaves to chance the matter of orientation. A baby, for instance, has an instinctive drive to suck, but it often takes a couple of hours of orientation before it can find the nipple. Likewise in the case of sex. An animal must be oriented to the act. In the wild this orientation is acquired by watching other animals copulate. Tarun and Raji had no such opportunity in the zoo. They were both sheltered virgins."

Throughout the entire next year—from August 1971 to July 1972 (Dr. Buechner did not come to the National Zoo until 1972)—there was more of the same unproductive behavior. It was now four years after the rhinos' first contact, and the prospect was daily growing less likely. One liaison took place on August 26, 1971, lasting from 2:52 P.M. to 11:55 P.M. During that time there was one mount that lasted 17 minutes and another for 10 minutes; ten additional mounts occurred but never for more than about five minutes. During these mounts the male at best occasionally only achieved partial intromission and sometimes ejaculated externally. And always the mounts were characterized by difficulty in locating the vagina, usually because the male was too far forward.

"The penis of the rhino is about three feet long," explained Dr. Buechner. "It is rarely in the right position. Mostly it's to one side or the other. In addition the initial tendency of the male is to move in close. So he has to learn to back up. With racehorses and other domestic animals, man can lend a hand. But with a big dangerous wild animal such as a rhino that's out of the question. So it's a matter of self-orientation."

And Tarun was nothing if not a slow learner. The summer of '72 was a-wasting. A year of great expectations had fizzled into a run of blanks. Melancholy was the keynote at Rock Creek Park.

Finally it was decided to make an all-out effort to achieve breeding. On July 11, 1972, Dr. Buechner, now heading the project, ordered the pair placed together for the first time after a long period of almost continuous, deliberate separation. He extended the time of their stay together at night and instituted a close watch to determine the nature of their nocturnal behavior. Convinced that it was quite safe to keep them together at night, Dr. Buechner secured approval from Dr. Reed, director of the Zoo, to keep the animals together throughout the entire night with the help of watchers from the Friends of the National Zoo. This, then, became the start of what is perhaps the most complete record of the sexual behavior of two individual large mammals in zoo history, attended by a team of observers that at one point aggregated nearly one hundred people holding three-hour watches and making detailed notes.

The first attempted breeding occurred on August 12, starting at 6:50 P.M., when Tarun mounted Raji. During the next fifteen hours, twenty-four mountings occurred, for twelve of which Raji stood well for Tarun. Partial intromission occurred at least three times and external ejaculation occurred at least five times, but Tarun failed to achieve full intromission and did not stay mounted for more than ten minutes at a time. Five more attempted mounts occurred after the last mount at 11:10 A.M. the next day, and fourteen other attempted mounts occurred during the fifteen hours of Raji's receptivity. By feeding time at about 3 P.M. on August 13, both animals were exhausted, and both slept almost continuously for the remaining daylight hours and through the night. Raji whistled occasionally during the onset of estrus, but not during estrus. No horizontal urination or flashing of the vulva occurred until she was in full estrus.

"It was heartbreaking!" exclaimed Dr. Buechner. "Here we had all this intense breeding activity and nothing happened. We had them together all through the night. Breeding started at about 7 P.M. and went on continuously even into the next morning. And it all came to naught!"

Nevertheless the procedure of keeping Tarun and Raji together, except for two hours at feeding time, was continued. Again the Friends of the National Zoo watched all night and the staff of the zoo watched by day.

"Suddenly, on the morning of September 30, 1972, with practically no prior indication of estrus being imminent, we were presented with one of the most beautiful sights it has ever been my privilege to witness," said Helmut K. Buechner, D.V.M., senior ecologist in charge of the procreation efforts of two of nature's rarest animals. "It was just getting daylight, 6:20 A.M., with a light rain falling. Someone brought me news that Tarun and Raji had just walked outside together and that immediately and without the slightest difficulty Tarun mounted the female and was still up on her. We dropped everything and raced over there to be present. Tarun remained mounted for 70 minutes—slightly longer than the average length of mounting time for the Indian rhinoceros. Raji stood well for him and there were periodic bouts of pelvic movement presumably followed by ejaculation. We continued the watch but no more mounting took place that night or the next day. Then we watched again when she should have come into estrus, 35-45 days later, but no mounting occurred, that is, she did not come back into estrus. Conception had apparently taken place sometime during those seventy minutes on the 30th of September, 1972. We watched all through the next year until July 1973 but saw no signs of estrus. Then we decided to separate them to make room for the baby. We still weren't sure but we were hopeful. He arrived at 1:55 P.M., January 1974, four hundred and eighty-seven days after his conception."

From the months-long pregnancy watch, executed by a one hundred-strong battalion of volunteers—high school students from Arlington, Virginia, and the University of Maryland, housewives from Chevy Chase, and others—was acquired a body of data which will go a long way toward saving a species of near-Paleolithic animal that verges on extinction. Volunteers, in the drab steel-barred enclosures of the Elephant House in Rock Creek Park, had taken wild-animal, endangered species breeding a giant step forward.

And the baby? Is it doing well?

"Oh yes," beamed Dr. Buechner, like a new father. "Go down and have a look at that little guy. His name is Patrick, after Daniel Patrick Moynihan, present U.S. ambassador to India; Dillon Ripley, secretary of the Smithsonian Institution, was ill in India, and Ambassador Moynihan took care of him there. So Mr. Ripley honored his benefactor by naming the baby rhino after him. My God, but the public loves that little guy! They watch his antics by the hour. Bumping horns with his mother . . . both of them racing around dodging each other . . . darting in and out of the two cages tossing their heads. And with all this he's still gaining four and one-half pounds a day just on mother's milk. But that's the way it is with rhinos: nothing grows as fast as a baby rhino."

The case history of little Patrick can be taken as an example of the enormous commitment with which all good zoos have applied themselves to the breeding of rare wild animals. And in the process zoo people have learned much that will be useful in the worldwide battle to save endangered species. But what of the other animals in the menagerie? Zoo lions and kangaroos and snakes eventually die in the zoo (indeed, deaths outrun births sometimes by two to one) and others must take their place in the public enclosures. What then of the breeding of the more common types in the zoo population?

First of all, zoo professionals say it is axiomatic that success in zoo breeding, no matter what kind of animal, is largely affected by good living quarters and right diet. Lions, for instance, have a reputation for being animals that will breed anywhere, even in a ten by ten steel cage with a concrete floor. But subtract proper medical attention from the list of requisite breeding factors, that is, let the lion's health deteriorate and the result will be a related decrease in fecundity. An unhealthy animal may *survive* in the zoo but it is not as likely to breed as will a healthy one. On the other hand, give that lion a natural habitat, or place it out among its accustomed pride and its breeding performance will be considerably enhanced.

The part that proper diet plays in reproduction performance is illustrated by a recent example in the London Zoo. Baboons are also excellent breeders in captivity, and London had an exceptionally good breeding colony of common baboon over a period of many years. Suddenly, however, its fecundity disappeared and it stopped breeding. It was discovered that, although the Zoo had always paid meticulous attention to the diet of these animals, somehow an essential B-vitamin had been omitted from their food. As soon as the vitamin was replaced the colony started breeding again.

Another instance of the relationship of diet to breeding is the koala, a tree-dwelling mammal that requires a diet of eucalyptus leaves. The leaf must be at just the right stage of growth. Cut the eucalyptus leaf from the koala's diet and it will not only stop breeding but may even die. This is why the Australian Government will not permit the export of koalas except to two zoos—those at San Diego and San Francisco—where eucalyptus leaves of exactly the right quality grow.

But successful breeding at the zoo does not derive solely from the two factors of housing and diet. It goes far beyond that into a complicated area of animal psychology and behavior that, as the example of Tarun and Raji demonstrates, requires not only long demanding observation and study but also simple common sense and experience. Each species of animal has its own special approach to the universal phenomenon of procreation. Some are notoriously easy breeders. "Our hippopotamus is always pregnant," says National Zoo's Dr. Reed. "I think she'd get pregnant if we kept the male somewhere at the far end of Rock Creek Park." And the same tends to be true of the lion and many other cats.

But other species need the conditions of social interaction and privacy afforded by the large enclosures, paddocks and free space of the wild-animal park. "The Père David deer, for instance, doesn't feel secure," explained Dr. Reed, "unless he's in a herd with a balance of age or sex. They need to relate in normal social units. Cheetahs, on the other hand, have to be kept out of earshot and noseshot of each other when not breeding—they won't breed if there's a continuing social relationship. Or take the sable antelope. They are never known to breed in front of anybody. We did a study on them and had to use a peephole."

There are other animals that require the excitement of fighting over a mate before they can become interested in sex. "Unless there's a junior male to challenge the older male, he won't do anything. You see, he really doesn't care about the girl but he doesn't want anybody else to have her, either."

And there are many that need a wide choice of individuals and will not mate with just any animal of the opposite sex which happens to be present. "These types have got to like each other first," said Dr. Reed. "I would say that some animals are a bit more selective than we are."

All of which means that zoos are hard at work to meet the challenges of breeding an ever-widening spectrum of exotic animal. And their efforts have been rewarded with a number of signal successes. In 1971, the Baltimore Zoo bred the first captive-born spectacled bear in the Western Hemisphere. San Diego Zoo has been successfully breeding chimpanzees since the 1940s and had second generation babies in the 1950s. In the last few years at least forty zoos have been able to rear orangutans, with Philadelphia Zoo having a particularly enviable record with the famous breeding pair, Guas and Guarina, the world's oldest captive primates, both of which are now 54 and gave birth to their eighth baby in 1955. The Bronx Zoo, among its many other outstanding accomplishments, has been breeding the rare pigmy hippopotamus since 1919, when the first captive birth took place, and has reared at least a dozen since then. And a single pair of Andean condors, the largest flying bird, with a wingspan of up to 12 feet, produced nine offspring between 1942 and 1952 while nesting among the 60-foot-high trees in the San Diego Zoo's huge aviary.

In recent years, with the advent of wild-animal parks such as San Diego's San Pasqual Valley facility, where with its 1800 acres of free space and the emphasis placed on breeding rather than on public viewing, notable success has been achieved with difficult breeders such as the cheetah. The Bronx Zoo, too, even though its breeding record in the limited acreage of its urban quarters is nothing to be ashamed of, is moving toward the establishment of a rural breeding farm with, according to some reports, a possible affiliation with the Catskill Game Farm in upstate New York. And the National Zoo has acquired the use of four thousand acres of Federal land at Front Royal, Virginia, the old Army Remount Station, where animals such as little Patrick will devote themselves solely to the reproduction of their species.

Despite all the progress that has been made since Carl Hagenbeck demonstrated the interrelationship of habitat with performance, breeding wild animals at the zoo is a science that is still in its infancy. "What we don't know could fill volumes," explained Dr. Buechner. "In the old days zoos had hardly any motivation to know anything about the breeding behavior of wildlife. There was what seemed an unlimited supply of it from the wilderness. But now with wildlife joining other treasured resources such as energy, clean air, good water, on the endangered list, we've got to get a move on. And many zoos are doing just that."

Dr. Buechner rose from his chair to show an instrument which reminded the visitor of an apparatus which, as a onetime newspaper reporter, he had once seen police use for surveillance of a suspected rapist. The suspect was making his way under cover of darkness from window to window in the courtyard of a large apartment house looking for a place to break in, while up on the roof police were following his every movement through a large telescope, despite the total absence of light. The secret of this maneuver was that the apparatus threw an infra-light on the culprit and thus enabled the roof police to observe him through a telescopic lens without his knowledge and to relay intelligence to an officer lying in wait inside the building.

"Yes, this night vision glass, as we call it, permits us to do something of the same thing," said Dr. Buechner, "although we are of course not police and we hope we are studying normal rather than aberrational sexual behavior. It is just one of the many technological aids that we are now using to advance our knowledge of the sexual behavior of exotic animals. We've been doing a lot of work with the sable antelope, for instance. We keep the male separated and then introduce him to a group of females and just watch. No, we're not peepshow artists—we're looking for patterns. And, with this gadget, I can watch at night as well as by day. One of the things we're trying to discover, for example, is whether he takes the dominant female first and if so, what his behavior is with her and with older and younger females. Another thing we are trying to check out is how soon after the male is introduced does the female come into estrus."

Isn't the onset of estrus determined autonomously, Dr. Buechner was asked. Did he mean to imply that contact of the male with the female brings the female into so-called heat?

"No, not yet. It's a little too early to make a definite decision. But it looks like a real possibility. It may be, for instance, that the sexual interrelationship is based on the male's ability to induce estrus into the female when she comes into his territory, instead of on her visiting the male's territory the moment she comes into estrus. This is the sort of the thing we can learn in studies of breeding at the zoo. And, in turn, it helps us to learn what is going on in nature."

When it is realized how great a part studies such as these play in the research programs of major zoos, a third factor, scientific investigation, must be added to good housing and proper diet as a requisite for achieving success in breeding at the zoo.

There is also a fourth factor to be considered essential to good reproduction performance—the all-round good health of the zoo animal. An animal that is bedeviled by sickness and disease is not likely to be a productive breeder. This is where the zoo veterinarian comes in. Since the time of Carl Hagenbeck, which marks the birth of the modern zoo and its emphasis on the relationship of breeding to psychological and physical health, the role of the zoo veterinarian has steadily grown in importance.

Hagenbeck himself was an amateur veterinarian of considerable accomplishment. Even though veterinary science has come a long way from the days when strangling was employed to euthanize a terminally sick elephant because only a few experts knew how to dispatch it with a gun, Hagenbeck's homespun therapies remain as basics of the practice. His approach might be likened to that of the old style country doctor or the practitioner of folk medicine who seems to be coming back into vogue. At any rate, one thing Carl Hagenbeck felt certain of: ". . . medicines often do more harm than good; the proper method of doctoring a wild animal is to place it in such wholesome conditions that nature brings her own remedy without artificial assistance."

For example, take the case of an Indian buffalo that developed an inflammation of the snout, accompanied by high temperature and much pain, especially when it was feeding. An examination revealed that an abscess on the snout was crammed with parasitic worms. Although it caused considerable suffering to the animal, a scientific cure was tried but was unsuccessful and hope of saving its life was given up.

"At this point an old Hindoo came upon the scene," reported Hagenbeck, "and, when we informed him of the various unsuccessful attempts to cure the buffalo, he undertook to do the job himself in a single day. We attached little credence to the Hindoo's professions, but, since everything had failed and all hope been abandoned, there seemed no objection to letting him try what he could do. On receiving our permission, he went away and returned a few hours later with a bundle of blossoming branches of some shrub with which I was then, and am still, quite unacquainted. All I can say is that the blossom gave forth a somewhat penetrating odor. We imagined that the Hindoo was about to make a decoction from these plants to wash out the sores—but no such thing. He merely tied the branches securely to the buffalo's tail. This so irritated the animal that it lashed its tail about, hitting itself over the snout in its endeavours to tear off the branches. The constant contact of the snout with the shrub very quickly produced a remarkable effect. I cannot say whether the worms in the abscess were stupefied by the odor, or whether they merely disliked it and endeavoured to escape from it. But certain it is, that without further trouble they all fell out of their abscess, and the creature was soon completely healed."

Although this method of healing might seem primitive by modern standards it was only one of a whole repertoire of simple techniques by which Carl Hagenbeck succeeded in keeping his animals in good health. Only in the case of infectious diseases did he resort to the more sophisticated veterinary procedures. Throughout all his long career he confined himself mostly to old and well-established healing procedures, often improvising intricate techniques for handling a particular problem: a kind of Albert Schweitzer to neglected animals languishing in the zoo-jungles of Europe. Once he took from the Copenhagen Zoo a polar bear that had been given up as suffering from a hopelessly incurable problem. Caged polar bears have a habit of twisting around on their hindquarters so that the claws in the back paws get very little use and grow immoderately long, often imbedding themselves in the flesh. In this case the claws had not only grown into the flesh but had gone right through and come out on the other side of the hind paws. Hagenbeck built an iron cage seven feet long, five feet high and one and one-half feet wide—just room enough to box the bear in—with a door made of parallel bars. He transferred the bear into this box, tilted it over and set it down on blocks—just high enough for him to get under it and at the bear's hind paws which were now resting on the parallel bars. In this way he was able to tie the hind paws down to the bars and then clip and extract the claws, as a podiatrist might remove a man's ingrown toenail, all without subjecting the animal to the trauma of anaesthesia or a struggle to tie him down. After he had removed the claws from the inflamed flesh he transferred him immediately to another small cage, the lower half of which was lined with zinc and filled with continuously running ice-cold water. For two weeks the bear was forced by the narrow confines of the cage to keep his hind paws in the ice-cold stream, but he was rewarded with a complete cure and Hagenbeck had a once-more healthy specimen.

On occasion country-doctor Hagenbeck was not averse to employing remedies even simpler than running ice-cold water. "Everyone who has had anything to do with animals is well-acquainted with the fact that they often have a strong predilection for alcohol and sugar," he pointed out. "Thus it is well known that race-horses are given sack to drink, or have their nostrils washed out with it, before they start in a race. Monkeys, too, are fond of wine, or of alcohol in any other form. Once when I was transporting seven elephants and a number of other animals through Germany the elephants were seized with colic. In order to cure them of this I gave them doses of rum. One of them, however, appeared to have had rather too much, for he became exceedingly hilarious and challenged his more sober neighbor to a duel. The jovial monster was disturbing the entire menagerie, so I saw that there was nothing for it but to repeat the dose, for the purpose of reversing the effect. I therefore supplied him with a large extra quantity of grog. He then became completely drunk, and soon fell into a quiet sleep."

Today veterinary medicine in the zoo has advanced beyond such primitive albeit useful techniques for the diagnosis and treatment of animal diseases and injuries. To a large extent this is due to the disappearance of the traditional animosity between zookeeper and veterinarian. Although many zoo directors have also been veterinarians, such as Charles Schroeder of the San Diego and Theodore Reed of the National zoos, for years the average zookeeper considered the veterinarian an ignoramus about wild animals. The veterinarian, on the other hand, generally regarded zoos as little more than cruel, unsanitary and unnecessary freak shows. But in the past few decades zoomen and vets have joined forces to make the zoo hospital a model of the most advanced practices in animal health service, including preventative medicine. An institution such as the Bronx Zoo, for example, performed surgical operations in 1972 that included repair of lacerated corneas, biopsy, tumor removal, fracture repair, gastrotomy, intestinal anastomosis enucleation of an eye, correction of dystocia, and caesarean section. In addition, a staff of seventeen specialists in pathology, nutrition, pharmacology, radiology, ophthalmology, parasitology, dentistry and other disciplines worked, in collaboration with chief veterinarian Emil P. Dolenseck, on research projects that ranged all the way from the use of white whale blood in the diagnosis and treatment of human autoimmune disease to the function of pectin in the eye of birds.

A good zoo is consequently now a place where animals generally live longer and healthier lives than they do in the wild. Nevertheless, deaths still outnumber births in the zoo by an average ratio of about two to one. There are a number of reasons for this, one of which is the fact that wild animals usually conceal evidence of sickness, an instinct which, in the wild, serves to ward off attack from their enemies. Consequently, by the time the zoo veterinarian becomes aware of an animal's illness it is often too late to save him.

Another reason for the preponderance of death over birth at the zoo is the fact that in captivity, breeding does not yet go as well as it might. Despite the fact that, as mentioned, great strides are being made in the science of breeding in the zoo, there is still much ground to be covered before births come apace of deaths, one of the main liabilities being that in many cases there just are not sufficient, compatible, or productive mates available.

Causes of death at the zoo are largely attributable to infectious diseases. Parasitism, circulatory disturbances, disorders of a neurological, metabolic and nutritional character, and trauma, either physical or pyschological, also increase the morbidity rate. Snakes, for instance, are particularly susceptible to emotional stress. "Snakes," as the saying goes in the zoo, "don't like people any more than people like them." Reptiles have a need to hide and that is why good zoos provide places in the cage where they can hide from people. Otherwise they are under constant stress and can, as it were, be "looked to death."

In the routine task of keeping zoo animals "feeling good," and therefore in prime condition not only as exhibits but as breeders, a veterinarian might handle a caseload of several thousand during the course of a year. Although there are many serious cases involving complicated surgery and treatment, most of the vet's practice is similar to the daily complaints of human beings—cuts, scratches, broken bones, rashes, stomach upsets, colds, as well as hysteria and depression. A male antelope may go into deep mourning over the loss of its mate, or a young monkey exhibit all the symptoms of a nervous breakdown due to overintense peer rivalry. Such animals are not likely to be interested in propagating their species; they must be treated as sick individuals.

Or a seal may suddenly stop eating, as was the case with one of a mated pair that had lived together in good health for a number of years. After the female had lost considerable weight, the keepers began watching it closely. The two seals were getting 20 butterfish each day but the patient was not even trying to eat. The male, however, was eating all the fish and throwing up from the overload. The female was now moved from the pool, treated with drugs and placed alone in a tank. After 10 days in isolation she began eating again— some 12 fish a day—and was returned to live with her mate, where she ate well, gained weight and became active again. No one was quite sure what exactly caused her return to health—perhaps it was the holiday from each other—but "certainly," observed the veterinarian, "not all problems developing in an animal collection are medical in nature. Social interaction, as manifested in the competition for food, apparently was the origin of the case of these seals."

So the zoo veterinarian, aided by the keepers who must eventually handle the animal, finds that his daily caseload presents him with a variety of problems that range from adenoma to zymosis in aardvark to zebra. A rattlesnake may need to have its teeth pulled or an elephant an orthodontal job on incorrectly growing tusks. With the drug-immobilizing modalities available today this is no longer an horrendous problem. The vet fires a hypodermic dart from a distance, immobilizes the animal and proceeds to his task in perfect security.

But what of the days before the immobilizing drugs? What did the zoo do with, say, a bald-headed tiger? There was one such, indeed, in the National Zoo forty years ago, who developed a shiny pate because of a severe condition of mange. Yul Brynner may be a sex symbol in the world of man, but a bald-headed tiger is not likely to bowl over the feline ladies, if for no other reason than that he is too busy scratching the mange off his crown. So the problem confronting the keepers was how to massage hair back onto the tiger's neck and head without getting clouted into the hereafter. They positioned themselves on the top of his cage, in the manner of Carl Hagenbeck at the underside of the polar bear's box, and showered the animal with a solution of sweet oil and sulphur. They also doused the places on the floor where he usually lay down to rest. The result was that they succeeded in getting the tiger to do his own massaging. Like any house cat that will clean itself of a foreign substance, the huge beast lay there hours on end moistening his paw with saliva and then rubbing it over his head and neck in an attempt to rid himself of the sticky liquid. Eventually he managed to massage the hair roots back to health and wound up with one of the most beautiful coats in the zoo.

Oddly enough, the success, however limited, that zoos have achieved in breeding as the result of research and health measures —even so primitive a measure as the bald tiger example—have created another problem. In the AAZPA Newsletter of March, 1974, vice-president John E. Werler states that ". . . We are well aware that a major factor in the reduction of wildlife is vanishing habitat. [However] A related problem unique to our profession is becoming increasingly evident—that of vanishing *space.*

The two oldest captive primates in the world, fifty-four-year-old orangutans, Guas and Guarina of the Philadelphia Zoo have bred eight offspring in their lifetime. *(Photo credit: Franklin Williamson. Courtesy of Zoological Society of Philadelphia)*

Breeding at the zoo took another big step forward when an okapi, a short-necked relative of the giraffe with zebra-striped legs, was born in 1973 at the San Diego Zoo. Discovered in 1901, there are only sixteen members of the species in American zoos. The Zaire government in Central Africa offers a limited number for sale at $100,000 each, but has had no takers recently. *(Photo credit: F. D. Schmidt, San Diego Zoo)*

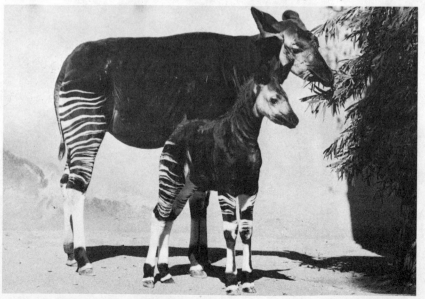

Spectacled Bear born at the
Baltimore Zoo in 1971, is first
ever born in the Western
Hemisphere. *(Photo credit
Ray Faass, Baltimore Zoo)*

Twin orangutans born at the
National Zoo, Washington.
*(Photo credit: Donna
Grosvenor)*

The first Indian Rhino born in the Western Hemisphere was born at the National Zoo in Washington in 1973. A large corps of volunteers, students, zoomen and scientists kept a round-the-clock watch over the mating, pregnancy and birth. *(Photo credit: Ray Faass)*

August 13, 1972

0854 — ♂ vigourous rubbing of ♀ hindquarters
0855 — ♂ kicking at female (trying to mount)
ATTEMPTED MOUNTING
♂ follows ♀ and rubs her with his head - constant contact
HD TO HD ENCOUNTER

♀ honking
♂ initiative and aggressive pursuit
♂ head swinging and rub-butting of ♀ hindquarters
♂ kicks ♀ with forefeet, rubbing her hindquarters ↓

0858 — ATTEMPTED MOUNTING   not accompanied with normal urination
♀ horizontal urination, as ♂ enters water pit
♀ honks during HD TO HD ENCOUNTER
♂ is in constant pursuit of ♀

0900 — ♂ enters indoor enclosure - ♀ waits at doorway
HD- HD ENCOUNTER
♂ walks with head alongside flank of ♀ as main form of pursu
Constant ♂ rubbing ♀ hindquarters with head and legs

0903 — both animals in inside enclosure
♂ head is against ♀ flank   - ♂ flehmen (no urine lapping) floor

0909 — MOUNTING
erection achieved
♀ head tossing
♂ is doing "pushups" on her back.
♂ leg quivering
blow noises   7""""
♀ runs away as ♂ achieves intromission partial
♂ ejaculation - ⊞ ⊞ (more ejac in the beginning - very
preliminary leaks?   not spurts   heavy however, as ♂ almost
♂ heavy salivation but 3 drip   reaches vagina)
♂ leg quivering
no ♂ times ♂ is able to lift penis to vagina (rather than erecting
and only able to bump between ♀ legs) — | | |
at each time, ♀ honk-snorts, then runs slightly
0916 — male is pushed off by ♀   erection ends   15 sec
0919 — ♀ horizontal urination (without normal urination - alone) 10 sec
    (waKing noises in a series   by ♀

♂ charges ♀
violent head - horn rubbing as ♂ charges

0921 -
♂ takes a dip in tank
♀ stands alongside tank
♂ flehmen in water tank and horizontal urination by ♀ 1 second
after flehmen.
♂ head tossing - water splashing in tank violently

0922½ -
♀ lies down to right of tree parallel with bars.
♂ head tossing - water splashing still

0930 -
♂ is out of tank and back to pursuing ♀
♀ small honk

0932 -
♂ licking tree flehmen 1
♂ kick with foot - rub with face ♀ hind flank

0933½ -
♂ ATTEMPTED MOUNT

III ejaculation spurts
♀ tolerates mount
♂ tail lifted - has female up against the wall
several efforts to find vagina (lifting penis up and down between ♀ legs)

0938 -
♀ runs off
♂ licking tree and nuzzles ♀ hindquarters
blow- snorting

0940 -
HD to HD ENCOUNTER
♂ constant efforts to follow ♀

0943 ↗
MOUNT
lifting and rubbing of ♂ leg on ♀ hindflank as well as
headrubbing always preceed mount.

0944 -
intromission

0944½ -
ANOTHER ATTEMPTED MOUNT
2½ - 3 minutes of mount
35 secs. of intromission

0949 -
♀ horizontal urination

0952 -
♂ is back in tank splashing around
♂ then runs into indoor enclosure
both honking and snorting
♀ exits to indoor enclosure - she blows as senses
male advance
HD TO HD ENCOUNTER
♀ honking and honk- snort

Debbie Bundy   0400-0700

0509   She returns to corner and sways forabout
a minute, then she urinates again- she then
paces back and forth along the swoll, with her
head held high

0513   Raises head and whistles

0515   Urinates. Circles the cage. then returns to corner.
She vocalizes several times while walking.

0517   She raises her head high, tenses and whistles.
she then returns to swaying movements.

0519.   She lifts her tail and urinates

0520.   She again urinates then lies down on her
right side in the corner. She whistles once
while raising her head high.

0522   She stands takes a drink, then enters the
closed cage. She stands in doorway about 1 min
then returns to corners and begins swaying

0530.   She whistles, then continues swaying.

0535   She moves over to the water, eats some hay (one mouthfull)
then urinates. She circles the cage twice,
vocalizing several times, then returns to corner

0540   She eats some more hay then goes into the
closed cage. She returns to open cage. Circles it
once. then walks from the corner, to the bars
and back to the corner fourtimes She whistles
twice while standing still in the corner.

0545   She walks from corner to bars twice more,
mawing loudly and swinging her head high. She
circles the cage twice more then returns
to the corner and sways and vocalizes loodly.

Excerpts from notes taken on "pregnancy watch" over Indian Rhino, Raji,
by volunteer from Friends of the National Zoo, Washington, D.C.

0550 She urinates and pacing and swaying continu

0553 She thp cage again and ojires a small houp, raising
her front two feet several inches off the flpar.
mowing continues

0555 She urinates again.. Vocalizations are louder
and more often (one every 3 ay seconds),
Pacing continues, her head is held very
low when she walks. her tail is curled
over her back.

0600 She backs up to the wall three times as
if to depocate, but there is no resut. She
whistles then continues pacing in or
near corner, moving her head up and down
rather than from side to side in swaying
movement.

0610. She charges the keeper as he walks past her
cage. She urinates then continues pacing.
She goes into the closed cage and leaves
it in less than 10 seconds

0612 She whistles very loudly and continues to pace
from corner to bars and beck again. She whistles
twice more, there is no 'mewing' now, She whistles
again. slight shift in abdominal position.

0615 She urinates a few drops and whistles her tail
is held high

0618 She lies down then stands at once. She backs up
to the wall but does not defaeate. She turns
and lies down, her tail twitches constantly.

The Siberian tiger is the largest of all the cats—the largest on record having weighed 847 pounds. Today there are more of this rare animal in captivity than in the wild. Accordingly, zoos thoughout the world are cooperating in a breeding program to keep it alive. All are pedigreed and the stud book is kept by the Prague Zoo. *(Photo credit: New York Zoological Society)*

"We have become extremely successful in breeding certain species. An increase in applied research into proper husbandry and nutrition is beginning to pay off in increased numbers of viable offspring. Laudable, though perhaps too long in coming, are recent efforts among zoos to pair single specimens. Cooperative pairing arrangements are having gratifying results in many cases. But the resulting surplus of particular species may soon put a strain on zoo exhibit and holding areas.

"What disposition will we make of last year's litters of tigers, for example, or this year's litters, or next year's? *The International Zoo Yearbook* reported five hundred and thirty-five lions and three hundred and ninety tigers born during 1971. This is almost half the total captive tiger population for that year. What became of those that reached adulthood? Even when occasional rare species are successfully bred in captivity, there remains the nagging problem of finding *space* to properly accommodate the expanding captive groups. How many zoos can properly house more than a couple of pairs or trios of tigers in their present facilities? Very few.

"The opportunity to relocate surplus stock in suitable captive situations is limited. As an example, Houston's first three successful litters of Kodiak Bears went to excellent facilities. However, subsequent crops were disposed of less satisfactorily, and we had found no source for our 1973 bears by the time the 1974 set was born.

"Selling blindly, we allow our animals to end up in foreign circuses, second-rate zoos, or in extreme cases even on the 'sportsman's' wall. Breeding animals simply for breeding's sake is a questionable practice. Thought must be given to the eventual destination of the offspring.

"Developing zoos need specimens for their new facilities. Beyond that, there are few additional outlets. The often-stated ultimate goal is to return zoo-born animals to the wild areas of their original ranges that are suitably protected from poaching and habitat destruction. Most habitat areas are shrinking alarmingly and almost all zoo-born species would require extensive training to survive in the wild, as evidenced by George Adamson's experience with lions . . . With certain species we have acted only as consumers, drawing more specimens from the wild than are even maintained successfully in captivity. We must concentrate on husbandry of these species . . . I suggest that those of us who are contemplating development of spacious animal-survival centers consider construction within them of multiple large enclosures for endangered animals. Instead of one pair or trio, such a center may accommodate half-a-dozen or more trios, each zoo specializing, as has not been recommended elsewhere, in which there is no outlet, seeing them become useless commodities. particular species. We must not raise large numbers of species for zoos can work together for our common goal: preservation of the world's wildlife."

10 *Superstars at the Zoo*

The directory of animals in the zoo ranges all the way from aardvark to zebra. The zebra is, of course, a well-known animal; but the aardvark, a large piglike African beast that burrows at night for termites . . . how many people have ever heard of an aardvark? Or, for that matter, an aardwolf, next in the alphabetical order.

In so large and representative a register as the *Bronx Zoo Book of Wild Animals* it is a long alphabetical journey just through the A's before an animal is reached that most people have heard of—the adder, the venomous viper which sent Cleopatra to her grave. Likewise through the rest of the Bronx Register, or indeed the register of any zoo. And of the easily recognizables only a handful of species could be labeled popular. Lions, of course, the "king" of beasts, are always a great attraction. Tigers, too—a species which, in fact, is larger and stronger than the lion—seem to fascinate endlessly. Monkeys, giraffes, gorillas, elephants, and, as Simon and Garfunkel put it ". . . orangutans . . . zebras . . . antelopes . . . turn on frequently . . . You gotta come and see at the zoo."

These then, are the species of animal which might be called the "stars" of the zoo. Throughout the world, in almost every animal garden in any era, much the same roster of wild animal has always been relied upon to provide the main attraction for the zoo-goer. But there are also the superstars of the zoo: specific individuals that, for one reason or another, manage to capture the fancy of the public in a special way.

Several years ago a poll was commissioned by a U.S. Government agency to determine the popularity of a certain zoo animal. Costing $15,000 and comprising a 192-page report, the study concerned itself with what was called "Public Images of and Attitudes Toward Smokey Bear."

Actually, the sponsors of that study could well have saved themselves their money. Most anyone could have told the U.S. Forest Service's Division of Cooperative Forest Fire Control, otherwise known as Smokey Bear Headquarters, that practically everybody in the country loved Smokey Bear. During one year Smokey's mail exceeded that of a very popular President of the United States, and required the assignment of his own postal zip code. As far back as 1952, only two years after his appearance on the scene, Smokey Bear had already become so popular that Congress had to pass a special law protecting his name from unauthorized use. At its peak, his free advertising alone was annually worth forty-million dollars; his comic book *The True Story of Smokey Bear* sold 1.5 million copies, and his mail was mountainous enough to keep three people working full time dashing off replies over his pawprint. At his home in the National Zoo, attendance records showed that Smokey Bear claimed the lion's share, so to speak, of the attention of the annual total of some 4,000,000 visitors.

The saga of Smokey Bear (he is mistakenly referred to as Smokey the Bear) is also a case study in the consequences of anthropomorphism. Without the enormous press agentry surrounding him that has built him into a human symbol, there is nothing so unusual about Smokey Bear. He is an ordinary American black bear (*Ursus americanus*), the kind that roams by the droves in the national parks begging handouts from tourists. And yet—and for a good cause—the anthropomorphic role he has been cast in has clothed him with sufficient humanity to place him permanently in the national folklore.

Smokey Bear, zoo superstar. How did it happen? One day in the hot summer of 1950, a huge conflagration broke out in the Lincoln National Forest of New Mexico and raged for five days and nights, ravaging some seventeen thousand acres. When the flames were finally extinguished, weary fire fighters found a badly burned little black bear, apparently abandoned by its mother, clinging to a scorched ponderosa tree. Gently they lifted the terrified animal from its perch, applied first aid to its burns, and then made a search of the surrounding area for its mother. When this proved fruitless, they turned the tiny cub over to the care of Ray Bell, a New Mexico game warden. Warden Bell, with the aid of veterinarians and his young daughter, nursed the cub back to good physical condition, named him "Teddy Hot Foot" and looked forward to one day turning him over to a local zoo.

Meanwhile, from Hollywood, all during 1943, Bambi, Walt Disney's sloe-eyed deer, had been beseeching careless Americans through U.S. Forest Service posters to stop destroying their forests by fire —such as the one that nearly snuffed out the life of a little bear in New Mexico. But after a year of leasing Bambi out, Disney wanted the deer back and the Forest Service was left with no one to tell its story. Besides, a deer, though popular, was hard to humanize in posters. So Uncle Sam set out on a search to find another animal to help him save the forests.

The Advertising Council, Inc., and the advertising firm of Foote, Cone and Belding came to the rescue. In 1945, in collaboration with the Forest Service, they created a poster bear, named him Smokey, and painted a Forest Ranger's hat on him, together with blue-jeans, shovel and bucket of honey. They then sent thousands of his pictures throughout the nation to warn people that: "Only *you* can prevent forest fires."

For the next five years Smokey Bear did his job well, even though he was only make-believe. People took his warnings seriously, even adults, and many acres of precious forest were saved from the ravages of unnecessary fire. Bears had always been close to man, performed in his circuses, ridden bicycles, put on boxing gloves, turned somersaults and generally seemed so *human* and, in fact, are relatively easy to train to appear human as compared to most animals. "Besides," says Mal Hardy, the U.S. Forest Service man who has been in charge of Smokey Bear's image for many years, "people will accept things from a bear that they won't think of taking from another guy."

But in 1950 when the story came out in the newspapers about the little bear that had been burned in the terrible forest fire, the Forest Service decided they had a real Smokey Bear! This ersatz poster character had been fine for what it was, but that was all it was—an "it." Now there could be a "him"—an authentic living being that had been through a forest fire. This real bear would give their story the extra dimension it needed.

So Teddy Hot Foot was renamed Smokey Bear, taken out of the old washing machine in which he liked to while away his cubhood days in New Mexico, and readied by Game Warden Bell for his debut at the National Zoo in Washington. He arrived in the nation's capital in a special plane with his picture, like the Presidential Seal on Air Force One, painted on the exterior. Waiting to greet him at his new home were photographers, newsmen and VIPs. It was a debut befitting the launching of a superstar.

Smokey was given a big cage all to himself at the National Zoo. His press agents began work and soon people were coming in droves to see the "real" Smokey Bear." Signs on the zoo grounds read: "This way to Smokey Bear." When he wasn't posing for newspaper photographers in his home at the Zoo, Smokey was riding in parades out on the city streets; if he couldn't make it to a broadcast in person, friends such as Bing Crosby, Dinah Shore and the Sons of the Pioneers would host for him on nationwide hookups. Kids by the thousands all over the country signed up as Junior Forest Rangers, received an "official" badge and ranger kit from Smokey, and took a pledge of conservation. For them Smokey Bear was no made-up or make-believe character. He was part of their lives; their letters to him prove that.

"I would like to be a member of Smokey's forest ranger team," began a letter from Gary Gjerstad of Vinton, Iowa. "Would you please send me a membership card and any other material that would be of interest to our third grade class."

It was the same request made by most of the other kids. But Gary's letter was different. It was written in Braille.

"I am a member of the third grade class at the Iowa Braille and Sight Saving School located at Vinton, Iowa," Gary went on. "Our class very much enjoyed the visit of Smokey [actually a fire prevention officer dressed as Smokey Bear] to our school recently."

Another from Eric Riggenbach, 9, of Williamsburg, Iowa, who once sent his first ranger kit back with a letter saying he was unworthy of it: "I was playing with matches while I was visiting my cousin's house. I threw the matches on the ground. A fire started to burn the grass and the trees and wildflowers. They called the fire department. They came to put it out before it reached our cousin's home or any home nearby. My Dad and Mom told me to send everything back. They do not think I should have any of it. I do not feel worthy of belonging to the junior forest rangers. P.S. I do wish I can be a junior forest ranger after that mistake. Is there anything I can do to earn the badge again?" Smokey promptly wrote Eric he would be reinstated after a three-month period of good behavior. Eric got his badge back.

Or again, from a kid who, neglecting to include a return address, became a little annoyed when he failed to receive a reply from Smokey: "Smoky, goddam you why dont you sent kit?" wrote James, a fiery little mountaineer, whose follow-up letter was postmarked Leaksville, N.C. "P.S. All the goddam other kids got one." Five months later another letter in the same scrawl came from Hendersonville, N.C.: "Smoky Bear, I moved now. Sent that kit or els . . ." The letter was signed with a dagger dripping "blod." (sic).

It was not too long before Smokey Bear's picture was hanging not only in nearly every subway, trolley, bus, school and other public place in America, but also on walls as far away as Mexico, Venezuela, Japan and Australia. In less than ten years Smokey Bear not only had an international fan club larger than could be dreamed of by Andy Hardy, Judy Garland or indeed any movie superstar, he also was the best-known zoo animal that had ever lived. Besides, with fire losses having been cut by ninety percent and a billion dollars saved in a single year since his prevention campaign started, Smokey Bear had become a virtual god and now could hand down commandments in "tablets" that read:

BREAK MATCHES
CRUSH SMOKES
BE *SURE* ALL
FIRES ARE OUT

Such was Smokey Bear's admirable public career as the symbol of conservation and ace salesman of fire prevention. But what of his private life in the zoo, if indeed, in the glare of such intense publicity, he can be said to have ever had one? Even as a superstar the six-foot cinnamon-tinted black bear took rather well to his ancient iron-and-stone cage, which was all the National Zoo, with its chronic financial needs, could offer him. Not that his cage was below par for an animal of his species. "It's adequate for a bear's needs," Zoo director Dr. Theodore Reed explained. "I'm sure one can raise as nice a family in a Victorian dwelling as in a suburban ranch house."

Dr. Reed was referring to the new quarters that were planned for Smokey some years back: a $50,000 moated enclosure designed to resemble the log cabin ranger station with which Smokey's TV image was associated. This never materialized, despite the fact that there was some sentiment in the U.S. Senate for Federal Housing Administration aid for a Smokey Bear dream house.

According to J. Lear Grimmer, assistant director of the National Zoo, who was then in charge of the bear, "Smokey knew he was something special. And he never extended himself too much for his peanuts, either. But even with all the attention he got from the crowds he was still a pretty lonesome bear."

In 1962, when Smokey was twelve years old—which is roughly half the life span of a healthy bear—it was decided to get him a mate. To some extent, that determination was prompted by concern for the bear's needs, but there was also the very large consideration that a son and heir would be required for continuity in the national fire prevention program. And, at twelve, it was getting rather late.

Fortunately for the purposes of media coverage an appropriate young female was found. Only one and a half years old—a May/September match—his prospective mate was a black bear; like Smokey, she was a native of New Mexico, and she was also an orphan. So the young female, named Goldie because of the mix of fine gold hair in her coat, was flown in to Washington with even greater fanfare than had been associated with Smokey's arrival. Goldie was accompanied by Ray Bell, the same game warden who had brought Smokey in. A motorcycle escort whizzed her from the airport to the Zoo. Newspapers, magazines, television, radio and wire services relayed news around the world that "Smokey Is Getting A Bride!" Even the Congressional Record reported the affair in a thousand-word speech entitled: "A Great Social Event," delivered by Senator Hubert H. Humphrey of Minnesota.

All through the winter of 1962–63, the world waited for the two to become acquainted with each other. To expedite the process, Goldie was placed in a cage adjoining Smokey's where they could at least sniff and touch each other between the bars. "With animals," Dr. Reed pointed out, "you just can't put perfect strangers together immediately, even if they're of the opposite sex. Most require a courtship period."

Finally spring came, and Goldie was ready. She was placed in Smokey's cage with high hopes that nature would take its course, and a new Smokey Bear would soon be on the way. Nothing, however, could have been further from reality. After noting the presence of his new cagemate with an apathetic nod of his head, the old celibate walked off to his own part of the cage, and, in the eleven years since, hasn't bothered to take a second look.

No one can say with certainty why the two never bred. Both were healthy animals and black bears are not known to be particularly shy breeders in captivity, although, of course, some individuals may have special problems. One guess is that Smokey never quite recovered from the trauma of his cubhood experiences (for years he would almost go berserk at the smell of fire). Another theory is that he was too advanced in age and accustomed to celibacy to be interested in sex when Goldie was introduced to him. Whatever the cause, the consensus among professionals is that Smokey Bear's behavior was extremely unusual.

The problem of a successor to Smokey Bear was solved in 1972 by the adoption of a young male cub—again an orphaned black bear from New Mexico. He was named Little Smokey and placed in a cage next to his foster parents. And there he waits eventually to take over his foster father's mantle.

Except that mantle may not have the bright sheen it once had. In his declining years the legend of Smokey Bear has taken some ecological reversals. New ideas about 'the role of fire in nature's scheme of things have lately come into vogue. In the April, 1973, issue of *Natural History*, Raymond B. Cowles, a biologist and professor emeritus at the University of California, told of the destruction by fire of the California town of Chaparral a decade ago. The Forest Service philosophy of fire suppression, and Smokey's stern warnings, kept all fires away from Chaparral, allowing the area's chaparral vegetation to grow rampant. "Without fires," wrote Cowles, "the clear areas in the pine forest became choked with thickets of spiny Ceanothus, chinquapin, and other shrubs, and the accumulating piles of fallen pine boughs." This meant, according to Cowles, that, because of a fuel buildup, an accidental fire was far more devastating than it would have been if natural or controlled fires had been allowed.

This theory has been taken up by other critics of the U.S. Forest Service, who claim that Smokey's old-fashioned approach to fire is actually damaging to the wilderness, upsetting to ecosystems, and causing unnecessary fires such as the Chaparral conflagration. Fire is nature's method of regenerating, they say. It recycles nutrients, returns phosphates, potassium and calcium to the ground and eventually even attracts wildlife into a burned area for the lusher new vegetation. When fires have been suppressed for decades, allowing dense accumulations of undergrowth, a fire can easily become a holocaust and destroy the highest trees.

So despite strong rebuttal by official Forest Service spokesmen that Smokey is not against fires, but only against careless handling of fires, his critics maintain that his message nevertheless comes across as indiscriminantly anti-fire. Moreover, the strength of his opposition is gaining such momentum that the old superstar's image is already taking something of a beating. Even the annual report (1972) from Smokey Bear Headquarters said, "It would have been easy for Smokey to have felt like he was in a hostile camp this past year. Almost any given month the newstands across the country displayed magazines and newspapers containing articles proclaiming Smokey as a liar."

And so, in his twilight years, the saga of Smokey Bear, superstar, may be drawing to a close. Now twenty-four and so arthritic he can hardly move his back legs, the old hero spends most of his time sleeping. Gone are the days when news photographers crowded round and plied him with sweets to induce him to allow "just one more." The keeper brings his ten-pound daily ration of fish, it's true, but often it's hours before he makes a move to touch it. "Sometimes he'll lie down and can hardly get up," says keeper William Rose. "People will come over and say, 'That's not the real Smokey, I heard he died years ago.' Then they see him make some little move and they say, 'Hey! I believe it *is* him. Gosh, he looks old and worn out.' "

Besides, there are new young stars that have come to edge Smokey out of whatever limelight still remains. He is still in that ancient steel cage that they have talked about moving him out of since 1957, but up on the hill in a gleaming new four-hundred-thousand-dollar mansion are two young giant pandas. "Important diplomatic gifts and zoologically among the rarest animals in the world," officials say. No longer do you see signs reading: "This Way to Smokey Bear." Everywhere you look in the Zoo, there are new signs saying: "To The Pandas." Some signs don't even need the word Panda, they just have an arrow and a picture. *Sic transit gloria*—even in the zoo.

A few still remember, though. On July 10, 1974, a Congressional subcommittee on agriculture approved a resolution declaring: "That it is the sense of the Congress that when Smokey Bear goes to that great honey tree in the sky it is just and fitting that he shall be returned home to his place of birth, Capitan, New Mexico, for proper disposition and a permanent memorial in or near Capitan among the cool green mountains where he was born."

"We're just getting ready, that's all," said Representative Harold Runnels, Democrat, of New Mexico, who sponsored the resolution. He added that he hoped Smokey Bear would live for many more years but that the four hundred residents of Capitan felt that a permanent memorial was the least the Government could give to the black bear who has been the symbol of the nation's fire prevention program since 1950. And who also earned the Government some 1.3 million dollars over the years in royalties from children's toys, books, records and other items.

Not too long ago—as recently as 1971, in fact—had anyone predicted that two native Red Chinese would soon be having millions of Americans queue up to catch an adoring look at them, he would have been considered a candidate for a psychiatric ward. Nevertheless that is precisely what did happen, starting on April 20, 1972, when crowds that would total 8,000,000 within eighteen months lined up for a quarter of a mile to ogle two newcomers from the People's Republic of China who were making their first public appearance in Washington. The creators of this pandemonium were, of course, two giant pandas.

The giant panda may look like a common bear (which really he is not) but he is actually about as rare as the black bear of the Smokey variety is common. His rarity is not the reason why he became a superstar of the zoo. The two new pandas that came to the U.S. did so as a result of the sudden thawing of Sino-American relationships occasioned by ex-President Nixon's visit to the People's Republic.

They were ideal candidates to benefit from all the extra-curricular hoopla. Added to his natural charisma and the fact that the few left of his species come from one of the remote places in the world—the nearly inaccessible peaks of Southwest China and Tibet—the giant panda is visually the perfect zoo animal. He looks like an outsized Teddy Bear, acts like a human being and cavorts like a freaked-out otter. As cuddly-looking as a big bunny, the panda has two jet black ears and two circles of black around his eyes that, on a snow-white face, give him the appearance of a circus clown. He waddles on all fours, turns somersaults, does flip-flops, plays hide-and-seek and, alone in all of the animal world, stands on his head like a Yogi. This he does to mark his scent, which, in the wild, he does by rubbing his ano-genital area on trees for the purpose of warning other pandas that they are now on his turf. He also does it on the wall of the zoo, instinctively, as dogs lift a leg on fire hydrants—territorial behavior carried over into domesticity.

When the giant panda eats his staple food, which is bamboo, he is a wonder to behold. Taking hold of a fresh, growing stalk he pulls it to the ground. Then he sits on his haunches with legs stretched out and, holding it in his prehensile forepaws, chomps away like a contented child munching on a candy stick. A visitor looks in amazement as this incredible animal consumes stalk after stalk of the tough, woody "poles," sometimes an inch thick, as easily as a human might chew on a Tootsie Roll. Nature equipped the panda for this spectacular performance by endowing him with an elongated wrist-bone which he uses like a human thumb to hold the stalks, and with mighty molars that crunch the bamboo to a pulp, whereupon it is delivered through a rough-lined esophagus to a thick-walled muscular gizzard-like stomach and an exceedingly short intestine.

The giant panda has, not surprisingly, always been a superstar at the zoo. As far back as 1937, when Su-lin, the first panda to emerge from China, arrived at Brookfield Zoo in Chicago, a panda rage swept the country. Panda toys, panda dolls and panda fashions sold by the millions. After that only two zoos, Bronx and St. Louis, were lucky enough to get pandas, and the last one in the United States died in 1953. When the Chinese Communists took over on the mainland in 1950, the U.S. Government, under the Trading-With-The-Enemy Act, forbade import of the animals along with everything else Chinese. As a result this country lost the opportunity of acquiring Chi-Chi, who, in 1958, was refused admittance here and then immediately was snatched up by the London Zoo, where she became a sensation. Moscow, too, despite its political friction with China, had no compunction about accepting An-An, and he came to be regarded with something of a reverence accorded to a recipient of the Order of Lenin. In Tokyo, two pandas that were given by Mao Tse-tung to commemorate a visit by the Japanese Premier took that city by such storm that a Dial-A-Panda telephone number was set up so that people could call in to hear them bark and bleat. With the pair in North Korea (both London's and Moscow's died in 1973) there are now only six in captivity outside of China, Hsing-Hsing and Ling-Ling, in Washington, being the latest to come into the Western world.

Hsing-Hsing (pronounced Shing-Shing) means "Bright Star" and Ling-Ling means "Cute Little Girl." Apparently the Chinese Communists are also aware of the power of their animal superstars to win human hearts. When the U.S. Government decided to renew relations with a regime that controlled eight hundred million Chinese, Premier Chou En-lai is reported to have told Mrs. Richard M. Nixon, "You have made us gifts of musk oxen. We'll load your plane up with pandas."

Accordingly, two were selected from the Peking Zoo, earmarked as gifts to the President of the United States and his wife, and therewith was set in motion the exchange of what was perhaps the most important diplomatic gift in modern times. On the U.S. side, a pair of rare musk oxen, like the panda, an animal that lives in a cold climate (Greenland and the Arctic) was requisitioned from the San Francisco Zoo for the Chinese. Perhaps the selection, on both sides, of animals associated with low temperatures was an unconscious symbolic recognition of the long freeze that was about to be thawed.

As soon as the gifts were announced—even before, in fact, as soon as the news was leaked—a political contest began in the U.S. for the possession of Hsing-Hsing and Ling-Ling. All three of the great zoos which had formerly had pandas in their collections—Brookfield, Bronx and St. Louis, in addition to San Diego, the country's largest—lobbied for the animals with all the intensity of politicians seeking votes. Governor Richard B. Ogilvie of Illinois, backed by Clement Stone, perhaps Nixon's biggest campaign contributor, pressed claims to the animals for their state. Ogilvie's office bombarded the press with copies of the urgent appeal that he sent to the President:

> Brookfield Zoo was an innovative pioneer in establishing natural settings for its animals, thus permitting them greater freedom and giving the public a better view of the natural behavior of the animals. The Zoo was also the first in the country—and the last—to have a panda, and the grotto in which they lived waits for new occupants. In 1958, the Zoo had completed arrangements to buy a panda, but this move was blocked by trade restrictions. Instead, the panda went

to London, where as "Chi-Chi" she is perhaps the most famous animal in the world. I respectfully urge you to select this outstanding zoo as the future home of the pair of pandas which will be your gift from the Chinese government.

And of course, the National Zoo's hat was automatically in the ring on the basis of its being the "zoo of all the people." Also on its side was the tradition that all state gifts of animals to Presidents go to the National Zoo. In addition, Washington's position was strengthened by the fact that the U.S. gift of musk oxen was to be formally presented to the Chinese by the National's director, Dr. Theodore Reed.

For a couple of weeks, resolution of the "Great Panda Squabble" lay in the balance. While governors, mayors, senators and representatives barraged the White House with pleas on behalf of their hometown zoos, the President kept his own counsel. Public Law 89-673, the Foreign Gifts Act of 1966, states that persons in governmental employ may not keep a gift with a retail value of more than $50. Nobody of course dreamed that the President would keep Hsing-Hsing and Ling-Ling in the White House backyard as the Kennedy's did Macaroni, Caroline's little pony. But then this was an unpredictable President and, with all the controversy surrounding him, there was inevitably more than customary suspense.

Another item that kept suspense at high pitch was the question of the sexual identity of the pandas. The genitalia of the female panda is almost indistinguishable from that of the male. This matter was discussed at the highest levels of the White House, according to *The New York Times.* "Eight days ago, for example," it reported on March 14, 1972, "while sunning himself at Key Biscayne, Florida, John D. Erlichman, Mr. Nixon's top domestic policy advisor, received a call from a zoologist who said he feared that the Chinese might send two males or two females . . ." This sentiment represented a feeling among some zoo people that despite the Chinese having named the animals "Bright Star" and "Cute Little Girl," what eventually arrived here might well turn out to be a "dealer's pair," that is, two pandas of the same sex. Such a pair would of course preclude the occurrence of what everybody was dreaming about: the birth of the first baby panda in a zoo outside of China.

Further concern developed in Washington when Milton, one of the two musk oxen that were scheduled to be delivered to the Chinese at the time of the President's visit, developed coughing spells and the sniffles, which caused his shipment to be delayed. When the pair finally arrived in Peking, both were so mangy-looking they could not be displayed to the Chinese people. Harrison Salisbury of *The New York Times* reported on June 4, 1972 (three months after the originally scheduled delivery date of the musk oxen) of dining with Mrs. Sun Yat-sen, dowager widow of the Republic's founding father and vice-chairwoman of the People's Republic. "To dine with Mrs. Sun is to be in a presence," wrote Salisbury. ". . . this vigorous woman still flashes a smile that has something of a schoolgirl's grace in it and her wit has not been dulled by the years. She took a cigarette from a green box. It was a Panda, she said—very mild all-Virginia tobacco with no sweetening or preservatives. That brought up the subject of the musk oxen in the Peking Zoo, which still have not been exhibited because they are suffering from a skin ailment. 'We got a bad deal,' she said with a laugh. 'That's Nixon for you.' "

Adding even more mystery to the brouhaha was the fact that, apart from the question as to who was going to get what kind of panda, their departure was now being delayed from Peking. Diplomatic rhubarb? Chou En-lai had had second thoughts? Mao Tse-tung had proscribed in a fit of late dogma?

No. Mrs. Nixon was ecstatic about the gifts and, as one official reported, according to the *Washington Post* ". . . Mrs. Nixon wants to announce everything herself. They're her pandas." The Chinese on the other hand had already accepted the two musk oxen and regardless of their condition they *were* already in China. The real reason for the delay was something more weighty than diplomatic protocol. Hsing-Hsing and Ling-Ling, like so many other wild animals which have been isolated from their adults, were absolute innocents about the mating process. So the Chinese, consummate diplomats, had delayed their departure to give the pair a sort of crash course in mating by letting them watch other pandas in action at the Peking Zoo before shipping them out.

By mid-March the giant panda competition was finally resolved. At a White House briefing on March 13, 1972, a spokesman said that, "The President and Mrs. Nixon had discussed the gift of the two pandas at Camp David over the weekend and that, since they were a gift to all of the people, they felt it was proper that the animals should set up housekeeping in Washington." Mr. Nixon also put an end to another nagging fear: Hsing-Hsing and Ling-Ling were a "true pair," the spokesman said (although he did not state how he knew) and the President had "every hope they would mate and flourish here."

And so, on April 16, 1972, Hsing-Hsing and Ling-Ling arrived in Washington accompanied by Dr. Ting Hung of the Peking Revolutionary Committee and Yang Chung, a panda keeper. The female, six months older than the male and having been in captivity longer, weighed one hundred and thirty-six pounds as compared with seventy-four pounds for the male. She was also considerably larger. They were installed in a hastily remodeled building, pending construction of a new $425,000 "panda palace" that was being rushed to completion on the site of the former Delicate Hoofed Animal Paddock, from which other rare but less-publicized animals had been removed. A special panda team, comprising three keepers, an associate curator and a round-the-clock security guard, was set up to look after the strangers—so strange indeed, that there is considerable controversy as to whether the giant pandas belong to the racoon family, the bear family or, since they have characteristics of both bears and racoons, a family of their own.

"The scientists at the Smithsonian and the National Zoo reviewed all the literature available," said Dr. Reed. "They concluded that the giant pandas and the lesser pandas belong together in a family of their own (*Ailuropoda melanoleuca*). But we really know so little about them we may have to change our minds."

By fall of 1973, the "panda palace" was ready. Even the Watergate Apartment complex would be hard put to surpass the new air-conditioned panda digs. Being solitary animals, both pandas have separate quarters. Each has a huge plate-glass-fronted "living room" through which the public can watch it eat and go through its daily routine of amusing itself—and the watchers. These living rooms are decorated in a style attesting to the pandas' preeminence in the Zoo's hierarchy: oak-panelled walls, potted bamboo plants, soft indirect lighting and "Swedish modern" furniture, especially in the form of a multitiered, railroad tie "sofa" on which the occupants can indulge the attitudes in posture for which they are so comically famous.

Leading off each living room is a "bedroom" or sleeping den, into which the superstars can retreat when they wish to be alone, which is quite often.

Outside of the ultramodernistic Panda House, which looks as though it might have been designed by Le Corbusier (although in fact it was designed by Faulkner, Faulkner and Vanderpool), slopes an acre of beautifully landscaped garden, divided by a cedar wall hedged with *Phyllostachys nuda* and *Pseudosasa japonica* into "his" and "her" sections—again out of respect for the pandas' love of privacy. Provision was made, however, for those moments when Hsing-Hsing and Ling-Ling might also want to remember they are pandas. Something called "moon gate," a circle of reinforced mesh overhung with a fanciful Chinese-style roof, was installed in the dividing wall so that they can woo each other through the openings. The whole spread, costing $425,000, is something like the kind of studio "cottage" that Louis B. Mayer might have lavished on Greta Garbo and Lars Hansen when he corralled them for Metro-Goldwyn-Mayer.

Here the tab was being picked up, not by MGM, but by Uncle Sam. And with it erupted another chapter in the Great Panda Squabble. A number of keepers, employees of the U.S. government at the National Zoo, claimed that excessive time and attention were being lavished on the two pandas. Unnecessarily large quarters had been assigned to them, which, they said, required the displacement of other animals. As a result, a rare antelope, the bongo, miscarried, and two rare white rhinoceroses, Bill and Lucy (named after Dr. William Mann and his wife) were sent on indefinite loan to the San Diego Zoo.

"It's not that we're against the pandas," said one keeper. "They're the only pair in this country and that's great. But the officials have gone overboard. Some of that money would have been better spent looking after what we already had and correcting the deficiencies—like the serious soil erosion. In my book the pandas are no better than other animals. If a family of five people can live in an air-conditioned house costing $40,000, I don't understand why they have to spend half a million dollars on two Chinese pandas."

July 1, 1950—Smokey Bear, an orphaned cub badly burned by a forest fire in New Mexico, is welcomed, after his recovery, to his job as chief propagandist for fire prevention in the U.S. Chief of the U.S. Forest Service, Lyle Watts, does the honors. *(Photo credit: U.S. Forest Service)*

May, 1974—Smokey Bear, after almost a quarter-century of service to his country, now a fading superstar at the National Zoo in Washington. *(Photo credit: U.S. Forest Service)*

...and

PLEASE

make people more careful!

Only you can prevent forest fires

1963—America's favorite zoo animal at the peak of his career—Smokey's basic poster of 1973 was seen by millions throughout the world. *(Photo credit: U.S. Forest Service)*

April 1972—Declining superstar retires to background as new favorites claim the spotlight: Chinese Giant Pandas arrive to become reigning king and queen of the zoo world. *(Photo credit: U.S. Forest Service)*

Ling-Ling ("Cute Little Girl") reclining on her wood log sofa in her $400,000 air conditioned home in the National Zoo. Along with a male giant panda, she was a gift to the United States from the People's Republic of China. *(Photo credit: Smithsonian Institution)*

Hsing-Hsing ("Bright Star") the male, whose name is pronounced "Shing Shing," is younger, smaller and less aggressive than the female. He likes to play in the garden, a finely-landscaped acre of which both have outside their house. His favorite game is pulling down bamboo stalks, which is the panda's basic food. *(Photo credit: Smithsonian Institution)*

Ling-Ling comes out into her garden whenever she can for a bath, Oriental style. *(Photo credit: Smithsonian Institution)*

The pandas have not mated yet—they are a bit immature. But that does not prevent them from getting a head start now and then. That's Ling-Ling in the foreground being a little coy. *(Photo credit: Smithsonian Institution)*

Ham, the "chimponaut," another fading superstar at the zoo. One of America's space pioneers, the first primate to go hurtling down the Atlantic Missile Range, the aging chimpanzee at the National Zoo no longer has crowds stepping over each other to ogle him in his cage. *(Photo credit: The National Zoological Park)*

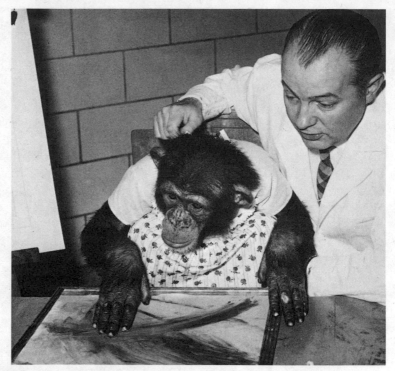

Arthur Watson, director of the Baltimore Zoo, with Betsey, TV superstar and famous painting chimpanzee. *(Photo credit: Afro-American Photo)*

Betsey with one of her finished paintings. *(Photo credit: Vernon M. Price, Baltimore Zoo)*

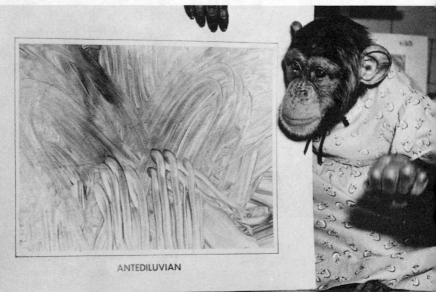

ANTEDILUVIAN

The Washington Post editorialized about "elitism at the National Zoo," basing its statements, in part, on the allegations of the keepers. This in turn drew a response from Dr. Theodore Reed, the Zoo's director, which in substance stated that the money came not from operational budgets but from unobligated money previously appropriated. Additionally, the two rhinos had been committed to San Diego Zoo long before there was any idea that there would be pandas in the U.S. and solely in the hope that the change would stimulate the rhinos to breed, which they did. He also said the inability of the female bongo to deliver her calf derived from physical reasons certified by veterinarians as in no way related to the transfer of the animal. Dr. Reed concluded his response by saying that the *Post*'s editorial and the newspaper articles on which it was based, "reflected less than a total understanding of a complex subject."

No doubt the subject of the pandas is a complex one, as Dr. Reed suggested, and perhaps his critics overstated their case. It is also true that old Smokey Bear is still padding around in his circa 1916 cage —no MGM studio den for him. It makes one ponder the eventual fate of Hsing-Hsing and Ling-Ling, given the whimsies of public favor and international diplomacy. In any case, for now and the foreseeable future, they are superstars of first magnitude, and not only because they are pandas. Hsing-Hsing and Ling-Ling are also living symbols of peace and new comity between the world's most populous nation and its strongest, on view day after day in the nation's capital where they are seen by millions of Americans from every part of the country. Had the richest nation in the world not found the time and the funds to present these symbols in a setting appropriate to their special importance, would it not have been an affront to the giver?

Meantime Hsing-Hsing and Ling-Ling go on being just plain pandas—playing with cakes of ice in their summer air-conditioned cages, knocking the daylights out of snowmen in their winter gardens, plopping like fat tipsy humans in their round wooden bathtubs, doing cartwheels, handstands and flip-flops, and when the occasion suits them, sitting down with a plate of diced chicken, raisins, carrots and rice in hand like some late night patron of Ruby Foo's.

"Look, she eats like a person," squeals a twelve-year-old boy, as

Ling-Ling polishes off her morning repast with a desert of bamboo leaves.

"I can't believe it!" exclaims a svelte New York fashion model. "I promoted a trip to Washington just to see them, and now I can't tear myself away."

"Neat!" exclaims a girl in braids.

And so it went day after day all through 1973 and into 1974.

Sometime in 1975, perhaps, when the pair becomes mature sexually, the U.S. may be able to achieve something no nation in the Western World has yet been able to do: breed a giant panda in captivity. The British sent their Chi-Chi to live for a time with Russia's An-An in Moscow, and the Russians did the reverse on one occasion. But neither international exchange bore, so to speak, any fruit. Some zoomen feel that the difficulty was that Chi-Chi's keeper had spent too much time with her as a baby, thus becoming so important to her that she lost interest in her own kind.

"This won't happen here," said Larry Collins, associate curator in charge of Hsing-Hsing. "We have three keepers for the pandas here: Dave Bryan, Curly Harper and Tex Rowe. So they are not likely to become attached to any one individual." "Besides," added Keeper Rowe, a slight Buffalo Bill of a man with a goatee and wide mustache, "that English keeper must have been a lucky fool. We know enough about pandas, especially lady pandas, to realize they're not such ladies. See those teeth marks there," he said, pointing to his cowboy boot. "That's a little present our little lady gave me."

Tex had gone into Ling-Ling's living room with her food. Since she was reclining on an opposite side of the room, he had assumed he was safe. Before he knew it she was at him and had pinned him to the wall. He was completely cornered by the wall on one side, a bamboo pot on the other and the panda in front. Ling-Ling grabbed his leg and sunk her teeth into the boot, just missing the anklebone.

"So I danced," Tex recalled. "I knew she hadn't hit the bone and I just kept on wiggling my leg so she couldn't get a good hold on it. She had my right leg in her hand and I kept kicking and waving my left. The people out there thought it was some kind of game. I *know* they thought I was dancing with that panda." For Tex, more than international relations hung in the balance.

By the very fact of their semblance to man it would seem reasonable that bears, such as Smokey, or pandas, such as Hsing-Hsing and Ling-Ling, would become superstars of the zoo. Primates, too, particularly the gorilla and the chimpanzee, belong in this group. One such, the baby gorilla, Patty Cake, born in Central Park Zoo in 1972, captured the hearts not only of New Yorkers but also millions of out-of-towners via network television. (For more about her, please see Chapter 11 about Central Park Zoo.)

The chimpanzee is also a public celebrity in large part because of his intelligence and his ability (plus willingness) to perform—to be a "ham." Indeed Ham was the name given to one of the most famous of zoo chimps: the primate who, as America's first astronaut, plummeted through space in a Redstone rocket on January 31, 1961. His first week at the National Zoo, after discharge from the aerospace program, drew crowds that stumbled over each other to have a close-up look at the new zoo superstar, the banana-eating trailblazer who had hurtled 5000 miles per hour on a suborbital flight four hundred twenty miles down the Atlantic missile range. Strapped to a couch in the capsule, like any proper astronaut, he had experienced free fall, increased gravity, re-entry—the works. He even pressed levers to make scientific tests while in flight. The entire world knew the name Ham almost as well as it knew the name of the President of the U.S. He was in all the headlines for weeks.

When Ham was given to the National Zoo in 1963, he was in top physical shape. There were no discernible aftereffects from his journey into space, such as the inner ear troubles reported by John Glenn and Alan Shepard. But Ham, like Smokey Bear, also never took a mate. "Too much handling by humans," his keeper said. "He's not real sociable as far as other chimps are concerned. He likes people better, he's been more associated with them."

Now seventeen-years-old, and still in good shape, Ham no longer draws the crowds. "Even with the sign posted on front of his cage telling who he is," said the keeper, "nobody pays him much mind. It is very seldom a child notices who he was. But I like him fine. He's a beautiful animal. Of course, he's very highstrung . . ."

So Ham, once a star of stars, is living out his twilight years in relative obscurity. No more trips, no more crowds, no more headlines—like an old trooper or soldier or fire-fighting bear, he's just fading away.

Other chimpanzees, though, are making headlines. In the Yerkes Primate Center at Emory University a young female chimp named Lana is learning to read and write a brand-new language called Yerkish, a name derived from the place where the studies are in progress. There, three-year-old Lana is rapidly mastering a sign language which is based on a computer that she can operate at will by pressing large keys on a console. On each of the variously colored keys are different symbols which represent basic words of Yerkish: please, banana, give, make, candy, etc. When Lana presses a key the symbol flashes on a screen overhead, which she can see, and is reproduced in English on a teleprinter in a control room.

First, Lana was allowed to casually play with the computer's keys. If she touched the symbol for candy, a piece of chocolate would drop into the vending machine and the symbol would flash on the screen. Soon she began to make the association with certain symbols and the corresponding reward. Then the experiment was advanced a bit and she was required to punch the symbol for words such as "please" before she would get the reward. Later, she had to learn a more complex task, such as pressing in sequence keys that would read: "please make machine give candy period" before she punched out her own reward. Further on in the experiments, the researchers reversed the process. They flashed on the screen parts of a sentence such as "please machine give . . ." and almost always Lana punched out the correct completion. When the researchers tried to fool her by jumbling the sequential order—for example, "give machine make . . ." —Lana generally wiped out the sentence by indignantly punching "period," therewith clearing the computer and screen.

Something akin to this has been going on in the zoo world since 1972—specifically at the Portland, Oregon, Zoo, under the supervision of its director, Philip Ogilvie. There, in addition to an assortment of monkeys, ostriches, giraffes, camels and elephants which are learning to pull chains and press lighted panels that deliver food, chimpanzees are learning the standard American Sign Language (ASL) for the deaf and mute. Groups of volunteers under expert direction sit in the cages with the young zoo chimps, talking to them, showing them signs, guiding their hands into correct ASL positions and rewarding them with goodies. Two of the young chimps, named Charlie and Jezebel, are already fluent in over two dozen ASL words that enable them to ask to be fed, tickled, picked up or chased. The experiments have already progressed to the point where the chimps are not only communicating with their human tutors in ASL but also with each other. On one occasion, a tutor who had been playing a chase game with Charlie, suddenly got tired and stopped. Charlie then made the "chase" sign to Jezebel and she immediately began running him around the cage.

Out of all this near-human performance of the chimpanzee may well come a new zoo superstar. Although part of the motivation behind the experimentation taking place at zoos such as Portland is a desire to alleviate the zoo inmate's boredom, the main thrust of the work is to study the animals in a social context surrounded by their peers. Scientific research in such a setting is considered by behaviorists capable of delivering more valuable results than if conducted on animals in isolation.

As for learning a language, who knows what chimp genius may one day emerge from all this work to open up new channels of communication between man and animal? An example of this may indeed already have occurred in the case of Betsey, of the Baltimore Zoo, who came upon the art scene in the 1950s as a painter of "abstract" pictures. Many zoo professionals considered Betsey's "art" as sheer gimmickry, not comparable in any way with serious art or even with the behavior studies of chimpanzees in connection with computers and other instrumentation. Other professionals, however, including some artists and anthropologists, claim that her work is at least comparable to paintings made by the average six-year-old child. And, indeed, in a joint showing held in Baltimore of paintings by six-year-olds and by Betsey, a number of works by the children and the chimp were indistinguishable.

Whether or not her work can be considered "work," much less art, the fact is that Betsey, who died in 1960, became not only a superstar in her own zoo but also something of an international celebrity. She demonstrated her talents on many television shows including several network programs. Her paintings were exhibited at an art gallery in London, along with those of Congo, a resident of the London Zoo, an event attended by a large number of artists and scientists including Salvador Dali, Sir Julian Huxley and Dr. Desmond Morris. And her canvasses, even during her short career, fetched a total of more than $3,000, which is considerably more than Van Gogh realized from his art during his lifetime.

Betsey, a white-faced chimpanzee, was born in 1951 in the back country of Liberia, West Africa. She was trapped by natives when she was only a few months old and sold to the Chase Wild Animal Farm near the port city of Monrovia, where she spent over a year in the camp stockade, awaiting sale and shipment. She was finally shipped out to Philadelphia in a collection ordered by an animal dealer. Arthur Watson, director of the Baltimore Zoo, looking for a female to join Dr. Tom and Dagmar, two other white-faced chimps in the Zoo, bought her and installed her at the Zoo as a gift of John R. Sherwood of the Sinclair Refining Company.

She arrived at the Zoo in 1953. Since the Baltimore Zoo at that time was one of those municipal installations that financially had low priority, Watson tended to experiment out of necessity with unusual ideas to generate much-needed income. Betsey, he discovered, had an extraordinary affinity for paint. Once exposed to it she would have nothing to do with the other traditional diversions of zoo chimps. In her play time she always went to her canvas, while cage-mates, Dr. Tom and Dagmar, amused themselves with clowning, tricycle riding, block play and the like.

Betsey started out almost as any child might with paint and paper. She was given the materials and coaxed a little; she experimented, made a huge mess at first and then gradually caught on to the general idea. Watson would place a wooden frame on the table in front of her chair and soak a large sheet of paper in water. The damp paper would then be set in the frame and several gobs of different colored paint placed on it. Betsey would study the materials for a moment and then go to work with her fingers (she was a finger painter, while Congo of London was a brush painter).

"In a short space of time her work improved immensely," said Watson. "She took to it naturally and didn't need coaching. She understood what was expected of her, that people were there to watch her and she obliged. And her paintings began to take on form, predictable patterns and a personal style. If you study them you can note the sweep of her lines. The strokes she makes are all large natural curves with no sudden stops or sharp lines. These are her individual signature. And strangely enough she gets some of her best effects from hanging positions. It is one of her secrets."

By this time Betsey had already become one of the best-known figures in her hometown of Baltimore. She had also become the butt —or least her painting had—of much criticism in the local press. Editorialized the Baltimore *Sun* of March 12, 1957:

Ape As Artist

Betsey, Baltimore's own particular chimpanzee, is enjoying a certain vogue at the moment. One of the oldest of drolleries in the world of art is tying a brush to a cow's tail, or putting a box of water colors in a baby's hands, or giving a trained seal some pastels and then surveying the results with the exclamation, "There is a Masterpiece of Modernism for you!" Betsey is in the Ancient Tradition.

But she may yet surprise us. It isn't surefire at all that this precocious ape will always produce "abstractions." Didn't some notable scientist, somebody like Jeans or Eddington, tell us long ago that given enough monkeys, enough typewriters and enough time, the chances were that eventually those monkeys would tap out the complete Works of Shakespeare? Why not vary the old painting gag with Betsey? . . . Provide her with a proper set of colors and see what happens. The chuckling school of look-a-monkey-can-do-it critics could be mightily surprised—at the end of some day they might find a beautiful copy of Botticelli's "Primavera" signed with Betsey's paw mark.

But Arthur Watson and Betsey persisted. Presently Betsey's fame spread around the world. Twelve of her finger paintings were put on display at the Institute of Contemporary Arts in London, along with twenty-four sketches by London's chimpanzee, Congo. Russian critics thought that the presentation in an art gallery of a chimpanzee's "sloshing" was obscene. The *Times* (London) tongue-in-cheeked the event with the observation that, "Ordinary artists have every reason to be worried and alarmed by the arrival of a competitor who is not only non-union, but enjoys the grossly unfair advantage of . . . possessing twice the usual number of hands. Artists have enough to do keeping the wolf from their own door without having to worry about excluding mandrills from the Leicester Galleries." And the United States Customs, citing the Supreme Court case of *United States vs. Perry*, in which the Court ruled that "everything artistic and beautiful cannot be classed as fine art," insisted on a duty payment for admission of Congo's work into this country. "Paint placed on a canvas by a subhuman animal with no rational mind or powers of imagination doesn't meet our test for works of art," the customs appraiser said.

On the other hand, Dr. Desmond Morris thought that the patterns produced by both chimpanzees were an important source of information in tracing the origins of human art. Their activities were "terrifyingly intelligent," he said.

Three international art figures now joined in the debate. Georges Mathieu, one of France's leading abstract painters and a champion of the "direct power of signs which do not refer to any reality," said that the question was whether Betsey was expressing herself directly or if she was simply painting in imitation of human painters. "Philosophically," he pointed out, "Betsey's work is interesting in terms of the Gestalt theory, if she creates signs which express her fears or pleasures. But in no sense could she be considered a member of the abstract school, although to profane eyes her work may resemble nonobjective painting. A chimpanzee could hardly go through an evolution which produced painters like Mondrian or Pollock. It's more likely that she's an objective realist."

Rudolph Springer, owner of West Berlin's best-known modern gallery, said that modern painting is the expression of movement. "Painting by a chimpanzee is very interesting. It shows the movement of an ape, the form of expression of a creature created by God. There is in Betsey's work a parallel to contemporary painting known as the theory of automatic painting. But an ape's painting can never be regarded as art," he added, "for every work of art needs the creative spirit of a human being." To which Betsey might have countered, "Male *human* chauvinist pig . . ."

The man who has painted with blowtorches, shaving sprays, hands, feet and most every other medium conceivable also ventured an opinion. "I would expect much better from a chimpanzee," said Salvador Dali, the famed surrealist. "Something more lucid; the method is no good. Putting the paint on the canvas for her and letting her dabble with her fingers, toes and elbows is all wrong. She should be allowed to select the colors and quantity and then be permitted the same freedom allowed to human abstract painters—to throw paint at a wall with a sponge or drop it in blobs on a prone canvas. This would be more scientific, for it would allow the chimpanzee the maximum of movement and action."

Letting a chimpanzee paint, or buying her painting is not a bad thing at all, according to Dali. The decadence of Western art that the Russians saw in the furor over a painting chimpanzee was amusing, he said. "Even though Betsey's paintings were very mediocre, even for a chimpanzee, they are considerably more creative than those resulting from the bureaucratic method of socialist painters.

"Anything that exists alive—or mineral—can be art. No one line is uninteresting. There is nothing wrong with accidents themselves. A human can create an accident that is almost animal. And an animal can create an accident that is almost human. But Raphael—or Dali—" he added, "produce accidents that are almost divine."

And so the controversy raged on; but Betsey kept on painting. And her life was a busy one for a zoo animal: Off to New York in a special compartment on the Congressional Limited for a Tonight Show TV appearance to demonstrate her technique . . . A new "studio" of her own in the Baltimore Zoo—a glassed-in cage where her ever-growing public could watch her at work . . . Endless promotional work with children and educational groups.

But as the crowds watched, year after year, the question was never definitively answered: could the finger-painting that fascinated so many people be called "art;" or was it simply that old attraction known as anthropomorphism—seeing an animal delightfully doing something that is considered properly the function of a human being? Or was it the expression of still another dimension that men unconsciously sense but as yet know little of? In Betsey's case the answer was never quite resolved, for she died within a couple of years of achieving her greatest fame. In this last, she was more fortunate than most of her human confreres, who, if indeed they ever achieve, fame and stardom, must usually wait until long after their deaths.

11 Yeas and Nays—Including the Case of New York City's Central Park Zoo

"THE ANIMALS ARE STRIKING BACK, AND MAYBE IT'S ABOUT TIME. FROM NEW YORK'S CENTRAL PARK ZOO, WHERE A POLAR BEAR SEIZED THE ARM OF A TORMEN- TOR, TO WYOMING'S YELLOWSTONE NATIONAL PARK, WHERE A BUFFALO TRAMPLED A TOURIST, MAMMALS ARE ON THE MARCH." So heralds an article by Kenneth Koyen in *Town & Country* of March, 1972, headed "Let's Abolish Zoos."

Among these mammals on the march, not the least strident are those two-legged members of the order that go by the name of *homo sapiens*. Undeniably well-meaning people, some of these individuals see every incidence of cruelty or neglect connected with zoos as an occasion to shout "free the animals from their cages"—though they themselves confine birds within a metal cage or big dogs inside a one- room apartment. Still others band together in "humane societies" de- voted to catching up stray dogs from the jungles of city streets and lodging them in tiny cages to await acceptance into the larger cage that constitutes the home of the new master. Other groups march on the zoo itself with placard, bullhorn, and leaflet demanding that the animals be sent back where they came from, which, in many cases, has become the site of a Holiday Inn, Uganda, and its surrounding complex of golf courses.

Mr. Koyen further states that no matter how well U.S. zoos may house their inmates or how tenderly they may care for them, all zoos, even the best, share one inescapable condition: ". . . they confine the inmates in spaces which are minuscule in contrast to the expanses of their native habitats. Not only are the areas constricted; the climate, the vegetation, and the very soil are usually hopelessly alien. Instead of a leafy bough, a gorilla must make do with a rubber tire or a chain. Buffalo, which roamed the Great Plains, stand torpid in paved pens. Zoos are, in short, jails. They are remote penitentiaries for prisoners without crimes."

Little invention is required to imagine the kind of reply that Dr. Charles Schroeder might make to charges of this kind. "Come and be our guest at San Diego Zoo, Mr. Koyen," the "grand old man" of zoos might well say. "Come see our alien climate, vegetation and soil. Have a look at the lions and leopards lolling in a sun as authentically subtropical as any that rises over East Africa; observe the koalas munching on our home-grown eucalyptus leaves that might well have been picked in their native Australia; see our nine-banded armadillo burrowing in earth hardly distinguishable from the soil of his South American jungle."

As for those buffalo which, as Mr. Koyen notes, once roamed the Great Plains, William Conway, general director of the New York Zoological Society, would perhaps point out that their descendants in the Bronx Zoo (where they stand in green paddocks, not paved pens) are standing there because that zoo helped save the species from extinction. Other leading zoomen might well add that it is a mistake to believe that captive animals desire the amount of space that, in the wild, nature compels them to cover in the search for food. Nothing is lazier than a lion, for instance. Once he has had his fill of food, a wild lion does exactly what he does in the zoo: sleeps for up to twenty hours a day. And very little space is required for that. Give an animal his food, a mate and the social group he might require, in addition to the main essentials of his natural environment, such as a place to swim if he's a marine mammal, a place to dig if he's a burrower, places to retreat, nest, climb,, and he can well adapt himself to limited space. And, mind you, this without loss of any of his natural skills.

Charges and rebuttals such as these have been going on between zoo-haters and zoo-lovers ever since the birth of the first public menagerie. One of the oldest, the London Zoological Society, had to weather enormous opposition from all kinds of "humane" groups before it was able to get started in 1828. Even today, let the slightest mishap occur at Regent's Park and off go the outraged letters to the editor of the *Times,* sometimes from solid citizens who had not lifted a finger to protest some of the more barbarous treatment of human beings that once marked British colonial rule. The same is true in the United States, where, for example, vandals recently broke into a cage at Central Park Zoo in New York and beat a fallow deer to death, thereby setting off a public clamor for closing of the Zoo.

Accordingly, having read numbers of outraged letters to the editor plus reams of editorials protesting cruelty in zoos, as well as having heard zoos defended in personal interviews with eminent zoo people, we sought out a professional zoo-watcher—a person whose job involves the prevention of cruelty to animals—to see how she felt about zoos.

Mrs. Sue Pressman is a zoologist in the employ of the Humane Society of the U.S., which, from its headquarters in Washington, D.C., acts, as it states in its literature, as a kind of "Ralph Nader of the zoo world." In 1971 Mrs. Pressman, a pert, dark-haired dynamo who once worked at the Boston Zoo animal hospital, started an investigation of U.S. zoos for her employer (HSUS) which took her to some one hundred and twenty commercial and municipal installations. I spoke with Mrs. Pressman on the telephone.

Pressman: "Surprised to hear me say I'm not against zoos?" said the rather musical voice at the other end of the wire. "People think that because we're a humane society, *ipso facto*, we're down on zoos. Not true. We're only against bad zoos, as we're against bad pet treatment, bad domestic animal management, bad legislation for wildlife and all the other inhumane conditions of animal life. But there are lots of things we're *for*, and one of them is good zoos. We think the zoo is a most important institution."

Interviewer: "Why would a humane society think that a zoo, even a good one, is important? What humane role could even the so-called best zoo possibly serve?"

Pressman: "Look, in a few years my thirteen-year-old boy will have a vote. So suppose we did get all the animals back to where they 'belong,' which is what most people mistakenly think we're trying to do? My boy doesn't approve of the way zoos are, so he's going to vote 'no' when it comes to money for them. So all the zoos are closed, no open-concept animal parks, nothing. The animals are back in the wild where they 'belong.' But the wilderness also has to be funded and protected. So if there's a knock on the door and he's an urbanite, as most of our kids will be, and somebody says, 'Hello, I'd like to collect a dollar for a tiger in the Indian preserve,' well, my boy's going to say 'What have you done for me today? Talk to me about parking meters in front of my house or the dog offal on the sidewalk.' That's what he'll be willing to give a dollar for. And unless he can see a tiger in a zoo being allowed its own dignity—where it can display what a tiger really is and not a pacing chunk of meat with stripes—then he won't want to save that thing in the wild. He'll not care unless he's had a chance to relate to that animal, know what it is, why it's here, what it does. Otherwise, who cares?"

Interviewer: "What, then, would HSUS consider a good zoo?"

Pressman: "The primary object of a zoo should be to educate people about the marvelous world of living things of which they as well as wild animals are a part. But in order to educate well, the animal must be maintained well and exhibited well. Otherwise the education is negative. As long as there is one animal caged without a positive educational purpose HSUS and all humanitarians have work to do. That was the objective of our zoo study."

In the course of that study, follow-ups of which are still going on, HSUS found a chimpanzee manacled to the bars of its tiny cage, an alligator trapped in a pool the size of a bathtub, fourteen lions in one cage, and a bear huddled in a packing crate for shelter. "Many of the zoos studied," the HSUS report declared, "were nothing more than animal ghettos."

But obviously cruel conditions were few. Most of the problems HSUS discovered had to do with the concept of exhibiting animals. Some eighty to ninety percent of the zoos investigated were merely displaying "stamp collections," that is, exhibiting one or two of everything, in quarters so small, bland and unimaginative that no visitor could possibly learn anything about the living habits of the animals. "Animals need more than cleanliness,," the HSUS report noted. "What can anyone learn about the characteristics of a lion while it is living in a 12′ x 12′ ceramic-brick cell, no matter how scrupulously clean it is kept?"

So HSUS guidelines concerning cruelty in the zoo zeroed in not so much on individual acts of deliberate maltreatment (although these were of course condemned) but rather on any condition that modified a captive animal's ability to display himself to his full potential. This was considered the cardinal sin that zoos could impose on their animals.

Pressman: "We found three major things wrong. First, when it was a municipal zoo the main problem was bureaucratic meddling, political interference that kept the zoo from functioning. Second most critical problem was archaic buildings that were no good for the proper display of animals even when they were first built. And yet the budget was always spent glueing the damned things back together. The third thing was the public's antiquated approach to zoos—you got to have an elephant and a tiger, otherwise it's not a zoo. This was the only place where the zoo director was guilty. It is his job to change that attitude and replace it with the new philosophy, to stimulate public interest in the zoo by getting people to want more than just gawking at an elephant or a tiger."

Interviewer: "Zoos claim they are on the bottom of the priorities list when it comes to money. What if priorities were shuffled a bit and zoos got more money to work with? Would that change the situation?"

Pressman: "The things we found wrong were not money problems, they were attitude problems. In fact, if you dumped tons of money on them it would only enhance them—more money, more political

meddling. Incidentally, you don't have too much of this political meddling where zoos are run by zoological societies such as the Bronx
or San Diego. What we concluded is that there has to be an absolute
change in zoo philosophy by most municipal zoos. And more than
that, the public must be informed about what we had learned, which
means that you've got to get off your duff and say, 'Why doesn't my
zoo look the way it's supposed to look . . why do we have these
problems of obsolescence, neglect and vandalism? With a modern
public attitude you wouldn't have so many people wanting to abolish
zoos."

   Interviewer: Can you cite an example of this type of bureaucratic
meddling, as you call it?"

   Pressman: Take a certain zoo in Texas. They built a huge model
for a gorilla exhibit—the kind that you show to banks for loans. By
the time the bid got picked up and the political pot got boiling . . .
well, the zookeepers joke with me now. 'We got the working model,'
they say, 'now we can look forward to the real thing.' Well, the real
thing turned out to be one-third the size it was meant to be. And the
zoo director can't tell the public the municipality was responsible for
bungling . . . he's not going to risk his job and you can't blame him.
So they got a midget version of the original design, the gorillas get
out of it all the time, they have to put up hamstringing things to
keep them in, and you're back to the obsolescence you started with.
No wonder much of the public has such a low opinion of zoos."

   HSUS's opinion of United States zoos found official expression in
a rating system that it established for itself as a result of its investigation. Group I incorporates all those zoos which, though not without
flaw, have more good than bad qualities. This would include such
top zoos as Bronx, San Diego, National, and others that have superb
staff, conservation and education programs, excellent medical and
research facilities, behavioral displays and community awareness.
Group II includes mostly major municipal facilities that have some
trained and qualified personnel but are hampered by municipal meddling. Here the good things are about equally divided with the bad
and the situation is static; they go along making only minimal progress if any. Municipal bid systems hamper purchase of animals, cage
design, educational and conservation services, even master plans. In

this category fall the great majority of American zoos: about seventy-five percent. Still, these zoos have the possibility for improvement, according to HSUS, and they get a Group II rating because the city would be more poorly served without the zoo. Boston and Baltimore, at different levels in this group, are examples of this rating. The third category, Group III, includes almost all the so-called "roadside" zoos, which often comprise no more than a single caged animal in a gas station or gift shop. And there is the smaller municipal facility, which employs no really aware zoo people; mostly the facility is run by the Parks Department, the Town Fathers, or a committee which does not have the money or prestige to attract sophisticated personnel. If there are any zoos that can, in Kenneth Koyen's words, "send mammals (including humans) on the march [against zoos]" these are the ones, for there are infinitely more bad things in them than good, and, in their current condition, they should unquestionably be phased out. Certainly, if they are near another major city zoo, they are not only a crime against animals but also a waste of money and should be abolished.

Pressman: "But you just can't leave the watchdogging of zoos to the little old lady in sneakers. It requires the pressure of an aroused public, and that comes from education. Mostly that education comes from seeing the animal exhibited in its full dignity, but sometimes it comes from the opposite. I'm in this work because I want to make up for all the animals I allowed to be humiliated in zoos. But that doesn't mean that just because there are bad zoos I want to abolish zoos. The truth is that the animal can do himself a service in a good zoo."

Interviewer: "You're not giving me the usual zoo position about wild animals living longer, healthier lives in the zoo, with less of the stress that comes from fleeing enemies or hunting food, are you?"

Pressman: "Not at all. The stress that comes from boredom in a zoo can cancel out the stress that is avoided by the elimination of enemies. In fact zoo-stress is now being recognized as medical pathology and being treated as such. What I mean in saying that an animal can do himself a service by being in a zoo is that in a good one, where you see him exhibited in his full dignity, he becomes an ambassador for his kind. Display a leopard with respect—as the regal beast he is—and people will admire him and want to protect him. They will think twice about wearing his skins. But if he is treated as of no account, as just an object to gawk at, then what difference does it make if you cut him up for a coat, or let his species disappear? So you see, a good zoo is good not only for the family of man but also for the family of animals. In our view, the yeas definitely have it over the nays when it comes to preserving zoos. Let's just upgrade them as fast as we can."

Mrs. Pressman may or may not have had in mind with her last statement New York City's Central Park Zoo and the prominent naturalist Roger Caras' vision for it, but they would seem especially to apply.

No zoo in the world receives the criticism that the tiny menagerie in New York's Central Park does during an average year. This is largely because people expect something more than ancient iron cages for lions and tigers in a zoo that is set in the nation's best-known park, to say nothing of being bordered by Fifth Avenue, considered by many the most fashionable street in the world's leading metropolis.

Yet this 9.6-acre menagerie is visited by more people than both the superb 252-acre Bronx Zoo, only thirty minutes away, and San Diego, the country's largest and most aggressively publicized zoo. Easy accessibility plus the fact that droves of visiting out-of-towners inevitably wander into Central Park on their sightseeing around New York accounts in large part for this small zoo's high attendance. There are other factors, though. First, the Zoo is an open one, and admission is free. Picnickers, strollers, tourists, lunching office workers by the thousands each day make moseying through the Zoo a part of their visit to the park. Undeniably there is some special charm in Central Park's unique mix of wild-animal and open public park, boxed in on all sides, as it is, by towering skyscrapers.

But in recent years the little potpourri of animalia that annually attracts some seven million people to zigzag through the pretzel vendors and Good Humor men who congregate under the Delacorte animal clock has been dealt what might seem some unkind blows. Posted on the cage of the fallow deer by an animal defense league is a sign offering a $650 reward for apprehension of the individuals who "beat the fallow deer in their cage." The sign served not only as a dramatization of public outrage at the Zoo's alleged negligence in protecting its animals, but also became a kind of a hang-tag on a campaign to phase the Zoo out. And the fact that one of the beaten deer died, allegedly from lack of timely veterinary atttention, only made the situation worse (it culminated in the city's appointing a consultant to revamp the entire municipal zoo structure).

What exactly is Central Park Menagerie—and menagerie is what it is still officially labeled—that people should become so embattled about it? In a sense it is one of America's landmarks, like the Kitty Hawk of the Wright Brothers or Samuel F. B. Morse's first wireless telegraph, for it is the first and oldest zoo in the country. Philadelphia Zoo may have been *chartered* earlier, but long before it got around actually to making exhibits under that charter, Central Park was already displaying wild animals. This was done informally by taking the animals out of their wooden pens and placing them in portable cages on the lawns. The well-known Arsenal building was already there, originally owned by the state and used as an ammunition depot in the Civil War but finally turned over to the City to become its first museum of natural history.

The early days of the Zoo were a page out of the picturesque history of nineteenth-century America. Seamen brought exotic pets to the bustling Port of New York from all the world and turned them over to the Zoo. There were international exchanges of animals between the Old World and the New World, as, for instance, the gift in 1862, during the height of the Civil War, of twenty-seven swans from the City of Hamburg, Germany, to the City of New York. Local citizens donated birds such as the bald eagle, America's national symbol, which is now going into extinction but which then was in plentiful supply throughout all of the Eastern states. On one occasion a donor brought in as many as twenty-three specimens of this majestic bird. Added to these donations were other specimens of local fauna such as raccoons, skunks, opossums, bobcats, deer, mountain lions, and bears.

Even the spoils of war made their way into America's first zoo. General William T. Sherman tarried long enough on his march through Georgia to seize three African Cape buffalo from the estate of some Confederate bigwig and pack them off to Central Park.

Likewise General George A. Custer, except that his trophies were American buffalo seized in the Indian wars before his adversaries dispatched him at Little Bighorn. By 1873, a year before Philadelphia Zoo opened its gates to the public, director of the Menagerie, William A. Conkling, was making his first formal report to the General Superintendent of Public Parks, famed designer Frederick Law Olmstead, from whom it was passed on to the Parks Commissioners.

This report is an interesting piece of Americana. It reveals that Central Park was acquiring wild animals from dealers—and from collectors such as P. T. Barnum—as early as 1868; by 1873, the date of its first formal report, the Zoo's permanent collection had grown to an impressive total of 581 specimens. Moreover, it was already breeding lions, leopards, camels, and hyenas right in the center of New York City. And to top its list of accomplishments, the Zoo was exhibiting not only giraffes and a Malayan tapir, but also a manatee (herbivorous sea cow) which, as the director noted, ". . . is expressly worthy of note, inasmuch as it is the first of the species exhibited in New York (and therefore the country) and the success of keeping it alive was hardly hoped for, owing to the difficulty in obtaining the proper food. The tapir is the first of its species ever imported to this country."

So that little "eyesore of a zoo," as some have called the present Central Park Menagerie, has an old and impressive history. It was contributing impressively to the zoo world, such as it was, long before the Bronx or San Diego were gleams in their creators' eyes.

Nothing of extraordinary note happened to the Zoo over the intervening years until 1934, when the old pens and sheds were demolished and the red brick buildings erected that stand in the park today. These were constructed under Federal Works Progress Administration (WPA) grants, those Great Depression "pump-priming" projects for rescuing the nation's battered economy which, among other enterprises, "improved" so many zoos. Although the buildings were modeled after standard zoo architecture of that period, today they are about as obsolete for modern animal exhibition as an old Brownie would be for filming the Indianapolis 500.

Nevertheless, that is what Central Park Zoo has been obliged to make do with over all these years. In conjunction with the Arsenal that flanks the Zoo on the Fifth Avenue side, the zoo buildings are considered official landmarks and their exterior structure may not be altered, no matter what the welfare of the animals occupying them may dictate. In addition, under existing city regulations no land is available in the rest of Central Park for expansion of the Zoo— 9.6-acres is what the Zoo has to work with and that is it. Here is a prime example of that type of municipal constriction to which HSUS's Sue Pressman referred. This kind of frustration, together with an operating budget and a civil service rating for animal keepers that scales them below ordinary laborers and makes for a perennial turnover of personnel, is demoralizing. Keepers, for instance, start at $8300, while a Parks Department laborer starts at $12,650. There are six senior keepers assigned to the Zoo, which means that the junior keepers generally have a long wait until there is a vacancy in the senior keeper category before there is any hope for advancement. As a result it is the junior keeper who is usually the first in line at civil service examinations for better positions in the Parks Department. Nevertheless, some of them do remain on year after year despite the low pay and bleak future, for, to some people, working with animals they love at $8300 a year is preferable to picking up litter at $12,650 a year. However, this does not especially attract the bright young college-educated person with ideas. The Zoo's budget may also be a contributing factor, aside from the fact that it is open until midnight as is the rest of the park, to incidences of vandalism such as the beating of the fallow deer. Security in a zoo is an expensive service, particularly in a location such as central New York City. But vandalism at Central Park is no worse than at most of the municipally underwritten zoos in Group II on the HSUS list, which is to say, seventy percent of the country's zoos. Nor are the Zoo's lion and tiger cages much different. After all, the National Zoo, which is an installation of the U.S. Government, only recently dismantled the ancient ceramic-tile-and-steel cages in which its big cats were housed. And even at this writing the animals are on loan to other zoos awaiting completion of more modern housing. The Bronx Zoo also still keeps some of its cats in cages circa 1916. As Sue Pressman explained, "We had to put Central Park in our Group III, the lowest category. But that's not because it's all that bad for what it is. Believe me we've seen plenty worse. Actually we considered it good enough to go in Group II (that is, with the 75 percent in which good things were about equally divided with the bad. The determining reason was that it is too close to the Bronx Zoo and, as Central Park Zoo is now, that represents a wasteful duplication. In Nashville, for instance, or Kalamazoo, it would go into Group II, because there is nothing like the Bronx close by. But even in New York City it could one day possibly go into Group I if it did something unique, such as getting a theme of its own."

So "hats off" rather than "Bronx cheers" would seem to be in order for the little menagerie that has persisted for well over a hundred years as a kind of national zoo, catering, as it does with its central New York City location, to a varied and immense cross section of the national population. Certainly it is to be regarded with the kind of respect that is generally reserved for landmarks on the American scene.

Today, however, this pioneer of zoos is hard-pressed to keep apace with fast-moving modern developments. By current zoo standards animals do not live in buildings; they live in natural habitats or open shelters. Central Park has little if any of these nor can its landmark buildings, as mentioned, be altered, and certainly not demolished, to conform to such philosophy. Zoos no longer emphasize the exhibition of animals on a one-or-two-of-each pattern, that is, in so-called postage-stamp style, but rather on a theme or specialization basis. Central Park's design has not only traditionally been structured to postage-stamp display but its collection, in keeping with conventional zoo philosophy, has always included large, high-care mammals such as hippos, camels, elephants, which are not only wasteful of its limited space but would also take up practically the entire zoo if natural habitat were possible. As for the education of the public, one of the major concerns of the modern zoo, Central Park does fall short. "That polar bear they have there hasn't been a polar bear since it was captured," says Sue Pressman. "The polar bear is an aquatic mammal. Ninety percent of its environment is water, ten percent land. At Central Park it's just the reverse, as it is in so many zoos: ninety percent rocks and a pool the size of a bathtub. How can anybody be educated as to what a polar bear really is in that kind of setup?"

Roger Caras, the noted naturalist, puts it more strongly: "People say that there is no educational experience in Central Park Zoo. Well, I would put it differently. I'd say the Central Park Zoo was a profound educational experience, that is, a totally negative experience. A kid does not go to that zoo without coming away with the impression that animals don't count, that there's no natural way of exhibiting them, that they have no place in nature."

Yet to bring Central Park up to its full potential as a zoo would entail changes that require formidable sums of money and a major uprooting of tradition. This is something that, up to now, has been inconceivable in a municipal zoo which still calls itself a menagerie, keeps its director at a supervisor level, retains a part-time veterinarian who also looks after hundreds of animals in two other city zoos and farms, and allocates so little money for animal management that concerned keepers often make improvements at their own expense.

With all of this there has been a continuous effort—sometimes well-conceived, sometimes perhaps not—on the part of a dedicated staff to upgrade the Zoo within the limitations of these handicaps. Says John W. (Fitz) Fitzgerald, a soft-spoken, native New York City resident who has worked at the Zoo for nineteen years: "It's what I inherited when I was promoted from senior keeper to supervisor eight years ago. The Parks Council—that's a private watchdog group—won't permit a change in the design of the buildings, nor will they allow additions to deface them. We've enlarged many of the cages on our own but even there we can't be too drastic without bringing them down on our heads.

"Also we've begun to phase out some of our larger mammals to make room. Just last week we shipped out our Nile hippos. Commissioner August Heckscher used to be appalled to see those gigantic animals lying there snoozing all day. But that's what they'd do in the wild anyway. Nevertheless he wanted them out and now they're gone, hopefully to be replaced by pigmy hippos. Our camel is gone, too. He was what's called a rogue animal—killed his mate. But we'd have moved him out anyway, because of his size. Same thing with others of the larger species. We're trying to adapt our collection to the limited space."

As it is today, the Zoo is divided into a lion house, which is a catchall name for a building that houses not only lions but other big cats, as well as baboon and gorilla groups in cages that are split into outdoor and indoor compartments. The antelope house, in which there are lodged two antelope and a dozen or more small and large mammals, is roughly of the same design, except that on one side it opens into big pens used by various hoofed stock. There are a monkey house, elephant house, bird house, small outdoor aviary, deer house, aoudad house, bear pen, and a seal pool surrounded by four monkey gazebos. On the periphery is the old Arsenal building, plus a big garage, a pony ride, and a large restaurant. On the other side of the Delacorte Clock, which on the half-hour displays a carousel of sculptured animal musicians, is the Children's Zoo, donated by one-time Governor Herbert H. Lehman. Excluding the Children's Zoo, which contains some two hundred domestic animals, Central Park has a wild-animal population of 101 species in two hundred twenty-six specimens of birds and mammals. A staff of about thirty, including the supervisor, services the main zoo.

"We never had a big collection in Central Park as it is today— less than one half of what they had a hundred years ago, if you leave out the Children's Zoo. But what we've had has been good, at least by conventional standards. Many visiting zoo directors have commented on the excellent condition of our animals. We're trying to do our small bit where we can. And there's no animal suffering here. People are appalled when they come here from a wild-animal park and automatically assume the lion is suffering because of the small cage. Our lions couldn't care less, I'm sure. They get all their meals, have their basic needs filled, and breed like rabbits. And the male roars regularly. You know what that means? It's a territorial thing—a lion roars to warn other males this territory is occupied. Now he can't hate his cage too much if he's roaring other males off, can he? We also have a female twenty-one years old who'd be dead in the wild long ago. The old wild lion is eaten live by hyenas, you know. And another thing—where in the world can you walk down a great city's most fashionable boulevard and hear a lion roar? You can here, right on Fifth Avenue."

Supervisor Fitzgerald stopped for a moment to answer the telephone in his tiny office near the elephant house. From one side came the cries, calls, and cackles of birds and small mammals lodged in the Zoo's "hospital" room; keepers barged in and out of his cubicle with complaints; at the office doorway stood two boys waiting to give him an injured sparrow they apparently had just picked up. The organization chart for Central Park obviously included no such thing as an aide to handle trivia.

"In addition to the old lioness," Fitzgerald continued, "we have other examples of longevity. Our two female gorillas are among the oldest in captivity—been here since 1943. And we have had excellent results in cheetah longevity: age sixteen, when the average is only about eight. Not only that, this menagerie, as it's called, has successfully bred wanderoos, ocelots—one of the toughest to breed —spotted and black leopards, and gorillas, the most famous of these, of course, being Patty Cake. We've done the best we could with our limited facilities. But even with the many mistakes that have no doubt been made, when we look at the breeding and longevity results we feel that, under the conditions, we can't be doing too many things wrong. Besides, it would take a major earthquake to change conditions here."

That "earthquake" did in fact erupt in April, 1974, when an aroused public, backed by newspaper editorials, reacted to the attack on the fallow deer by calling for the closing of the Zoo. The city administration responded by retaining Roger Caras, a well-known author, naturalist, and conservation authority, to undertake a study of the role and function of the City Zoo, together with the changes required in housing its animals. A visitor reminded Mr. Caras of the official view that, considering its breeding and longevity results, Central Park was not really all that bad, no worse in fact than any number of municipal zoos. If it had not been for the death of the fallow deer. . . .

"As it is today almost everything at Central Park is bad," replied Mr. Caras. "And this has no reference to the fallow deer. Vandalism can happen in any zoo, particularly in these distraught times. That zoo teaches little but cruelty, neglect, and indifference. One of the main functions of a modern zoo is to show people how animals live in their natural habitats and the relationship between animals and man, with the objective of fostering a keener appreciation of life itself. Otherwise keeping a zoo becomes not only an act of cruelty to animals but also to man, and there is absolutely no reason for its existence. Now, where, in heaven's name, is there anything in the setup at Central Park that justifies its existence as it is now? Breeding . . . longevity? Nonsense! A lion in captivity under the most miserable conditions will deliver you a barrelful of cubs every year. You can't give them away. Even people have sex in the most awful prisons, in concentration camps. Does that mean that those installations are good? As for longevity, people have hung on for years in hospitals with the most God-awful diseases. Look, I certainly favor a long and procreative life for a zoo animal, but if that's all a zoo can present to the public about its animals—that they can copulate and hang on to life for a long time—that zoo has fallen far short of its responsibility."

But, the visitor suggested, has not the staff at Central Park, hamstrung as it has always been by downgraded personnel and lack of funds for improvement—has not a corps of dedicated men and women made some commendable moves on their own iniative toward naturalizing some of those admittedly awful habitats? Keepers have been reported, for instance, as having contributed their own money and independent efforts toward dressing up cages in ways that city budgets did not allow. Newspapers have told how Zoo personnel had even cajoled construction workers on the new subway being built under the park into carting up excavated rock for use in the cages.

"Well-intentioned improvements, no doubt," said Caras, a giant of a man limping around his artifact-filled living room as a result of an accident sustained on a recent African photo safari, "but most of them ill-advised. What are rocks doing in a fallow deer's enclosure? Fallow deer don't live on rocks or on asphalt either, for that matter. Aoudad, yes, but not fallow deer. And those horrible cemented-over rocks in the polar bear's cage. A mountain of cement with a birdbath at the bottom. A polar bear never sees rocks or cement. They live at sea level. Their habitat is an iceberg. You just can't go on piling bad things on top of things that were abysmally wrong to begin with and expect them to work. Or go and look at the eland and the zebra—open plains animals. . . ."

"That, incidentally," interrupted the visitor, "is where the Zoo feels it has made one of its more progressive moves. In its effort to phase out the larger mammals and turn the space over to compatible mixes of smaller species, they've eliminated the camel, bison, and elk and made the five small pens they formerly occupied into three larger ones. Now they have zebra in one pen, eland in another and, in the third, a mix of llama, tapir, and capybara, a compatible group of animals that coexist in South America. It's considered perhaps their prize display: a geographical mix rather than a postage stamp exhibit—the first time at Central Park."

"Well, what do you see in these rearranged pens?" asked Caras. "Hoofed animals such as the zebra run on soft sod or grass. So you put them on asphalt!"

"But they maintain that's the only way the place can be kept sanitary," said the visitor. "The conformation of the land does allow drainage, they say, so a dirt floor would become foul with urine and feces and would be a source of infection, disease, and hoof trouble."

"Nonsense! I've seen many paddocks with dirt floor as flat as a pancake and they still manage to keep them clean. The real truth is simply that asphalt is easier to clean. All you need do is to turn a hose on it. Besides, if those pens in Central Park are really so unique that they are not feasible for dirt floors, then you just don't exhibit animals that require dirt floors. That's the kind of subtle cruelty I'm talking about. If you owned a horse you wouldn't put him on concrete all day unless he had rubber shoes on. The most complicated anatomical structure known is the front hoof of a horse. If a man's foot were capable of taking the punishment that a horse's hoof takes, it would be as large as a tennis court. Well, a zebra's foot is about the same as a horse's. So you take that foot and put it on asphalt because dirt is not as easy to clean. Why do that to a zebra? If you can't give them the natural floor they require then you just don't exhibit zebras.

"Another thing—and this goes for the eland and those other animals in the so-called South American compatible mix. If South America looked anything like that, there's not much hope for it. There is absolutely no place that you can stand there where you don't see a brick building or steel bars in the background. There is no eye-line, no perspective, no place where the animals are not in a dungeonlike atmosphere. I walked through there the other day with Morris Ketchum, the architect for the Bronx's World of Birds House. Morris volunteered to come with me that morning. He's a nice man and there isn't any way to pay him, yet he came out to advise me. I said, 'Morris, what are you going to do about this?' He said, 'Look, there are two parallel people walks. If you eliminated this walk and removed those bars, greened up this old garage building and rearranged the focus of this shed so that you view the animals from the inside of the building instead of from the outside, you'd see those animals in a natural setting.' In ten seconds, with a little imagination and innovativeness, the problem of natural setting is solved without altering the basic structure of the landmark buildings."

But does not the fact that the Zoo has the most minimal veterinary care (it was three days before the zoo veterinarian got to the fatally beaten fallow deer, according to the ASCPA), does not this require maximum caution against sickness, such as the use of asphalt floors instead of dirt even at the sacrifice of some naturalness?

"Let's look at the record. I was told when I assumed responsibility for rebuilding the Zoo that there was no hospital, not even any isolation facilities. A sick animal had to stay where he was, sick or not, infecting everything around him. New animals coming into the Zoo couldn't be quarantined in isolation—"

"Couldn't they go up to the Animal Lab at Flower Fifth Avenue Hospital?"

"Hoof stock? They don't quarantine animals at that hospital. Any animal bought for that Zoo comes right into the collection whether he's sick or not. 'Where' it is asked, 'where could we possibly have a hospital or isolation area in this zoo? Where is the space? And what about money?' "Okay. I take a quick walk through the Zoo, first day on the job. There's a nice big red-brick building erected in the 1930s containing an eight-bay garage, each bay big enough for the Pierce Arrows and Packards they drove then. Now with Chevies and Fords, everybody who works in the Arsenal knows somebody who can put his car down there. An eight-bay garage was made out of a zoo building for the convenience of a few office workers. So all the talk about no room for hospitalization or isolation is a lot of poppycock. It's been there all along. Dump three or four of those Fords out of there and the Zoo could have had a hospital and isolation space years ago.

"Another example of the kind of mentality that has bedevilled all of the municipal zoos—I'll not name names—but walking one day past a cage containing two badgers—two very secretive animals—I noticed how absolutely bare it was. Just two animals in a wet steel-

and-cement box with paint peeling on the walls. So I said to the director, 'Why don't you put a log in there for the animals? Maybe they want some privacy. Maybe they'd like to go behind the log, crawl over it, anything to break the monotony. That's no way to keep animals—for their sake, or even ours. Put a log in there.' He replied to me, with some degree of vehemence, 'Two years ago I put in a requisition to the City for a log and I'm still waiting for it to be delivered.'

"So I said to him, 'Why don't you go across the street when they're cutting down a tree and get yourself a piece of wood? Why don't you give a workman a cigar to bring you a piece of wood, or take the morning off and go out and steal a log? What in hell do you mean, two years? Do you expect Abe Beame to come through the door and say, 'Mr. Director, here's your log. Sorry I'm late.' With notable exceptions, that kind of approach to zookeeping is spotted throughout the municipal zoo administration."

Much of the criticism of Central Park could of course be also directed at any number of other U.S. zoos, particularly the municipally operated ones. Antiquated approach to animal management, lack of veterinary facilities, obsolete housing, archaic exhibition techniques, bureaucratic apathy—all can no doubt be found in quantity among American zoos, as the HSUS, of which Mr. Caras is a vice-president, discovered in its 1971 study. Indeed, officials of the Association of Zoological Parks and Aquariums, of which Mr. Caras is also a member, welcomed HSUS's criticisms and urged their members to work with HSUS to improve all zoos in the U.S.

"But in the case of Central Park we were aware of the special situation that zoo was in," explained Sue Pressman. "Hampered by the landmark building problem, stymied by an enormous, top-heavy city parks administration that looks on the Zoo as a necessary evil, made to look bad by the presence of a superb installation like the Bronx so close at hand, we felt that it hadn't done all that bad. You can't expect Central Park to be a miniature Bronx Zoo. And you can't expect its director to be a Bill Conway (Bronx's director) or its staff to be Bronx Zoo curators, when you take into account the level to which the City downgrades them. After all, the New York Zoological Society (Bronx Zoo) is a kind of gray eminence, with Rockefellers, Phippses, Schiffs, Astors, and Fricks on its board. Bill Conway wouldn't have stayed at Central Park one day under the conditions with which Central Park's staff has to operate."

Interestingly enough, at the very moment Central Park was undergoing its greatest criticism from one segment of the public because of the death of the fallow deer, it was also endearing itself to another and more populous segment by virtue of its new superstar: the baby gorilla Patty Cake. And Patty Cake herself set the stage for even more controversy.

The first baby gorilla born in metropolitan New York City came into the world at Central Park Zoo on September 3, 1972. For some time its sex was unknown, such often being the case with newborn of large, unapproachable wild animals. But most zoo personnel assumed it was a male and it was tentatively named Sunny Jim. The new baby, male or female, created an immediate sensation. In the weeks that followed, the crowds that came to gape at the newcomer and her parents were so large that police barricades had to be set up. Television and newspaper reporters were omnipresent, artists and photographers camped in front of the cages, animal behaviorists spent endless hours observing and taking notes, celebrities came, gawked, and signed autographs.

At length it was determined that the baby's sex was female. This prompted the New York *Daily News* to sponsor a contest for a name, whereupon a Staten Island fireman, among thousands of contestants, came up with "Patty Cake," an anthropomorphism that no doubt endeared him to the public but made zoo purists shudder.

At any rate, it was a name to contend with. One Central Park keeper said, "Since the day when she was named, there are only two questions asked at this zoo: 'Where's the bathroom?' and 'Where's Patty Cake?' "

The parents of the new Shirley Temple of the animal world were both wild-caught in Equatorial Africa in 1965 and came to the Zoo in 1966 when both were about one year old. Handsome specimens, each of them, they were obtained by the Zoo from dealer Henry Trefflich as low bidder on the City's request for a breeding pair of lowland gorillas which, at that time, were not on the endangered species list. The male was named Kongo and the female Lulu, and they were placed together in a corner cage of the lion house, where one visitor, almost daily, watched them grow to beautiful maturity.

Central Park Menagerie, circa 1898. (Courtesy of New York Public Library Picture Collection)

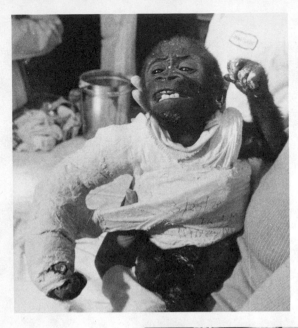

Patty Cake with her arm in a cast. The limb was broken in a struggle between her parents over custody of the infant. *(Photo credit: New York Daily News)*

Back in her cage at Central Park after recuperation at the Bronx Zoo from her broken limb, Patty Cake now lives without either parent. *(Photo credit: New York Daily News)*

Six years later, at the unusually early age of seven, they were the parents of a superstar.

"The spectacular thing here was that against all past performances Patty Cake started out being raised by her parents," said Zoo Supervisor Fitzgerald. "Most captive gorillas reject their young. Out of about seventy-five gorillas born in captivity only five mothers have raised their young. Maybe the first birth is sometimes confusing and frightening. Maybe some Zoos didn't give the mother a chance—that is, they got scared by what they thought was abusive behavior on the part of the mother and took the baby away. I don't know—I guess gorilla mothers might sometimes seem rough by human standards; nobody knows too much about them yet. But Lulu herself was very tender—she even cleaned the baby's nails, gave her a kind of manicure. After ten days or so she began going through all kinds of maneuvers to teach the baby to hang on. And some of the things she did looked pretty scary. For instance, she'd pick it up and put it on her head. Many people felt she didn't care, thought she was just having a good time bouncing the baby around like a rag doll. But if you watched closely, you'd see that she'd wait for a second and make sure those little fists tightened up before she moved. The gorilla baby must be taught to hang on because in the wild the mother's got to have arms and legs free to climb to safety while the male defends against enemies. So we felt that this so-called abusive behavior was an educational process to toughen up the baby. After the mother's head, the baby graduated to the neck and back. You could see Lulu duck extra low going through the door from one cage to another with the baby on her back. At first she'd allow it to crawl only a foot away before she'd grab it; a little later she permitted a greater distance. When it got a little older she began putting the baby up on the bars and it started to climb. But she'd always be right there ready to catch it if it fell. It was beautiful to watch—really remarkable maternal behavior."

"What about paternal behavior?" a visitor asked. "How did Kongo react to the domestic situation? Was he in the cage with her?"

"Yes, after the first two weeks," said Fitzgerald. "Lulu was very protective about Kongo's curiosity. She'd let him come over and put a finger on the baby. One time, when she was about four months old, Kongo did manage to get Patty Cake and he was running around the cage holding her in his palms. As though teasing Lulu. She kept chasing after him, howling and screaming. But he finally got tired, put the baby down on the floor and walked away, as if to say, 'See—I can do it if I want to.' Actually Kongo was very gentle with the baby. That's the nature of the gorilla."

When Patty Cake was six months old, in March, 1973, an accident occurred that—as a result of massive coverage circulation-minded newspapers, wire services and other media gave the little gorilla—caused a nationwide gasp of alarm. Patty Cake had her arm broken. The real story was not quite as the media saw it.

Said Veronica Nelson, a young keeper who at this writing is taking care of Patty Cake: "The news media would have liked to have it a dramatic bloody mess—a struggle between mom and pop for the custody of the child. It was nothing like that. It was a simple accident. Kongo was in one part of the double cage, Lulu in another, and between them was a partition of narrow bars. Lulu had Patty Cake in her arms and when Patty reached in between the narrow bars to touch her father, Lulu suddenly pulled her away. But Patty's arm got caught in the narrow bars and broke. It was a freak accident. No one ever realized that those bars were narrow enough to catch that tiny arm."

If there was an error in planning the gorillas' expanded family cage, certainly this time there was no negligence in getting an injured animal veterinary attention. Patty Cake was rushed off to New York's Flower Fifth Avenue Hospital, where her arm was set in a cast. Bronx Zoo made its hospital facilities available for post-cast care and she was shipped off to that zoo, where they took off the heavy cast and placed her arm in a light, sling-type affair to await recovery.

Once Patty Cake was at the Bronx Zoo a new battle over the fate of a zoo superstar was begun. Many professionals thought that in view of the limited facilities at Central Park, she should remain at the Bronx. Others felt that, whatever was done with her, she should certainly never go back to Central Park.

Said Roger Caras: "Philosophically I agree that animals as difficult as gorillas don't belong in a place like Central Park. I'm not sure they belong in places like the Bronx Zoo either. I'm not sure any zoo should exhibit all the apes, and Bill Conway [Bronx's director] and I could argue that for hours. He's got gorillas—I don't know why, and they're nothing to write home about. But there's every reason to believe that she wouldn't make it at Central Park with her parents. Conway said, 'If you take this gorilla back she will not be able to return to her parents. No matter what you do she won't be able to be raised by her parents.' "

In an attempt to resolve the impasse, the City consulted a developmental biologist, Dr. Ronald Nadler, of the Yerkes Primate Research Center in Atlanta. Dr. Nadler spent some time studying the case and submitted a report opposing the removal of the gorilla family from Central Park.

"Obviously the conditions at Central Park could be improved," said Dr. Nadler. "But under the financial conditions they have they are doing very well. It must be remembered that gorillas are an endangered species, and it would be well to allow two proven breeders to live as they are now. Pick them up and move them to the Bronx and that might disrupt them so that they will never breed again."

And so on June 10, 1973, after a two-and-a-half-month stay at the Bronx, Little Orphan Annie was brought back to Central Park. For five days she was kept isolated in a little room in back of the Zoo office under the care of Veronica Nelson. Veronica had raised Gertrude, a baboon which had been separated from her family for five months and then successfully returned to them. Patty Cake was nursed on bottles and tender loving care. The whole staff looked forward to the possibility of her re-acceptance by her parents, for if successful it would have been the first time such a thing had occurred for gorillas in captivity. Gorillas have much more complicated personalities than other primates. They have different dietary needs, are terrestrial, and need each other as well as keepers and "keeping."

"Take these two parents, for instance," said Veronica Nelson. "Lulu is capable of very involved behavior. When she didn't want Kongo to handle the baby she went through some very intricate ploys to put him off. She'd scream at somebody outside the cage in an attempt to get Kongo's attention off Patty Cake. Or she'd suddenly pick up a twig and go through a whole scene of examining it intently and when Kongo came over to see what was going on, she'd give him the twig instead of the baby. Compared to her, Kongo is very immature. She's really the dominant one in the family. When she gets her rage up, he goes and sits in the corner and pouts for four hours, knowing he'd better watch his step or she'll let him have it. It's like

Lulu has two babies to take care of, Kongo and Patty. Even though they're both the same age they were awfully young to be parents."

For five days after Patty Cake's return to Central Park Veronica Nelson took her up each morning to her former cage to reacquaint her gradually with her prospective home. She sat in the cage with her, fed her, played with her, let her climb up and down the bars. But Patty Cake was not allowed to see her parents nor they her—the shock might have been too great. Finally, on June 15, it was decided that she might be ready for the reintroduction.

"At 11:18 A.M.—I remember the precise moment," said Miss Nelson with all the solemnity of a royal nurse recalling the baptism of a French dauphine—"Lulu was brought in from outside and put in the cage next to Patty Cake. When she looked through the bars and saw the baby she screamed and the baby screamed, both at the top of their voices. Fitz [Supervisor Fitzgerald] then ordered the door between them opened and Lulu ran right over to the baby. But Patty was sort of whimpering and cowering. Lulu knew that if she grabbed the baby it would be terrified—at least that's the way it seemed because it was exactly what had happened with the baboons when we reintroduced their baby. Lulu just hovered over her like she wanted to grab her but didn't know what to do. Finally after running back and forth indecisively she swooped in, grabbed the baby and whipped her up to her belly. Patty Cake clung to her and about twenty minutes later we let Kongo in. He went over to her and nuzzled the baby and that was it. It was like Lulu's first scream was a scream of recognition—'My baby, my baby!' It was incredible, beautiful."

Patty Cake remained united with her parents in the Central Park cage for about six months. There was a first birthday party on September 3, 1973. Visitors came in droves, the press was back in force, the little gorilla was once more the pride and joy of New York.

But one element had not been taken into account. The sexual foreplay of gorillas is something to behold. It goes on for hours with ranting and raving and violent athletics that combine adagio dancing, heavyweight boxing, primal therapy, and half-nelson locks. And gorillas do not have "heat" periods as other animals do; like humans their sexual desire can turn on at any time. This meant that Patty Cake's presence in the cage with her parents could not be timed to breeding periods. Consequently she was in constant danger, because of the close quarters, of being stepped on, wedged into corners, or accidently injured. She simply was not able to be sure of getting out of the way. So for safety's sake, she was removed with Lulu to the cage adjoining Kongo's.

"But after three weeks Lulu just went crazy with desire," said Veronica Nelson. "She couldn't think of anything but Kongo. So we decided to let her go back to him and put Patty Cake in an adjoining cage with a young chimpanzee for company. Patty is able to observe her parents from there and can learn from them, but that's not as good as being in the cage with them. We so much want her back with her parents. But what else can we do? We've been promised a new gorilla cage by the Friends of the Zoo and from whatever the City . . . forget the City. . . . When she was returned to her parents right away we were going to have a new gorilla exhibit, and as usual nothing ever happened. The only improvements ever made in this zoo are made by Fitzgerald and the senior keepers themselves. It's a shame, really a shame."

So Patty Cake, New York City's superstar, darling of the *Daily News*, premiere tourist attraction of the Big Apple, is once again separated from her parents. "It's as Bill Conway said," repeated Roger Caras. " 'Patty Cake won't be raised by her parents.' I agree. No one's ever found out how to exhibit gorillas very well. Except perhaps San Diego, where Albert, the big silver-back male, has the run of that big pit. Or maybe Gerald Durrell on the Isle of Jersey in the English Channel with that big circular closed-in space where people walk around the outside."

So, in the final reckoning, the problem of Patty Cake and her parents (and Lulu is pregnant again) may be nothing more than a question of space. That "shame" of which Veronica Nelson spoke— the City's apparent apathy, the imprisonment of "landmark" animals in a landmark building that cannot be altered, the downgrading of dedicated keepers—all this might well be resolved by a little money, a large dose of imagination, and an authority to make things move. Oddly enough, Central Park may finally get the things it needs by way of Roger Caras, the man who is so down on the present zoo; that is, by way of Caras and that dead fallow deer.

Roger Caras is a big, blunt-spoken fellow with the energy of a Robert Moses, New York City's ex-commissioner of bridges, tunnels, and parks. Also something of a look-alike for Moses, Caras can display a list of accomplishments nearly as long as the ex-commissioner's: author of more than two dozen books on wildlife and conservation, African photo-safarist, former movie executive (Stanley Kubrick's "2001: A Space Odyssey"), television and radio broadcaster, lecturer, vice-president of HSUS, president of the Holy Land Conservation Fund, board member of the Arizona Sonora Desert Museum—name it, particularly in the wildlife world, and Mr. Caras is likely to be a part of it.

Now Roger Caras adds to that list the role of consultant to the City of New York for the rebuilding of its municipal zoos. To this point a reader has seen what Central Park once was and what it is as of this writing. Caras's appointment backed with authority should indicate what Central park can be.

"First, let me make it clear," Caras said, "I am not hired by the City of New York nor am I paid by them. The typical bureaucratic snafus precluded that. I advise the City but I am paid by a foundation which Parks Commissioner Edwin L. Weisl, Jr., prevailed upon to foot the bill. That's a good start towards having the City's zoos run by a private zoological society which, in my opinion, is the only way to effectively operate a zoo."

Mr. Caras did not elaborate, but he doubtless had in mind that good zoos, rather than being run by a political bureaucracy are usually operated by a broad-based membership of private citizens, such as San Diego or Bronx Zoo, who especially care about the best for zoos. But in New York City this might not be desirable, since as a zoological society, Central Park would have to solicit membership and that could be harmful to the Bronx—robbing Peter to pay Paul, so to speak, by building one zoo to the detriment of another. Moreover, the option to charge an admission, another means of support, is not available to Central Park; the Zoo occupies a thoroughfare through the park and a fee cannot be exacted from the people for use of their park. These two factors, added to the inability to expand because of the landmark question, are important obstacles to rebuilding Central Park.

"But I have already talked to people about money and had some pledges particularly for the initial architectural and artistic renderings," said Caras. "I've also found $50,000 'buried,' which I have access to now. But we must find a way so that the money never gets into the hands of the City, because it would never come back to the Zoo. It will have to go into some kind of cultural foundation or zoological society."

"In other words, Central Park is trending toward a zoological society-operated zoo?"

"That's certainly not an unfair projection, although I'm not saying that's what is going to happen."

"But the improvements, whatever they might be, are those going to be paid for out of City funds?"

"No. There's no money for that. It will have to be raised from private sources."

According to Caras, the case for Central Park is nevertheless an excellent one. The Zoo is potentially a first-rate educational facility that even now is visited by an estimated seven million people annually, and, eventually, that can rise to ten million. But its success depends upon three things: proper administrative personnel—innovative, imaginative, communicative; a good curatorial staff, including professional veterinary care for the animals; and—the largest single factor—reduction of the variety of the collection and increase in the facilities for this reduced variety.

"Plans are now afoot, for instance, to reduce the entire primate collection from about ten species to just five," said Caras. "You know the monkey house—the keyhole-shaped monkey house? Well, envision this. You go in the door at the bottom of the keyhole. Instead of having a broad aisle down the center, with nasty, filthy little cages on each side of the room, you deflect it to the right. And as you walk along the wall, on your right is a series of back-lit graphics of animals. You will pass four cages, in the entire stem of this keyhole, four cages, each one of which has good depth, is planted, and is a habitat environment. One contains a member of the *Lorisidae*, which is way down at the bottom of the primate line—you'd probably need red light there by day because they're nocturnal animals. Second cage contains a colony of *Lemuridae*—ring-tailed lemurs, they breed very well in captivity. Third cage would probably have a small, old-world monkey colony, and the fourth an example of new-world monkeys. Now here are four cages so far, but all would be four times the size of the present cages. Come now to the big, open, top-of-the-keyhole. The floor is ripped out, the ceiling is ripped out. You're standing on two levels and here is a great column, about 20 feet across, and in this large circular thing is your gorilla colony. One anthropoid ape, one old-world monkey, one new-world monkey, one loris, and one lemur, and that's your total primate collection, now down from about fifteen species. Not going to have gibbons, chimpanzees, or orang-utangs; not going to have ten kinds of monkeys."

"Is there any particular reason for that special collection?" asked the visitor.

"Sure. It gives you a good range of the primates. The only missing thing is what you bring in yourself: *homo sapiens.* The building is now beautifully used—great big round rotary exhibits. The ceiling can be ripped out so that you can go way up and give them things to climb on. And this exhibit will go through the back wall of that circle, which is now nothing but a dingy window but will become an archway. There's about thirty-odd feet of space before you come to the wall that separates the Zoo from Fifth Avenue."

"What about access to outdoors?"

"For gorillas only. There's just no way at present of doing it for the other primates. The gorillas would pass through the archway and into that 30 feet at the end of the park which is all masked in trees. Those trees are part of the present landscape. We wouldn't have to destroy any part of the park, or touch any landmark features. Right now that area is completely unseen and unused by the public, and it's a green area with trees."

"Speaking of gorillas—what about Patty Cake? How, if at all, does she fit into the new plans?"

"Because of her publicity she should be the focus of the new gorilla exhibit. The gorilla exhibit I'm proposing is so large the chances are she'd be perfectly fine in there with her parents. We may find her a husband, and we'll be able to breed her in there."

"With her parents? Exhibit her with her parents?"

"I don't know. But they have five gorillas in Central Park and gorillas live in large, family-related groups. You can put ten together and, as long as they're not all crunched together in the middle of rough sexual play between male and female, there'll be no effect on Patty Cake."

"What about the bird collection? Are there any plans for it and the bird house?'

"We'll probably keep most of the birds. As for the bird house, it's now being used by the Transit Authority as storage space in the construction of the new subway spur at 63rd Street and Fifth Avenue. They will be out of there in two or three years and when they've left we'll redo the whole thing. Right now the interior is keyhole shaped, same as the monkey house. You walked in and came to this broad central plaza at the big end of the keyhole, so big you could hold a square dance in there. Plastered up against the wall were these narrow cages, about 8 feet high, and 5 feet deep, and then this great expanse of ceiling. These were birds behind *bars*! They're as thick as your wrist. They could hold back King Kong.

"Imagine now walking into this same building and stepping into a cage—a *people* cage— that runs from one door to the other, back and forth, over a bridge, to be used by older or elderly people. Envision the entire rest of the building, all the way up and past the now-false ceiling, clear up to the top, one huge habitat flight cage with a waterfall at one end. There's a stream that snakes back and forth underneath the raised walkway that you are on—a swamp at one end and the waterfall at the other, with one side of the slate roof removed for southern exposure and the sunlight pouring in. Who said that in a zoo the animals belong in cages and not the people? Why not put the people in?"

"Any other plans?"

"The business of the hoofed animals. Certainly I don't want hoofed animals standing on asphalt. And I don't think there should be any hoofed animals by themselves. There should be one hoofed animal enclosure and only compatible species included.

"The cat situation is also deplorable. There is no possible way that Central Park could exhibit jaguars, leopards, or mountain lions. They are just too athletic. They have to be in cages, or they would have to be in Central Park. The mountain lion can jump twenty-five feet. You cannot possibly find room to contain athletes of that calibre. So the extremely athletic cats have been improperly or inappropriately placed in Central Park Zoo. They had a jaguar and they have leopards there now. Cheetahs also should not be in Central Park Zoo, because there's not room for them to do their athletic thing, there's no physical possibility for the necessary space to secure them without caging. So you come down, really, to two cats—lions and tigers. They're very attractive for two reasons. Lions because they live in prides—and you can get a pride of lion. Tigers are very attractive because, although they don't normally live in groups, they will live together all right in zoos. They can be together all winter, they love the winter. They're a far northern animal, not a tropical animal. Siberian tigers breed very well in captivity, and they're available. Plenty of them now in zoos, but not in the wild. You should see the cats out in the snow. They love snow. In Northern Alberta, Canada, the second week in December is freezing cold. I saw tigers up to their bellies in snow, frolicking, rolling in it, enjoying themselves, chasing each other. No weather New York has is too mean for a tiger."

"Without any buildings at all?"

"Buildings are optional. The cats should have structures to retreat into in sleet and rain."

"You include lions—lions can take that kind of cold weather too?"

"Less, but to some degree. So I would think that a way of handling cats in the Central Park Zoo is to have only two species: tigers and lions, a pride of lions and a small group of year-round active tigers. It makes more sense than a bobcat in one cage, a lynx in one cage, a jaguar in another cage, and a tiger in another one. That's a stamp collection, it's not zookeeping."

"There are a number of bears in the present Zoo and all that space, particularly the polar bear enclosure, which you remarked was 'phonied over white cement' to give the appearance of snow. And that 'birdbath' of a pool . . . what would you do with the bears?"

"I would suggest that the entire bear exhibit be gutted and that one species be decided upon, that one to be exhibited in the largest and most sensational possible quarters appropriate to the species. If we think it should be polar bear, then the quarters should be ninety percent water and there should be underwater viewing ports. There's no point in having animals go under water if you can't see them when they're there.

"Then there are other lesser proposals. For instance, the seal pool needs a filtration system. I want the restaurant out of there. It's utterly inappropriate, that big ugly circus-like restaurant, serving rotten food, in such limited space. We don't have room for that kind of luxury, or lack of luxury, I should say. Much better use can be made of that space than a glorified hotdog stand."

"How would you get around the fixation on the landmark status?"

"That circus pavilion is no landmark. Here's something else. The most popular building, in any zoo, one building that continues to draw people—and I've been to scores and scores of zoos—is the reptile house. Reptiles can be properly exhibited in Central Park because they don't require much space. You can have many different kinds in a very limited space. And they are animals that are relatively foreign to people in an urban setting. You could get an absolutely fantastic reptile exhibit into any one of those buildings."

"What would you do with the pony ride?"

"Turn it into a deer park. If you want a pony ride in Central Park, fine. But just don't have it in the only space the Zoo can expand into. I would take it over and make it into a deer park."

"Would you include the place where the fallow deer are caged now?"

"Probably."

"That would include the inside buildings that the deer retire to?"

"Yes—but get rid of the deer cages. I would remove those cages and move the people over to where the cages now are. You will have come in now past the deer park. The deer house will have been cleaned out and the wall on the Fifth Avenue side greened by planting and rock structure within the zoo grounds. You will see your hoofed animals—maybe an African Plains group—in a natural setting. The service building for that would be what is now the deer house. You walk with that on your right, looking into what is now the aoudad area, plus the bird area, plus the broad walk that is there now, and it all becomes another big habitat with the building in the background greened out."

"When, for all of this?"

"The initial proposals for the monkey house and the hospital have already been accepted, and I would like to see them completed by December 1975. The bird house would have to wait several years. As I've said, that building would not be available because of the subway construction. The other ideas would be implemented in a staggered kind of arrangement. You can't tear the whole Zoo down all at once. You have to do it in stages."

"And that's your vision of Central Park as it could be?"

"Right. First and foremost, the humane treatment of animals; two, a positive educational experience for the people; three, whatever conservation good can come of it—and conservation can come in several forms. It can get people to vote right and act intelligently toward the natural world, if they go through a natural and decent educational experience. It can be a breeding center for rare species, although I don't think this will ever be a major element in Central Park. And as a result of these other things, it would be a first-rate recreational facility for a city that sorely needs it."

It is also to be hoped that into Mr. Caras' vision of what Central Park might one day become can be incorporated the best elements of what it once was and what it presently is. All of the tradition that persevered over the years, all of the dedicated personnel who strove so willingly to make the most of an enormously difficult situation should certainly be made a part of the New Zoo. Including, Patty Cake—and soon her new sibling—who belongs to the millions of people who love Central Park.

12 Zoo of the Future—For Example, The Bronx

"The zoo of the future is an environmental park," William G. Conway, general director of the New York Zoological Society says. "It should be, among other things, a repository for vanishing species. From beginning to end it should be a series of experiences for the city dweller that reacquaint him with the beauty of the wild environment and make him realize that the world is not made of concrete and cubes. The zoo of the future should have fewer buildings. Those lovely old Victorian cubes—such as you see here at the Bronx—should disappear. And soon they will be doing just that."

"How would that be possible in a temperate climate such as New York City's?" inquired the writer seated, indeed, in a comfortable, circa 1890 office in one of those lovely old Victorian cubes.

"Bury them," replied the general director. "Our next building will be invisible."

Despite its reputation as a citadel of conservatism, derived mainly from the aura about the distinguished families who sit on its board, the New York Zoological Society (NYZS) is in fact one of the zoo

263

world's most daring innovators. Perhaps invisible buildings were not beyond possibility for an institution such as the Bronx Zoo.

"That is, as invisible as we can make it," resumed the general director. "We're using an earth facade to hide the side of the new building and we'll be greening it out. All that the public will see are plants and trees. It's not new—it was done by Hagenbeck in 1907. But it should be done more."

William G. Conway, at forty-five, is one of the most respected zoo directors in the world. Basically an ornithologist, with special interest in zoo exhibition techniques and conservation, Bill Conway has himself captured and exhibited a number of interesting birds, including the first mossy-throated bell bird and the first James's and Andean flamingos ever displayed in a zoo. Tall, with a tweedy look and a slow easy baritone, Conway became director at Bronx in 1962 and general director in 1967. His voice is heard in movies as narrator of many television wildlife films, and he also functions as head of a great cultural foundation—one of the greatest and most influential—for that is what many people consider the New York Zoological Society: a cultural enterprise established by such people as Theodore Roosevelt, Madison Grant and Henry Fairfield Osborn, and currently trusteed by Astors, Phippses and Rockefellers.

Founded in 1895, the NYZS has, in the zoo world of the past, always played the role of innovative leader. Aside from having pioneered some of the most forward-looking zoo exhibits, it also led the move for fewer animals better displayed that finally convinced many major United States zoos to eliminate postage-stamp type collections and install breeding and compatible groups. It showed the way for zoos to become potent forces for conservation. It established one of the finest aquariums in the world, in addition to setting up the Osborne Laboratories for Marine Sciences, which studies marine organisms. It was the first to develop a major educational program; it led all American zoos in scientific research. With its Center for Field Biology and Conservation it also became the only zoo in the Western Hemisphere to have significant conservation programs beyond its fences. Recently, for instance, it played a major role in having Amboseli made a national park in Kenya; at this very moment a NYZS researcher is on the back of an elephant watching Indian rhinos in Nepal, another researcher is working with Komodo monitors in Indonesia, still another making studies of Colobus monkeys in Uganda. The list of the Society's extra-curricular wildlife projects also includes restocking national parks with rescued American bison—the first successful example of reintroduction of wildlife —and reviving interest in whale conservation through its studies and programs. The popular "Song of the Humpbacked Whale" is a creation of the NYZS.

Such has been the role of the NYZS in the zoo world of the past. As to the zoo of the future, its voice is no less authoritative. The message that it sounds repeatedly is that the focal concern of the zoo of the future must be environment and conservation. Practically all of its efforts—exhibition, breeding, care, education, research— are so directed.

"The situation is critical," says Conway. "The prospect is for more and more habitat to disappear. Most Asian faunal communities will be gone in the next two decades. Destruction in South American forests is proceeding at a terrific rate; only a few of those wild animals will be saved. Now, add to this the prospect of human famine, which will most certainly occur in our lifetime—no question about it. This will make the pressure even on protected areas such as national parks so great that it is questionable whether many of them will be able to survive. I don't think starving peoples will permit in their areas national parks that could be used to grow food, or that government will maintain vast preserves that might produce revenues from commercial exploitation. The places where wild animals come from are getting smaller and smaller, while the possibility of almost all the large, slow-breeding mammals going into near-extinction is getting larger and larger. In the not-too-distant future the only place that you will find many species of the world's wildlife will be in zoos.

"Look at it another way. One out of ten of all Americans lives within a two-hour drive of the Bronx Zoo. The same concentration of urban population exists in other areas of the country. So it is the urbanite who controls the vote and it is he who will decide the fate of the Grand Canyon, Yellowstone Park and the Everglades— not the rural populations living in those areas. But the zoos are also in the cities and the only contact that most urban dwellers have with wildlife is at the zoo. So, again, you can see how important the zoo of the future is when it comes to educating Americans to preserve their natural environment."

Bill Conway swung around in his chair and leaned back. He hesitated a moment and then pointed at the window over his shoulder. "I take it you've been to Yankee Stadium at one time or another," he said. "Well, if you haven't I can tell you it's just a few blocks down the street from this Zoo. The City has appropriated fifty-five million dollars to renovate that stadium—and the scuttlebutt has it that it will cost eighty million before it's finished. Yet, even in its poorest years, attendance at the Bronx Zoo has always topped Yankee Stadium. Or take the arts. How disgraceful it is that there's a National Foundation for the Arts giving millions for the preservation of Dutch and French paintings, but no federal agency to give a dime to zoos for the preservation of precious wildlife. Think about that."

According to Conway, in order to fulfill its role of environmental park, the zoo of the future must specialize. It must concentrate on what it does best and not simply present motley "animals round the world" displays. And these specialty exhibits must be spacious. Moreover, it is not enough merely to exhibit animals, even on a specialty basis; the presentation must relate animal to man.

Bronx's newest exhibit—to be completed within the next few years—will meet most of these criteria of the zoo of the future. First, it will occupy a forty-acre area, a space nearly as large as the whole of the Philadelphia Zoo and itself a one-sixth chunk of the Bronx's own acreage—an enormous commitment for any metropolitan area zoo. Moreover, the new exhibit will specialize in tropical Asia, with emphasis on the relationship of man to animal in that area, as indicated by its name: "Man and Animal in Tropical Asia."

"I try to avoid using the words 'major breakthrough' indiscriminitely," said Conway. "But here I feel compelled to use them. Our new Man and Animal in Tropical Asia exhibit *will* be a major breakthrough, a giant step forward toward the model zoo of the future."

Bill Conway leaned back and thought for a moment.

"Let's take a look at something else at this point," he said. "Right outside this office is our Baird Court. Three old buildings—those vintage Victorian edifices—will be done over and greened out by trees and plants to house what we consider another important component of the zoo of the future. A zoo, if it is to fulfill its responsibility, must be, as I said, an environmental park. Accordingly, in the Baird Court, we will have an environmental education center. This center will glorify the works of man as our World of Birds glorified the work of nature. And the reason we will use these warm old Baird buildings is because they're so human. They will suggest man's past, while at the same time pointing to his future."

Here, as Conway described the new environmental education center, now in the planning stage, human beings will be exhibited to themselves. Visitors will go through exhibits in a special conveyance, much as they did in the moving chairs at the Westinghouse exhibit in the last New York World's Fair, a technique which will individualize the message. They will stop and look into displays, coming from back projectors and other media, of, say, various aspects of primate life. On the other side, at the same time, other visitors will be looking through and they will see exhibits of the human eye, that is, of the eye of the person that is looking through from the other side. They will see, for instance, a live human hand next to a primate hand, since people will use their hands to actuate displays. In addition there will be exhibits of various aspects of human behavior that will enable visitors to identify the kinds of people they are looking at. The aging process in humans, the difference between boys and girls, the courtship behavior of *homo sapiens* as compared to other animals will all be demonstrated right on the spot by graphics.

"It will be a living interpretative approach dedicated to the idea of getting man to understand himself as an animal," explained Conway. "This is something new for the world of the zoo, which had always committed itself only to the job of educating man about other animals. Here we will be trying to enable man to understand himself through animals as well as animals through himself."

"Will this be done on a level that will enable various age groups to comprehend it?"

"Absolutely. Now to get back to the Man and Animal in Tropical Asia exhibit. I'll give you an example of something that we will be doing there. One of the great contributions of the zoo to environmental education is its potential for *individualizing the animal*. If we look at a herd of deer in New York State, they're all ciphers:

deer one, deer two, deer three. Go down and kill a deer in Central Park and you'll discover that it is a special deer and that killing it will cause a bigger outcry than perhaps the slaughter of the entire cipher herd. A hippopotamus on the Nile is just a hippo, but you come to the Bronx Zoo, that's Pete. The mother of Patty Cake is Lulu; the father, Kongo. More people can probably tell you who Hsing-Hsing and Ling-Ling are than who Chou En-lai is. The major contribution of the oceanariums to the conservation of dolphins and whales was the individualization of dolphins and whales. If you're just killing dolphins and whales, that's one thing. But if you're killing the relatives of Bubbles or Flip or Shamu, you better watch out. This is enormously important. And it is the zoo that individualizes animals."

"How are you going to do that in the Tropical Asia exhibit?"

"You've often heard whites say something awful about blacks: they all look alike. And I have a black friend who tells me, 'All you honkies look alike—it's a good thing you wear a mustache, Conway.' Well, right now we are gathering for our Tropical Asian exhibit a marvelous series of facial portraits of orang-utans taken in zoos all over the world. We're also collecting a series of portraits of Indonesians of various types. And the thing that becomes evident at once is that the orangs look a lot more different from each other than do the Indonesians. You can tell Orang Briggs from Orang Henry a lot easier than you can Mr. Baharani from Mr. Suhatar. Immediately the animal becomes an individual and not a cipher. It was Konrad Lorenz, the recent Nobel laureate, who demonstrated that geese recognize each other by their faces and that if a goose puts its head under water as its mate comes up the mate might attack it unless it puts its face up."

"I always thought it was some other sense that was used for identification," said the visitor. "Some kind of radar or olfactory mechanism."

"No, it's the face. They recognize by vision. When I was capturing James's flamingos in the High Andes in 1960, I could walk by their enclosure with lots of other people watching them and their heads would come up and identify me. Animals individualize man and each other. So one of the things we will try to do strongly in the Tropical Asian exhibit is to individualize the animal."

"Would you, then, call this an environmental orientation center?" "No. It's an old idea used by museums for over half a century. Most people will not go into one place to get orientated by a lot of museum-type exhibits and then come out and go to another place to see the animals they've been oriented to. The interpretive displays must be right there where the animals are, so that they may be viewed when the visitor's interest is high. And the animals must be shown interpretively. I don't care what orientation is done, if zebras are shown as we show them: on a blacktop yard in front of a brick building—that's never going to be any good, no matter what orientation you do. Our zebra exhibit will be closed and replaced. If you do not connect environment with the animal you're being nothing less than medieval, like our God-awful monkey house which I hope we'll have closed in two years. If you show apes and monkeys sitting around in what amounts to a bunch of tiled bathrooms, doing exactly what humans do in tiled bathrooms, that is terrible and it relates them not at all to their environment."

Perhaps of no less importance will be the zoo of the future's breeding activities. Indeed, many zoos have for some time engaged themselves in significant breeding programs that have made them producers rather than consumers of wild animals—even of rare and endangered species. Recently the Taiwan Government announced that the Formosan deer had become extinct. Almost at the same moment the Bronx Zoo's herd of Formosan deer had increased to fifty, making it the largest single remaining group, some of which it was urgently trying to place with responsible parties. It also had, after the Duke of Bedford's, the next largest herd of Père David deer in the world. Deer are like humans: the sex of their offspring is about evenly distributed between male and female. But unlike most humans, they are a harem species, one male mating with many females. Every zoo that has a successful breeding program for harem-species animals thus winds up with an excess of males for which mates cannot be supplied, and which are, therefore, useless. In the wild the problem of the excess male is taken care of by predators, sickness and old age. But in the zoo the males live to advanced age and are difficult to keep because their courtship patterns require them to fight. They are even more difficult to get rid of, inasmuch as other zoos have the same problem of female shortage.

"This puts us in a terrible bind," said Conway. "Père David deer are not paintings you can hang on museum walls and forget about. If you stop breeding them they go senile and die. But if you continue breeding them you wind up with enough to fill all U.S. zoos. Here is an animal that is rarer than a Rembrandt—there are 750 known Rembrandts, and only 640 Père David deer—but in five years we will have such an excess that we might have to 'recycle' our Père David deer to our Siberian tigers, that is, actually be compelled to feed the rarest deer in the world to the rarest tiger in the world."

All of which has caused the custodians of America's zoo treasures to re-think their philosophy of animal collections. What with ever-growing problems of space, of breeding, of the trend toward specialization in collections, the zoo of the future will tend to be more national, even international, with "annexes" often located far beyond their city fences. It had not yet been announced, Conway informed the visitor, but he felt that he could reveal that the Bronx Zoo will soon have animals going down to St. Katherine's Island, off the coast of Georgia. There the Zoo will build an installation purely for conservation purposes. Endangered species will be bred and sufficient numbers held so that when restocking in the wild becomes possible the supply will be there. In some cases a gene pool will be set up for certain species so that replenishment of those groups can be assured. The entire operation will be non-public, an eleven-mile boat ride being required to reach the island.

The zoos of the future—and some are already laying the groundwork—will also work jointly with each other in breeding activities. In this connection the National Zoo has invited Bronx to participate in its future Front Royal, Virginia, breeding farm, and Bronx has extended the same offer for its St. Katherine's Island installation. Thus Washington's little rhino, Patrick, may one day be producing his own baby rhinos off the coast of Georgia if that environment seems more favorable to him. On the other hand, the Bronx Zoo's Przewalski's horse Berthold may be doing stud duty in the backwoods of Virginia.

Climatic and topographical conditions will dictate the disposition and placement of zoo animals in the zoo of the future more than they ever have since Carl Hagenbeck tried to simulate natural habitat in the urban precincts of Stellingen, Germany. The New York Zoological Society, Conway told the visitor, is looking at places in Florida, where climatic conditions make better sense for gorillas than does New York City. Wild sheep and goats, on the other hand, belong in areas such as the Rocky Mountains—and the Zoo is exploring a program there. It is also thinking about setting up special collections for wild horses, wild asses, zebras and other animals, all with the idea of appropriate environment and conservation in mind.

"With all these far-flung installations, the Bronx Zoo would, in effect, become a kind of national zoo, would it not?" suggested the visitor.

"Yes, that is a direction where the zoo of the future is heading," said Conway. "A series of interlocking agreements between zoos that permit them to take advantage of each other's special assets. The Bronx Zoo rarely sells an animal today; we loan it out to some other zoo and vice versa. Right now, for instance, we can only manage about ten Siberian tigers. But one day we may want to have a group of fifty. So we have some out on loan and we get some of their offspring with which to build that eventual group. Also, placing them around is insurance against being left with none in the event of a local disaster. And the same situation prevails reciprocally. Cincinnati has snow leopards here because we have an outstanding record in breeding snow leopards. In this respect zoos will trend more toward national rather than regional orientation."

Many of the zoo world's more revolutionary concepts have traditionally emanated from the "conservative" NYZS think-tank ensconced in the drab environs of East Fordham Road, the Bronx. Indeed, elements of "the zoo of the future" already exist in the present at Bronx Zoo.

For instance, the spectacular four-million-dollar World of Birds (WOB) exhibit which opened in June 1972 as a gift from Mrs. Lila Acheson Wallace, co-founder of *Reader's Digest* and a trustee of NYZS. It is hard to conceive of any ornithological exhibit of the future outdoing the World of Birds even though the WOB is mounted in a temperate zone with all the disadvantages of bad climate and unnatural habitat. It became possible because environments natural to hundreds of exotic birds displayed in twenty-six exhibits—rain forest, African jungle, swamplands, arid scrubland, and others—were all skillfully simulated in this most advanced bird exhibit in the world. This meant that birds could be presented in natural settings that not only show what they look like, but also what they do and how they do it. And all of it in a building set on a patch of land hemmed in by the roaring traffic on a street named East Fordham Road, the Bronx.

Designers of the World of Birds building (Morris Ketchum, Bill Conway and members of the Zoo staff) must have taken to heart Heini Hedinger's dictum about cubes: "Cubes," said the animal behavioral psychologist, "are a shape completely alien to nature. Architects have confined all animal life, from fish to giraffe, from snake to gorilla, in this particular spatial form. In zoo architecture it is not the simplest and the cheapest type of building which should be given primary consideration, but rather the type of building which comes nearest to meeting the animals' biological requirements. The cube, indeed a straight line of any kind, is unbiological." One would indeed be hard put to find a cube or a straight line, except for the walkways where the *humans* move, in the complex of silolike structures that together comprise the WOB building. Indeed, with its sweeping, unarranged curves and spirals, the WOB house outdoes even Frank Lloyd Wright's Guggenheim Museum in eschewing cubes and straight lines.

"This is where we decided to out-museum the museums," said Bill Conway as he led the visitor into a labyrinth alive with a symphony of bird sound. "But these shapes are not just shapes. These are exhibits; the exhibits were planned first and then clothed in these contours. So that no matter how attractive and unconventional the shape may seem, it is first of all completely functional."

Inside the World of Birds, the visitor goes through a unique experience. Exhibits are grouped together in a number of halls, each having its own story to tell about such matters as bird reproduction, bird geography, behavior, nest-building and tree-top life. Many of the exhibits have no barriers between the birds and the visitors. Except for a low, unobtrusive railing restraining the visitor from actually joining the birds, one can in effect walk into a number of completely open-fronted environments where colonies of the most fantastic looking birds go freely about just as they might in the environments they came from. The birds, too, willingly remain inside their open-fronted aviaries; they prefer the high light levels and lush plantings inside their exhibits to the deliberately darker sterility of the public corridors. In this respect they certainly are not, in the metaphorical sense, birdbrains.

The two largest exhibits, the African jungle and South American rain forest, carry the barrierless approach even further by actually bringing the visitor *into* the display. Here one goes up twelve feet on a walk-in viewing bridge and enters the two indoor forests, while birds of many kinds surround him. An added attraction to the South American rain forest exhibit is the sight and sound of rain, lightning and thunder—all ingeniously simulated by the Bronx's technicians—crashing over the nearly one hundred hummingbirds, tanagers, trogons, barbets and other exotic birds that live in the rain forest. The experience seems to combine a mixture of the past, the present and the future.

The journey with the Zoo director continued down past the bowerbirds, where the male had built a bower of twigs and decorated it with blue-colored items to attract the female; it went on past the burrowing owls, the warblers, thrushes and cardinals that live in the New England forest. Stilts and black rails of the swamps were seen; quail finches, larks and sunbirds from the arid scrublands of East Africa winged back and forth. From the upper level one could see bird life in the treetops: bright green quetzals with long trailing tailfeathers, paradise tanagers with coloring that looked as though it had been dabbed on by an abstract painter, Peruvian manakins with spectacular red heads. Finally, having looked in on birds that live in the Alps above the tree line and those that live on the forest floor, the visitor emerged into the New York sunlight.

"And this is just the public area," said Bill Conway. "Down below, as you will see, we have our own breeding and hatching areas where a complete file is kept on every specimen. Each bird gets its own number and all of its vital data go on a file card that is kept in a central registry. The Bronx was the first to install such a comprehensive system of keeping track of its birds.

"Out back in the open, a non-public area, we are completing a complex of buildings and paddocks that will be devoted exclusively to the propagation of endangered species of birds. It is just a start. But this kind of thing is essential if zoos are to fulfill their responsibility toward saving endangered species in the future. We'll have more of the same down on St. Katherine's Island.

"And we are already doing with our birds what I mentioned before, that is, spreading our collection out, as zoos must and will do in the future with others of their animal populations. See those turquoisine parakeets there. Those are an endangered species and they are bred by one of what we call our field associates. These are private aviculturists, some of whom have rather significant collections. Young Winston Guest, for instance, has the largest collection of waterfowl in the Western Hemisphere out on his Long Island estate and he's one of our most active field associates. We've selected what we consider the most concerned people and we lend our birds out to them for breeding and raising. This way we greatly expand our collection at practically no loss in space.".

The Rare Animals Range Exhibits, opened in June 1974, is another step forward on the Bronx Zoo's march toward the zoo of the future. Called R.A.R.E., the new range comprises three large moated areas, each an acre or more in size, devoted to three of the rarest animals on earth—the Père David deer, the European bison (wisent), and Przewalski's horse. All three of these species are extinct in nature and exist only in zoos and preserves. The mission of R.A.R.E. is not only to help save these wildlife treasures by breeding them in a protected area, but also to display them in a way that enables people to appreciate them and thus themselves become a motivated force in saving other endangered species from extinction.

The visitor was next taken on a tour that proved a living history lesson in man's ability both to destroy and to save wild animals.

"This range is not completed yet," said Conway as he stopped his zoocart on the road beside a large, sloping green paddock. "It's part of the old range—we've got to use the past to get to the future. But those fences that you now see will all disappear when those new-planted trees come up. In about two years you will see nothing but green when you look into these ranges. There's one of our Przewalski's horses coming up that slope. There are only 206 of him in the world, at last count. Let's see if we can get him up here for you."

Two styles of zoo housing:
1) Kodiak bear in old style stone-and-iron cage with cement floor at Baltimore Zoo. *(Photo credit: Ray Faass, Baltimore Zoo)*
2) Lowland gorilla peacefully asleep on grass in moated enclosure at San Diego Zoo.

Exterior of ultra-modern World of Birds House at Bronx Zoo. *(Photo credit: New York Zoological Society)*

Interior of World of Birds House at Bronx Zoo. One of the exhibits, the rainforest, has nearly 100 birds flying freely within the exhibit. The hummingbirds flash in and out of the falling waters as they bathe. They readily accept the presence of people and tamely fly near visitors. A viewing bridge brings the visitor into the rainforest to observe the birds without intervening glass or wire. Other exhibits are just as spectacular. *(Photo credit: New York Zoological Society)*

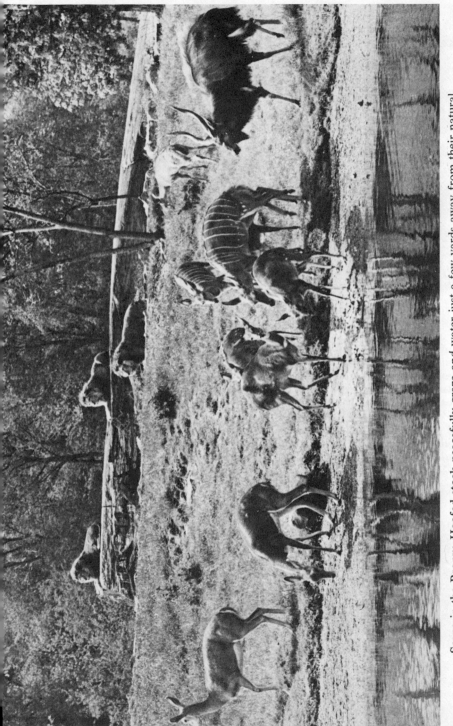

Scene in the Bronx: Hoofed stock peacefully graze and water just a few yards away from their natural enemy, the lion. At the Bronx Zoo the hunter and the hunted are separated by well-landscaped moats. *(Photo credit: New York Zoological Society)*

Architect's model of the National Zoo's future Lion and Tiger Complex, construction of which is expected to be completed by 1976. There will be two enclosures for tigers and one for lions, each containing rocks for climbing, trees, heated grottos, and watercourses. The entire complex will be surrounded by a water moat so that visitors will be able to view the animals without obstruction, and the individual enclosures will be separated from each other by dry moat. *(Photo credit: Faulkner, Fryer & Vanderp)*

The author pays a visit to Joan Embery and her performing elephants at another model of future zoos—the San Diego Wild Animal Park. *(Photo credit: Stanley Livingston)*

The Przewalski, or Mongolian wild horse, was first described on the basis of a skin and skull brought from central Asia by N. M. Przewalski. The first live specimens brought out of the wild were three young animals kept on a Russian estate in 1900. A year later Carl Hagenbeck captured twenty-eight animals in Mongolia and distributed them to various collections; it is from this group that the present captive stock is descended. At the present time the Bronx has three of the known existing population, a male and two females, received from Catskill Game Farm in 1968. Two more young animals will soon be added to the herd and it is from these that the Zoo hopes to develop a breeding group in the R.A.R.E.

"And here are our wisent, our cave paintings (a reference to the paintings of European bison which were made by primitive man in the caves at Lascaux, France). We have thirteen, the largest herd in America. There they are down there."

"Down there" was in the shade of an old Bronx elm tree sooted by the endless stream of exhaust floating in from East Fordham Road. And yet here was an inspiring sight. Wild animals whose Old World ancestors had been the subjects for the very beginnings of man's art now snoozing in the shade of a New World tree that, sooted or not, provided a blanket of security over their existence. The last wild wisent was killed in the Bialowieza Forest of Poland by a poacher on February 9, 1921. Now because of the work of zoos such as the Bronx, which saved the American bison from extinction, the wisent has been able to be returned to the wild. In 1956 a small herd was introduced into the Bialowieza Forest, where, latest figures show, it has increased to about one thousand.

In the third and last range on this tour of the future were the Père David deer. Called "ssu-pu-hsiang" by the Chinese, which means "four characters that do not fit together"—a reference to its having the antlers of a deer, the feet of a cow, the neck of a camel, and the tail of a donkey—the Père David deer was made known to the Western world in 1865 by the French Jesuit missionary, Father Armand David. He also discovered the giant panda. During the Boxer Rebellion in 1900 the last Chinese imperial herd was destroyed and the six hundred forty deer that are living today are descendants of eighteen animals acquired by England's Duke of Bedford and bred at Woburn

Abbey. At last count the Bronx Zoo had thirty-one, including five new fauns.

"Here they are now—watch those bulls," said Conway. "They're all forming their harems for breeding. There's a lot of argument between them, and this is good, because it's quite natural. Look at that one running a doe. Each one is trying to maintain his own harem. This one's got a harem down here and that one's got a harem up there. That's the way it would happen in the wild. See—there's one standing guard and ready to fight for his harem. You don't see this sort of thing in many zoos. Watch that bull who is nosing those females forward. He's testing them . . . to see if any are ovulating and ready for breeding. And notice how muddy the males are—they get down in the mud wallows at this time of year—and see how thin they are from fighting and breeding. That one up there's a little gimpy. Looks like he's had a fight. Did you see him horn her? He feels tough. Now, what we have to watch out for is what we call "spikes," those young bucks you see there. Right now they're all right. They're young enough so that the big bucks won't bother them. But next year we've got to get them out or the big males will kill them. It's with these fellows that we have the problem of disposal that I mentioned."

The zoo of the future. It was as though time had been rolled back to give the visitor a view of the past which, at the same time, was also a look at the future—those noble old wisent, resting serenely in a New York City park; that herd of Père David deer doing on East Fordham Road what their ancestors must have done for eons in the ancient forests of China . . .

The final portion of the visitor's odyssey was the Bronx Zoo's World of Darkness, considered by many to be the most futuristic of all the Bronx Zoo's exhibits. There, the mysterious creatures of the night are brought out of the "dark closet" of ignorance into the light of understanding. Alligators, aardwolves, bats, blind cavefish, frogmouths, owls, sloths, and other creatures whose normal life cycle revolves around the hours of darkness are seen going through their rarely observed nighttime activities.

Although zoos have long collected nocturnal animals (sixty percent of the world's land vertebrates are active only in the dark), they have generally been unable to exhibit them because of the animals' aversion to light. When light bright enough for human vision was used, the animals, reacting as though it were daytime, simply went to sleep; when too dim, the public saw nothing.

Accordingly the Bronx Zoo began experimenting with light of different colors—red, blue, blue-green—in addition to variations in its intensity. An owl, for instance, can see a white mouse on dark soil in less than one-millionth of a foot-candle of light while a human requires up to a hundred times that amount. Other nocturnal animals require different intensities of light; still others—most, in fact—are colorblind to red light. The sum total of the Zoo's research, including the kind and intensity of light that the public required, resulted in the World of Darkness exhibit, which duplicates the natural environment of nocturnal animals by reversing the day-night cycle. When it is daytime *outside* the building it is nighttime for the animals *inside*. And yet the light, though dim enough to provoke the animals into their natural actions, is still bright enough to permit the visitor to see them. After the building closes for the day, the lights are turned up to create "day" and the animals go to sleep.

The building itself, low and cavernous with steeply sloped walls sheathed in black mortar and black granite chips, is appropriate to its theme. Going past a sign posted at the entrance which warns the visitor to keep his voice low and refrain from running or making sudden movements, one enters through a "light lock" that permits his eyes to adjust to the darkness. He then proceeds through three main halls: Forest at Night; Wings in the Night; Refuge Underground.

In the Forest at Night he can peer into an owl exhibit from behind any of three glass panes—red, clear and blue-green. When he stands behind the red pane, the viewer is almost invisible to the owls. From behind the blue-green pane, he sees the owls as other owls see them, and from behind the clear he sees the owl as he might ordinarily see him, that is, under the full range of the spectrum. Over in another part of this hall, tree snakes, owl monkeys, and slow lorises slip in and out among the shadowy cypresses and stumps on the floor. Further on the visitor finds himself groping about at a nearby swamp, attracted there by a swelling frog chorus and the roar of a bull alligator.

"Daddy, where are you? I can't see," calls out a child to its parents

. . . "Why don't they make it day so they'll sleep?" brightly suggests a woman wearing dark glasses . . . "Oh,'² gasps a teen-age boy as he watches a boa advancing vertically up a tree trunk in search of prey. "Slimy. Spooky."

In another hall—Refuge Underground—the visitor sees burrowing creatures such as foxes, armadillos, pack rats and lizards in their caves and burrows. Further on he peeks into a tropical cave with stalactites, which drip water, and stalagmites, which backdrop several species of bats and toads. A stream runs through the cave and continues outside, where the bats swoop and sloths hang from the forest branches. Down below, pacas and agoutis, and tinamous slink across the forest floor.

"Daddy, I can't see," persists the child. "Why don't they make it day?". . . A man with briefcase exclaims, "Crazy things you never dreamed existed. Did you see those big eyes staring out at you?". . . "Are you there?" inquires a gray-haired lady, glancing nervously back toward her husband. "What's that thing scurrying about on the floor? I just saw him hanging from the tree a minute ago." . . . "Come here and look at those bats clustered up there!" commands a braided, bespectacled girl to her companion. . . .

In the Wings in the Night Hall the much-maligned bat, a mammal, is presented along with birds such as owls and frogmouths. A visit to this exhibit does much to increase understanding of a creature that is so important an element in nature's ecosystems. One learns, for instance, that many species of bats, far from taking live prey, actually subsist on fruit. For the first time it is discovered that all bats do not look, as supposed, like flying rats; some, such as the brown bat, seem more like furry little rabbits with wings. In the World of Darkness they hang upside-down in groups, sparring with each other like so many kittens—or so it appeared. The Chinese have long held bats in high esteem: the bat is a symbol of happiness, good fortune and longevity. A trip through the World of Darkness nearly always alters fixed attitudes about one of the most feared and despised of nature's creatures. As Helen Hayes, the actress, told Bill Conway after her own trip through the Bronx Zoo's bat exhibit: "I didn't want to go in there for anything in the world. But I'm glad you made me look at those bats. I'm not so sure that I'd now want to have one for a personal pet, but by the time I got out of there I was fascinated with them. And I must admit that they are extraordinarily interesting and even attractive creatures."

Leaving the World of Darkness, one comes upon a sign:

In this building you have been introduced to the World of Darkness, a world that represents only one part of the totality that is nature. The continuing increase in human environmental destruction is rapidly suffocating the world of nature. Therefore the future of all wildland and wildlife depends upon education, human protection and interest, and ultimately upon you."

In the end, after a traveler has touched bases in all the fascinating corners of the zoo world, both in its past and present and in its vision of the future, after he has gotten to know something of the animals, the people, and the places, the Simon and Garfunkel song seems especially appropriate:

> Someone told me
> It's all happening at the zoo
> I do believe it,
> I do believe it's true.
>
> It's a light and tumble journey
> From the East Side to the park . . .
> What a gas! You gotta come and see
> At the zoo.

Indeed, "you gotta come and see" all the exciting things happening at the Bronx, the San Diego, the Baltimore and the National zoos. But there are other zoos throughout America that are in many ways equally as interesting as these. The author regrets that they also could not be included in the book, but pleads extenuation on the grounds he did not set out to offer an encyclopedic presentation of zoos, but rather a story of the phenomenon of the zoo and some of its representative animals, people, and places. Nevertheless, he cannot finish without at least making brief mention of some other U.S. zoos and their outstanding exhibits.

Brookfield Zoo (15 miles outside of Chicago), Brookfield, Illinois.

Owned by Cook County Forest Preserve District and managed by the Chicago Zoological Society. Opened in July, 1934. Has a total of 1,789 specimens on 200 acres, with an annual attendance of 2,000,-000 and a budget of $3,250,000. One of the most imaginatively housed zoos in the world and the first U.S. zoo to use the free-enclosure concepts developed by Carl Hagenbeck. Famous for a long line of rare animals, including the first giant panda ever exhibited in the Western world.

Fort Worth Zoological Park and Aquarium, Fort Worth, Texas.

Managed by the Park and Recreation Department, with Fort Worth Zoological Society operating all concessions. Opened in 1923. Has 36.5 acres for 2,578 specimens, with an annual attendance of 1,000,-000 and a budget of $370,000. One of the more innovative zoos in the U.S., it presents classical music concerts to visitors in the manner of certain European zoos. Noted particularly for its fish and aquatic mammal collection.

Los Angeles Zoo, Los Angeles, California.

Managed by Recreation and Parks Department, assisted by the Greater Los Angeles Zoo Association in fund raising, animal acquisition, research and library. Opened in 1966 on site of old Griffith Park Zoo, the new zoo has 2,635 specimens on 113 acres, with an annual attendance of 1,750,000 and a budget of $2,300,000. Backgrounded by California hills and sub-tropical plantings, zoo displays a representative collection in five continental areas: Africa, Australia, Eurasia, North and South America. One of best education departments in the world.

Arizona-Sonora Desert Museum, Tucson, Arizona.

Owned and managed by Arizona-Sonora Desert Museum, Inc. Founded in 1952. Has a total of 605 specimens on 187 acres, with annual attendance of 316,380 and a budget of $759,500. Specializes in fauna of the American desert, with outstanding scientific, educational and breeding record. Considered by many to be one of the models for the zoo of the future. For its size certainly one of the best zoos of the present.

Philadelphia Zoo, Philadelphia, Pennsylvania.

Owned and managed by Philadelphia Zoological Society. Opened in July, 1874, second oldest after Central Park Zoo (1864). Has a total of 1,069 specimens on 42 acres with an annual attendance of 1,139,436 and a budget of $2,283,000. Guas and Guarina, its 54-year-old orang-utans, are the oldest anthropoid apes on exhibit in any zoo, being also grandparents of offspring at other zoos. Zoo has one of the most outstanding displays of large sea mammals, including toothed whales in sea tanks.

Portland Zoological Gardens, Portland, Oregon.

Owned by City of Portland and managed by Portland Zoological Society, which is responsible for total operation, including concessions, railway, care of animal collection and landscaping. Opened in 1958. Has a total of 483 specimens on 12 acres, with an annual attendance of 650,505. Avant-garde behavioral studies being made on zoo animals, particularly as regards their learning ability. Animals learning to feed themselves by manipulating electronic equipment.

St. Louis Zoological Park, St. Louis, Missouri.

A municipal zoo managed by Zoological Commission, with St. Louis Zoo Association operating gift shop, raising funds, buying animals and giving birthday parties. Opened in 1903. Has a total of 2,882 specimens on 83 acres, with an annual attendance of 3,000,000 and a budget of $1,550,000. One of the best-run municipal zoos in the country; made famous throughout the continent by Marlin Perkins's TV show, "Wild Kingdom." Fine general collection.

Milwaukee County Zoological Park, Milwaukee, Wisconsin.

Managed by Milwaukee County Park Commission, with Zoological Society of Milwaukee County assisting in advisory capacity. Has a total of 7,086 specimens, including 5,129 fishes, on 184 acres, with an annual attendance of 637,893 and a budget of $2,024,512. Opened in 1892. America's newest zoo, built from scratch after abandonment of old one. The latest in zoo architecture, control devices, feeding techniques. Animals are displayed on a geographical basis.

In addition to those listed above there are other U.S. zoos that have many good things to offer. Moreover, there are corporate-owned wild-animal parks—such as Busch Gardens in Tampa, Florida, owned and managed by Annheuser-Busch Inc; and Catskill Game Farm, Inc., in Catskill, New York, owned and managed by Mr. and Mrs. Roland Lindemann—that are the equal of the best municipal- or society-operated zoos. The drive-through animal parks, too, cannot be overlooked, some of which, such as Lion Country Safari and Jungle Habitat, have been described in detail in this book. For those who wish to have a look at zoos other than those already mentioned, whether in the U.S. or any other part of the world, information can be obtained by going to the local library and consulting the zoo directory. In the end, though, "you gotta," as Simon and Garfunkel suggest, "come and see" for yourself.

Index

Aardvark, 205
AAZPA. *See* American Association of
    Zoological Parks and Aquari-
    ums
Accidents, 53, 54, 222. *See also* Be-
    havior, public
Acclimatization, 148, 149, 165, 166,
    176
Administration. *See also* Personnel;
    Salaries
    Bronx Zoo, 263–264, 271
    Financing, 85-86, 266
    Central Park Zoo, 241, 256–257
    Henry III, 27
    National Zoo, 153–154
    Safari Zoos, 121–123, 126, 133
    San Diego Zoo, 94–98, 99
Admission charges, 47, 99, 123, 138
African Lion Safari and Game Farm,
    123
Akeley, Carl, 173
Alexander the Great, 20
Alpacas, 105
American Association of Zoological
    Parks and Aquariums, 161,
    166, 249
Anaconda, 31, 33
Animal Kingdom, Inc., 123
Anteaters, 40–41
Antelope, 106, 201
Antelope, sable
    breeding, 195, 196–197
Anthropomorphism, 32, 66–67, 214,
    215, 221–222, 250. *See also*
    Performing; Names, naming
Aoudad, 82
Apes. *See* specific apes
Ardrey, Robert, 55
Aristotle, 20–21
Arizona-Sonora Desert Museum (Tuc-
    son), 281
Armadillos, 232
Attendance figures, 99, 238, 266
Audubon magazine, 128
Auroch (wild bison), 25
Aztecs. *See* Mexico

Baboons, 64, 127, 129
    Breeding, 194
Badgers, 248–249
Baltimore Zoo, 195
    Accidents, 53–55
    "Betsey" (ape), 225
    Environments, natural, 56–57
    Feeding, 39
    Housing, 44
    Penguins, 56–61
    Recycling program, 67–68
    Vandalism, 47, 48–49
    Veterinary care, 42–44, 45–46
Barnum, P. T., 16, 142, 240
Bath, Lord, 124
Bats, 278
Bear, Smokey. *See* Smokey Bear
Bears, 108, 260. *See also* Koala bears
    Breeding, 195, 203
    Grizzly, 108
    Himalayan, 53–54
    Kodiak, 44
    Polar, 27–28, 47–48, 199, 242, 246
Bedford, Duke of, 71, 79, 269
Bell, Ray, 211, 207, 208
Benchley, Belle J., 95–96, 99
Bestiarii, 23–24
"Betsey" (chimpanzee), 225–228
Bieler, Charles (San Diego Zoo), 118
Birds. *See also* specific birds
    Baltimore Zoo (penguins), 56–61
    Bronx Zoo (World of Birds), 272–
    274
    Capturing, 183–184
    Central Park Zoo, 259
    Diseases, 162
    Montezuma's collection, 32
    Import restrictions, 163
    San Diego Zoo, 107, 113
Bison. *See also* Buffalo
    European (wisent), 186, 274, 275
    Wild (auroch), 25
Blackbuck, 106
Boas. *See* Reptiles
Brayton, Adrian (Baltimore Zoo), 65,
    66

Breeding, 160–162. *See also* Conservation; Feeding; Health; Housing; specific animals
  at Bronx Zoo, 269, 274–275
  at Central Park Zoo, 240, 245
  "Firsts" in captivity, 185–186, 195
  Habits in zoos, 194–195
  Overpopulation, 202–204, 269–270
  Rhinoceros (National Zoo), 187–193
  in Safari zoos and Wild Animal Park (San Diego Zoo), 115, 117–118, 134–135, 196
Bronx Zoo
  Attendance, 265–266
  Breeding, 195, 196, 269–270
  Environments, natural, 266–267, 269
    Catskill Game Farm, 196
    Rare Animals Range Exhibit (RARE), 274–275
    World of Birds, 271–274
    World of Darkness, 276–279
  Evaluation, 236
  Housing, 241, 263–264, 269, 272
  Man and Animal in Tropical Asia (exhibit), 266, 267–268
  New York Zoological Society, 263–265
  Outside-zoo projects, 264–265, 270–271
    St. Katherine's Island, 270
    Front Royal, Virginia, 270
  "Patty Cake" (gorilla), 252
Bronx Zoo Book of Wild Animals, 205
Brookfield Zoo (Chicago), 186, 280. *See also* Pandas
Buck, Frank, 102. 160, 164, 174–176
Buechner, Dr. Helmut K. (National Zoo), 177, 187, 189, 190–193, 196–197
Buffalo. *See also* Bison
  African Cape, 106
  American, 106, 265
  Indian, 198
Bullfights, 24, 25, 31
Byzantium, 26

Caesar, Julius, 24
Cage-less zoos. *See* Safari Zoos; Wild Animal Park (San Diego); Environments, natural (under specific zoos)
Camelopard. *See* Giraffe
Camels, 78, 105, 149
  Capturing, 181
Caras, Roger, 238, 242–243, 245–249, 252, 255–262
Cassanova, Lorenzo, 140, 141

Cassowary, 103
Cats. *See* specific cats
Catskill Game Farm, 79, 116, 196, 275
Central Park Zoo, 64. *See also* Health, veterinary care; "Patty Cake"
  Environments, natural, 247–248, 257–262
  History, 239-240
  Housing, 240, 242–244, 246–247
  Personnel, 241
  Vandalism, 47–48, 233, 238–239, 245
Charlemagne, 26
Chase, Charles P., 166
Chase Wild Animal Farm, 226
Cheetah, 259–260
  Breeding, 117–118, 134, 195
  Capturing, 182
  Endangered, 115
  Importation, 162
Children's Zoos
  Central Park, 244
  San Diego, 102
Chimpanzees
  "Betsey," 225–229
  Breeding, 185–186, 195
  Capturing, 179
  "Ham," 223–224
  Intelligence, 223, 224
  "Lana," 224
China
  Ancient, 17, 18
  Modern, 18, 214–219
  Mongol Empire (Kublai Khan), 28–30
Chippenfield, Jimmy, 124, 125
Christian era
  Charlemagne, 26
  Emergence of zool. garden, 26
  St. Gallen (Switzerland), 26
Circus, Hagenbeck's, 138, 144, 150
Cobras, 41, 62
  In Striptease act, 52
Cockatoo, 100, 102
Cody, William, 15
Collecting. *See also* Buck, Frank; Expeditions; Hagenbeck, Carl; Trading
Capturing. *See also* specific animals
  Drives, animal, 173
  Drugs, immobilizing, 177–179
  Rocket net, 178–180
  Running down, 180–182
  Trapping, 171–172, 173, 183
  Early history, 16, 20
  Insurance, 176–177
  Restrictions, 116–117, 151, 162–163, 168, 175–176
  Transporting, 140-141, 157–159, 176–177, 200

Wild Animal Park (San Diego),
116–117
Columbia (S.C.) Zoo, 133
Commodus. *See* Rome, ancient
Condor, Andean
Breeding, 195
Coney, 19, 109
Conkling, William A. (Central Park
Zoo), 240
Conservation, 15, 67, 90, 105, 168,
177, 203–204, 263, 265, 270–
271. *See also* Endangered spe-
cies; Smokey Bear
Breeding, 89, 186–187, 193, 196,
269, 273–276
in Safari zoos, 133, 134, 135
Education (public), 68, 265, 267–
268, 274
outside of zoos, 264–265
Turtles 85–86, 87
in Wild Animal Park (San Diego)
106, 111, 115, 118
Contests, animal, 27, 30. *See also*
Spectacles, public; Rome
Conway, William (Bronx Zoo), 232,
249–250, 252–253, 263–278
Cowan, Bob (San Diego), 111–112
Cowles, Raymond B. (U. of Calif.),
212
Crandall, Lee (Bronx Zoo), 99
Crowcroft, Dr. W. Peter (Brookfield
Zoo), 186–187
Curare. See Flaxedil

Dailley, G. D. (African Lion Safari),
123
Darwinism, 87
Dealers. *See* Trading
Deaths, animal, 118, 135, 200–201.
See also Massacres; Vandalism
Deer, 261
Fallow, 82, 261. *See also* Central
Park Zoo, vandalism
Formosan
Breeding, 269
Mouse, 155
Père David, 29, 71, 186, 274, 275–
276
Breeding, 194–195, 269–270
Diseases. *See also* Health
"Blackhead," 96
Bright's disease, 176
Hoof-and-mouth disease, 133, 162,
188
Malaria, 60
Newcastle's disease, 162
Disney, Walt, 126, 207
Dog
African hunting, 104
to Control other animals, 129

Domestication, 17
Hearst, Wm. Randolph, 77–78
Hunting with, 28–29
Dolan, Dr. James M., Jr. (San Diego
Zoo), 116–118
Dragons, Komodo, 157, 264–265
Drives, animal. *See* Collecting, capture
Drive-through zoos. *See* Safari Zoos
Dromedaries. *See* Camels
Drugs, immobilizing. *See* Collecting,
capturing; Health, anaesthetics
Dunn, Leon (Baltimore Zoo), 53–55
Durrell, Gerald, 89, 255

Eaton, Dr. Randall (World Wildlife
Safari), 135
Ecology. *See* Human/Animal relation-
ship
Education. *See also* Conservation
Early (Alexander the Great), 20
Bronx Zoo, 265–269
Central Park Zoo, 242–243, 245,
257, 262
Role of modern zoo, 64–65, 90, 234,
237–238
Safari Zoos, 135
Egypt. *See also* Hatshepsut, Queen
First zoo, 16
First public zoo, 20
Spectacles, 21–22
Elephants, 20, 27, 44, 97–98, 199
African, 109, 186
Asian, 109
Baby, 129
Breeding, 186
Capturing, 172, 181–182
Performing, 35
Embery, Joan (San Diego Zoo), 113–
114, 122
Emotional problems in confinement.
See Health
Employment, in zoos. *See* Personnel;
Salaries
Emu, Australian
Nesting habits, 103
Endangered species. *See also* Collect-
ing; Conservation; San Diego
Zoo
Early history, 25
Cheetah, 115
Formosan deer, 269
Koala bear, 109
Muhlenberg turtle, 85–86
Orangutan, 186
Oryx, 105
Panda, 214
Parakeet, turqoisine, 274
Père David deer, 71, 186, 270, 274
Przewalski's horse, 274–275

Endangered Species (*Cont'd*)
    Rhinoceros, white, 115
    Tapir, Malayan, 102
    Wisent, 275
Endangered Species Acts, 133, 160
Entertainment. *See* Performing; Safari Zoos, show business aspects; Spectacles, public
Environments, natural. *See* Safari Zoos; Wild Animal Park (San Diego Zoo); specific zoos
Escapes, animal, 62
Ethnographic exhibitions. *See* Hagenbeck, Carl; Human zoos
Expeditions, 16, 151, 173–174. *See also* Collecting
    National Geographic/Smithsonian, 154–160
Extinction. *See* Endangered species

Faas, Ray (Baltimore Zoo), 65
Falcons, falconry, 26, 29
Faust, Charles R. (San Diego Zoo), 113, 132, 136
Feeding, 38, 39, 40, 41–42, 188
    Breeding, relationship to, 193–194
    Public, 40, 43
    Special food, 40, 42, 108
    Transporting (animals and), 140, 157–158
Fennec, 104
Financing of zoos. *See* Administration
Fitzgerald, John W. (Central Park Zoo), 243–245
Flamingoes, 100, 101, 162, 268
Flaxedil (drug), 177
Flight distance, 114–115, 132
Ft. Worth Zoological Park and Aquarium, 280
France
    Royal menagerie (Versailles), 33, 35, 71
Free-roaming animals, 43–44, 78. *See also* Safari Zoos; Wild Animal Park (San Diego Zoo); specific zoos (Environments, natural)
Friends of the Central Park Zoo, 255
Friends of the National Zoo, 191, 192
Front Royal (Virginia), 196, 270

Gailey, Janet (Baltimore Zoo), 56–61
Games. *See* Contests, animal
Gardens
    San Diego Zoo, 94
    Versailles, 34
Gary, Ben (Baltimore Zoo), 44–45
Gaur, 157–158
Geese, 17, 268

Gibbons, 100
Giraffes, 16–17, 22, 105, 172
    Breeding, 160
    Capturing, 165, 181
    Importing, 161–163
Goats (as animal food), 140–141
Goats, Tahr, 82, 106
Gorillas, 95, 113. *See also* "Patty Cake"
    Breeding, 185, 245, 258
Great Adventure Amusement Park, 136
Great Britain, ancient
    Contests, animal, 27
    Henry I, 26
    Henry III, 26–27
    Tower of London, 26–27
Great Britain, modern. *See also* London Zoo; Bedford, Duke of
    First drive-through zoo, 124
Greece, ancient, 20
Greyhound, 16–17
Grimmer, J. Lear (National Zoo), 210
Grosvenor, Gilbert, 159
Groves, Frank (Baltimore Zoo), 39, 51–52, 62, 84
Guanaco, 105
"Guas" and "Guarina" (orangutans), 195
Guest, Winston, 274

Hagenbeck, Carl. *See also* Health, Veterinary care; Housing, environments, natural
    Capturing techniques, 173
    Circus, 138, 144, 150
    Education, 138–139
    Ethnographic exhibitions, 142–144
    Expeditions, 139–141, 159–160, 275
    Stellingen Zoo, 71, 148–149, 264, 270–271
    Trading, dealing, 139, 148
    Training techniques, 144–148
Hagenbeck, Carl-Heinrich, 150
Hagenbeck, Dietrich, 150
Hagenbeck, Gottfried Claas, 138
Hagenbeck, Heinrich, 150
Hagenbeck's Circus, 138, 144, 150
"Ham" (chimpanzee), 223–224
Hand-rearing, 62–63, 253
Hardy, Mal, 208
Hatari (film), 179–180
Hatshepsut, Queen, 16–17, 124
Health. *See also* Diseases; Housing, inadequate
    Anaesthetics, 177–179, 202
    and Breeding, 194, 197
    Emotional, 201–202, 135, 237
    and Longevity, 244, 245

Quarantine, 162–163, 165
in Safari zoos, 135
while Transporting, 176–177
Veterinary care, 46–47, 179, 200–201
Baltimore Zoo, 42–44, 45–46
Bronx Zoo, 200
Central Park Zoo, 243, 248, 252
Hagenbeck, Carl, techniques, 197–200
Hearst, William Randolph, 30, 72–83, 124
Hearst, William Randolph, Jr., 76–78, 79, 81–82
Hediger, Heini (Zurich Zoo), 49–51, 272
Hellabrunn Zoo (Germany), 186
Henry III (Gt. Britain), 26–27
Hippopotamus, 103
Breeding, 194
Capturing, 172, 177
Hippopotamus, pigmy
Breeding, 195
History of Animals (Aristotle), 21
Hoof-and-Mouth disease. *See* Diseases
Horn, Trader, 160
Horse, Przewalski's wild, 106, 187, 270, 274–275
Housing. *See also* specific zoos
Environments, natural, 84, 86, 88, 232–233, 263–264. *See also* Safari Zoos; Wild Animal Park; specific zoos
and Breeding, 194, 196
of Hagenbeck, Carl, 148–150
"Hsing-Hsing" (panda). *See* Pandas, National Zoo
Human/Animal relationship, 237–238, 245–246, 266–267
Human zoos, 31, 32–33, 126, 142–144
Humane Society of the U.S. (HSUS), 233–238, 241–242, 249
Hummingbirds, 107
Hunt, Don, 164–166, 182
Hyena, 104
Hyrax, 109. *See also* Coney

Iguanas, 84
Impala, 118
Importing. *See* Collecting
Imprinting, 58
Indians (American), 31
Infirmaries. *See* Health, veterinary care
Injurious Animal Act, 163
Insurance. *See* Collecting
International Animal Exchange, 164–166, 182

International Zoo Yearbook, 185, 203
Italy, renaissance, 30–31
Bullfights, 31
Contests, 30
Human zoo, 31

Jaguars, 162
Johnson, Osa and Martin, 173
Jungle Habitat, 121, 126, 127–131, 165
"Jungle Junction," 121, 130–131

Kangaroos, 104
Kenwood St., 900 S. (Baltimore). *See* Reptiles
Ketamine (drug), 178
Ketchum, Morris (architect), 247–248
Knowles, Richard (San Diego Zoo), 101, 100–110
Koala bears, 109–110, 194
Kodiak bear. *See* Bears
Komodo dragon, 157, 264–265
Koyen, Kenneth (writer), 231–232, 237
Kruger National Park, 127, 178

Lacey Act, 162
"Lana" (chimpanzee), 224
Lascaux caves (France), 17, 275
Lebau Brothers, 175–176
Legislation. *See* Collecting, restrictions
Lehman, Gov. Herbert H. (Central Park Children's Zoo), 244
Leopards
Clouded, 155, 157
Breeding, 245
Snow
Breeding, 245
LeRoy, Warner, 136
Lifespans. *See* Health, longevity
"Ling-Ling" (panda). *See* Pandas, National Zoo
Lion Country Safari, 122, 125–126, 133–134, 135
Lions
Breeding, 162
Housing, 244, 260
Popularity, 205
in Safari Zoos, 135
Training, 144
Llama, 43, 105
London Zoo, 47, 194–233. *See also* Pandas
Longevity. *See* Health
Lorenz, Konrad, 268
Los Angeles Zoo, 280
Louis XIV, 33–35
"Lulu" (gorilla), 250–255

M 99 (drug), 178
Mack, Dave, 84, 85, 86, 88, 90
Man and Animal in the Zoo (H. Hediger), 49
Manatees, 240
Mann, Lucile (Mrs. William), 154–159
Mann, Dr. William M., 153–159
Marco Polo. *See* China, Mongol
Maryland Herpetological Society, 85
McCrane, Marion (National Zoo), 63
Massacres (of animals)
  Pre-historic, 15
  Renaissance, 30
  Roman, 23, 25
Medicis, 30–31
Men and Beasts (Hagenbeck), 138–139
Ménagerie du Parc (Versailles), 34–35, 71
Menageries, 33
  Alexander the Great, 20
  Bedford, Duke of, 71
  Charlemagne, 26
  Chinese, ancient, 18
  Florence (Italy), 30, 126
  Hagenbeck, Carl, 138–139
  Haroun al-Raschild, 26
  Hatshepsut, Queen, 16
  Hearst, William Randolph, 76–79
  Henry III, 26–27
  Kublai Khan, 28–30
  Montezuma, 32–33
  Papal, 31
  Ptolemy Philadelphius, 22
  Ptolemy II, 22
  Roman, 24–25
  Schönbrunn, 71
  Solomon, King, 18
  Versailles, 33–35
  William the Conqueror, 26
Mexico
  Aztec, 32–33
  Modern, 33
Mice, as animal food, 38–40
Milwaukee County Zoological Park, 282
Monkeys, 180, 199
  Capturing, 180, 184
Monkeys, Colobus, 265
Montagu, Ashley, 56
Montezuma, 32–33
Morris, Dr. Desmond, 226, 228
Mortality. *See* Deaths
Moscow Zoo. *See* Pandas
Mount Kenya Safari Club, 164
Muhlenberg turtle, 85–86
Mynah birds, 65–66, 153–154

Nadler, Dr. (Yerkes Primate Research

Center), 253
Names, naming, 66, 207, 250
National Geographic, 159
National.Geographic-Smithsonian Expedition, 154–160
National Zoo
  Breeding, 56
  Rhinoceros, 187–193
  Collecting for, 154–159
  Environments, natural
  Front Royal, Virginia, 196
  Evaluation of, 236
  Feeding, 38, 49, 41–42
  "Hsing-Hsing" and "Ling-Ling", 217–222
  at Night, 68–69
Nelson, Veronica (Central Park Zoo), 252, 253–255
Net, rocket. *See* Collecting, capturing
New York Zoological Society (NYZS). *See* Bronx Zoo
900 South Kenwood St. (Baltimore). *See* Reptiles, Kenwood St.
Nocturnal activity, 68–69. *See also* Bronx Zoo, World of Darkness

Ocelots
  Breeding, 245
Octavian Augustus. *See* Rome, ancient
Ogilvie, Philip (Portland, Ore., Zoo), 224
Orangutan, 186, 268
  Breeding, 195
Oryx, 186
Osborne Laboratories for Marine Sciences, 264
Ostrich, 106–107, 141
Oxen, musk, 216, 218

Panama-California International exposition (1916), 94
Pandas, 18
  Breeding, 222
  Brookfield Zoo (Chicago), 215, 216–217
  Classification, 219
  Feeding, 41, 215
  London Zoo, 215, 222
  Moscow Zoo, 215, 222
  National Zoo ("Hsing-Hsing" and "Ling-Ling"), 217–222
  Attack on keeper, 222
  Housing, 219–221
  Lobbying for possession, 216–219
  Popularity, 186, 221–222
  Rarity, 214
  Tokyo Zoo, 215
Parakeets, turquoisine, 274

Parrots (San Diego Zoo), 107
"Patty Cake" (gorilla), 62–63, 66, 186, 223, 250–255, 258
Peacock, 19–20
Pegelow, Nancy (Baltimore Zoo), 43
Penguins, 56–61, 60
Père David deer. *See* Deer
Performing, 35, 102, 108–109, 149, 207–208
Training
"Betsey" (chimpanzee), 225–229
Chimpanzees, 224–225
Hagenbeck, Carl, 144–148, 150
Personnel, 44, 55–57, 61, 67, 110–112, 135, 241
Petting zoos, 102, 130
Philadelphia Zoo, 56, 195, 239, 281
Pliny the Elder. *See* Rome, ancient
Polar bears. *See* bears
Porcupines, 103
Portland (Ore.) Zoological Gardens, 224–225, 281
Preservation. *See* Conservation
Pressman, Sue (HSUS), 233–238, 241, 242, 249–250
Prices (of animals). *See* Trading
Profits, profit-making. *See* Safari Zoos; Trading, prices
Przewalski's horse, 106, 187, 270, 274–275
Ptolemy Philadelphius, 22
Ptolemy II, 22
Public, behavior of, 47-51. *See also* Central Park Zoo, vandalism
Safari zoos, 127–128, 129–130
Puma, 162
Pythons, 161, 183

Quarantine. *See* Health

Rabbits. *See* Coney
Rare animals. *See* Endangered species; Bronx Zoo, Rare Animal Range Exhibit
Rare Animals Range Exhibit (Bronx Zoo), 274–275
Ratings (of zoos), 236–237, 241–242
Reed, Dr. Theodore H. (National Zoo), 186, 194–195, 200, 210, 211, 217, 219, 221
Regent's Park Zoo. *See* London Zoo
Reptiles. *See* also specific reptile names
Bites, 51–52
Capturing, 172–173
Emotional stress, 201
Feeding habits, 38–39, 41
Kenwood St., 900 S. (Baltimore), 83–91

Popularity in zoos, 261
Restrictions, import. *See* Collecting; Trading
Rhinoceros, 109, 161. *See also* Breeding
Capturing, 181
White, 115
Ricciuti, Edward R., 128
Ringling, John, 97
Rome, ancient. *See also* Spectacles, public
Commodus, 24–25
Julius Caesar, 24
Octavian Augustus, 24
Pliny the Elder, 24
Roth, Dr. Ted (Baltimore Zoo), 42–44, 45–46, 161–164, 176–177, 179–180, 181–184
Rothschild, Walter, 71
Rowe, Tex (National Zoo), 222
Ruhe, Inc., 161, 164
Runnnig down. *See* Collecting, capturing

Safari zoos, 111, 121–136. *See also* Conservation, breeding
Automobiles, 131
Bankruptcy, 133
British, 124–125
Conservation, 134
Evaluation, 128–131
Expansion, 126
First, 124
Personnel, 135
Profits, 122–123, 126
Safety, public, 127–128
Show-business aspects, 121–125
St. Gallen (Switzerland) Zoo, 26
St. Katherine's Island (Bronx Zoo), 270
St. Louis (Missouri) Zoological Park, 281
Salaries, 135, 241
San Diego Zoo, 195, 236. *See also* Wild Animal Park
African Plains, 104–105
Aviary, 107
Botanical collection, 94, 100
Bus tour, 100–110
Children's Zoo, 102
Environments, natural, 95, 232
History, 94–99
Housing, 100, 101
Skyfari ride, 102
San Pasquale Agricultural Reserve. *See* Wild Animal Park (San Diego)
San Simeon (Calif.), 30, 74–81, 124
Schmeltz, Lee (National Zoo), 87, 90

Schönbrunn Zoo (Vienna), 71, 161
Schroeder, Dr. Charles R. (San Diego
    Zoo), 93–99, 102, 174, 200, 232
Scripps, Ellen, 95
Seals, 97, 102, 138, 201
Sernylan (drug), 178
Serval, 104
Shanahan, Terri (Baltimore Zoo),
    65–66
Sheftel, Herbert, 126
Sheftel, Stuart, 126
Shipping. *See* Collecting, transport
Signs, signage, 64–65
Shinners, Bob, 84, 85, 86, 89–90
Sladen, Dr. William, 56
Sloth, 63
Smithsonian Institution, 154
Smokey Bear, 206–213
Smuggling, 87, 90, 162
Snakes. *See* Reptiles
Solomon, King, 18–20
Specialties (of particular zoos), 56–57
Spectacles, public
    Egypt, ancient, 21–22
    Rome, ancient
        Bullfights, 24
        Combats, w/humans, 23–24
        Contests, animal, 23
        "Hunts," 23
        Massacres, 24–25
Spreckels, John D., 97–98
Starvation (human), 265
Stellingen Zoo (Hamburg), 148–149,
    264, 270–271
Striptease act. *See* Cobras
Suicide (human), 50
Sutton, Dr. George, 57

Tapir
    Capture, 177
    Malayan, 102
Territorial imperative, 55, 56, 61, 114–
    115, 187, 214–215, 244
Themalon (drug), 177
Thompson, Frank M., 166
Tigers, 146, 202, 205, 260
    Bengal, 107
    Breeding, 118, 129
    Siberian, 107, 129, 271
Tokyo Zoo. *See* Pandas
Tower of London, 26–27
Trading. *See also* Collecting; Expedi-
    tions; Hagenbeck, Carl
    Early history, 19
    Dealers, 164–170, 175
    Prices, 89, 161–162, 166
    Restrictions, 160
    Rare animals, 161–162
Training. *See* Performing

Transporting (animals). *See* Collect-
    ing, capturing
Trapping. *See* Collecting, capturing
Trefflich, Henry, 166, 175, 250
Tucson (Ariz.) Zoo. *See* Arizona-
    Sonora Desert Museum
Turkeys (as animal food), 32
Turtles, 85–87, 88–90

Vandalism. *See* Central Park Zoo;
    Public behavior
Van Dan Brink, Franz M., 164
Versailles (menagerie), 33–35, 71
Veterinary care. *See* Health
Vicuna, 105
Voyeurism, 48–49, 50

Wallace, Lila Acheson, 271
Walt Disney Wild Animal Kingdom,
    126
Wanderoo
    Breeding, 245
Washington, D.C. Zoo. *See* National
    Zoo
Water mocassins, 87
Watson, Arthur R. (Baltimore Zoo),
    47–48, 67–68, 226
Wegeforth, Dr. Harry M., 94–99, 176
Weisl, Edwin L., Jr., 256
Werler, John E., 202–204
Whales, 265
Wild Animal Park (San Diego Zoo),
    111–119, 131, 195–196. *See
    also* Breeding; Collecting; Con-
    servation
Wild Animal World, 126
Wilson, Mary (Baltimore Zoo), 45
Wisent (European bison), 186, 274,
    275
Wisnieski, Anthony, 84, 85, 89, 90
Woburn Abbey. *See* Bedford, Duke of
World of Animals, 126
World of Birds (Bronx Zoo), 271–274
World of Darkness (Bronx Zoo),
    276–279
World Wildlife Safari, 126, 134, 135
Wolf, 25
Wolf, South American maned, 103

Yak, 106
Yerkes Primate Center, 224, 253

Zeehandelaar, F. J., 167–170
Zebras, 247
    Capturing, 181
Zurich (Switzerland) Zoo, 49, 50–51